Resource-Based Theory

Creating and Sustaining Competitive A

Resource-Based Theory

Creating and Sustaining Competitive Advantage

Jay B. Barney

Delwyn N. Clark

OXFORD
UNIVERSITY PRESS

Great Clarendon Street, Oxford OX2 6DP

Oxford University Press is a department of the University of Oxford.
It furthers the University's objective of excellence in research, scholarship, and education by publishing worldwide in

Oxford New York

Auckland Cape Town Dar es Salaam Hong Kong Karachi
Kuala Lumpur Madrid Melbourne Mexico City Nairobi
New Delhi Shanghai Taipei Toronto

With offices in

Argentina Austria Brazil Chile Czech Republic France Greece
Guatemala Hungary Italy Japan Poland Portugal Singapore
South Korea Switzerland Thailand Turkey Ukraine Vietnam

Published in the United States
by Oxford University Press Inc., New York

First published 2007

British Library Cataloguing in Publication Data
Data available

Library of Congress Cataloging in Publication Data
Data available

Typeset by SPI Publisher Services, Pondicherry, India
Printed in Great Britain
on acid-free paper by
Biddles Ltd., King's Lynn, Norfolk

ISBN 978–0–19–927768–1
ISBN 978–0–19–927769–8 (Pbk.)

1 3 5 7 9 10 8 6 4 2

PREFACE

Resource-based theory is an efficiency-based explanation of sustained superior firm performance. The purpose of this book is to provide a comprehensive overview of resource-based theory from its origins to the current state-of-the-art research. The book starts by describing the history of resource-based theory, its fundamental tenets, how it has and can be applied, and outlines ongoing efforts to extend and refine this theory of persistent performance differences.

The content of the book is organised into four parts. **Part I** includes three chapters which provide an introduction to resource-based theory. In Chapter 1, the historical development of resource-based theory is outlined, and key terms in the theory are defined and discussed. Chapter 2 examines the relationship between strategic factor markets and competitive advantages in product markets. Chapter 3 focuses on the attributes of resources and capabilities that enable some to be sources of sustained competitive advantage.

Part II applies resource-based theory in analyzing the ability of four organizational resources and capabilities to be sources of sustained competitive advantage. The resources examined include organizational culture (Chapter 4), trustworthiness (Chapter 5), human resource practices (Chapter 6), and information technology (Chapter 7).

Part III shifts the unit of analysis from the competitive implications of specific organizational resources to the analysis of the competitive implications of specific strategic alternatives. Three corporate strategies—vertical integration (Chapter 8), diversification (Chapter 9), and mergers and acquisitions (Chapter 10)—are examined.

Part IV presents an overview of the current state of resource-based theory. A summary of the empirical research testing resource-based theory within strategic management and other management disciplines is provided in Chapter 11. Finally, opportunities for extending and expanding resource-based theory in future are proposed in Chapter 12.

Many of the chapters in this book are based on previously published materials taken from a wide variety of articles, book chapters, and books published over the last twenty years. Some chapters draw on several such sources, while others have been written specifically for this book. In each case, care has been taken to use the common language, definitions, and assumptions that have emerged in resource-based theory over these twenty years. In this sense, the contents of this book represent both the history of resource-based theory and its current state of development. It also helps define what we think are some of the important next steps in the evolution of this theoretical perspective.

Acknowledgements

The authors would like to thank the following for permission to reproduce published material: co-authors of paper extracts including: Asli Arikan (Chapters 1 and 11), Margie Peteraf (Chapter 1), Mark Hansen (Chapter 5), Patrick Wright (Chapter 6), Francisco Mata and William Fuerst (Chapter 7), Gautam Ray and Waleed Muhanna (Chapter 7), Heli Wang (Chapter 9), and Tyson Mackey (Chapter 11); and publishers including Blackwell Publishers (Chapters 1, 3, and 11), the Academy of Management (Chapters 4 and 9), Elsevier (Chapter 11), INFORMS (Chapter 2), Pearson (Chapter 9), the Management Information Systems Research Center (Chapter 7), and Wiley (Chapters 1, 5, 6, 7, and 10).

Special thanks also to many exceptional colleagues, students and friends who have contributed to numerous interesting and insightful conversations on resource-based theory over the years; to Kathy Zwanziger for excellent editorial support; to Oxford University Press, UK, for professional assistance with this publication; to Fisher College of Business, The Ohio State University, and the University of Waikato Management School, for institutional support; and to our families for being a constant source of love and inspiration.

A special note on the cover. After rejecting several suggested covers, Professor Barney happened across a piece of work by a young, but very promising artist/engineer—Isaac McFadden. Isaac's agents negotiated hard for the rights to this brilliant multi-media piece, but in the end, they agreed to let his work be included on the cover of this book. We both take great pride in introducing Isaac's talent to the world.

Jay B. Barney and Delwyn N. Clark

October 2006

CONTENTS

LIST OF FIGURES

Part I

Resource-Based Theory

1 The strategic management question and the emergence of resource-based theory*

The field of strategic management, like other social science disciplines, is organized around a central research question. That question is: 'Why do some firms persistently outperform others?' This question does not presume that there will always be persistent performance differences between firms. Sometimes firms do not outperform others; sometimes performance differences are short lived. Rather, this question only suggests that it may be the case that, in some situations some of the time, persistent performance differences will exist between firms. It is these differences in firm performance that strategic management scholars seek to understand.

At the broadest level, two explanations about why some firms persistently outperform other firms have been developed in the literature. The first, and older of the two, was originally articulated by Porter (1979, 1981) and draws heavily on the structure-conduct-performance (SCP) paradigm in industrial organization economics (Bain 1956). This explanation focuses on the impact that a firm's market power has on the ability of a firm to raise prices above a competitive level (Porter 1981). If entry into industries where firms are exercising market power is restricted by various barriers, then these performance differences can persist (Bain 1956).

* This chapter draws from Peteraf and Barney (2003) and Barney and Arikan (2001).

The second explanation of why some firms persistently outperform other firms focuses less on industry structure and market power, and more on the differential ability of some firms to more effectively and efficiently respond to customer needs (Demsetz 1973). This explanation draws heavily on neoclassical price theory (Foss and Knudsen 2003) and suggests that if it is costly for less efficient and effective firms to copy more efficient and effective firms, that the superior performance of these latter firms can persist (Rumelt 1984).

These two explanations of persistent heterogeneity in firm performance are not necessarily contradictory. Market power explanations apply in some settings, for example, when a firm is operating in an oligopoly (Gale 1972) or as a regulated monopolist (Bain 1941). Efficiency explanations apply in other settings, for example, when the level of competition in an industry is relatively high and when industry level barriers to entry either do not exist or are not effective (Cool, Dierickx, and Jemison 1989). Efforts to apply efficiency models of sustained superior performance in oligopoly or monopoly situations are likely to lead to poor firm performance; efforts to apply market power models of sustained superior performance in more competitive industrial settings are likely to lead to poor firm performance.

While not denying the importance of understanding the role of market power in explaining the existence of sustained superior firm performance in some industrial settings, this book largely ignores these explanations. Rather, this book focuses on efficiency theories of sustained superior firm performance and especially on one particular efficiency theory—resource-based theory. In this sense, the purpose of this book is to describe the history of resource-based theory, its fundamental theoretical tenets, how it has been and can be applied, and the ongoing efforts to extend and refine this theory of persistent performance differences.

Some theoretical antecedents of resource-based theory

Resource-based theory, like any theory, draws on prior theoretical work in developing its predictions and prescriptions. In the case of resource-based theory, important prior theoretical work comes from at least four sources: (*a*) the traditional study of distinctive competencies, (*b*) Ricardo's analysis of land rents, (*c*) Penrose (1959), and (*d*) the study of the antitrust implications of economics. Each of these prior theories is briefly discussed in turn.

TRADITIONAL WORK ON DISTINCTIVE COMPETENCIES

For sometime now, scholars have tried to answer the question, 'Why do some firms persistently outperform others?' Before more economic approaches to answering this question began to dominate this discussion (beginning with Porter 1979), this effort focused on what were known as a firm's distinctive competencies. Distinctive competencies are those attributes of a firm that enable it to pursue a strategy more efficiently and effectively than other firms (Learned et al. 1969; Hrebiniak and Snow 1982; Hitt and Ireland 1985, 1986).

Among the first distinctive competencies identified by those trying to understand persistent performance differences between firms was general management capability. General managers are managers in firms who have multiple functional managers reporting to them. Typically, general managers have full accounting profit and loss responsibility in a firm. And when they do not have this responsibility, general managers are likely to lead cost centers. Whether profit center or cost center managers, general managers can have a significant impact on the strategies a firm decides to pursue and on the ability of a firm to implement the strategies it develops.

Given the impact that general managers can have on a firm's strategy, it naturally follows that firms that have 'high-quality' general managers will usually outperform firms that have 'low-quality' general managers. In this context, choosing high-quality general managers is the most important strategic choice that can be made by a firm, and training high-quality general managers is the most important mission of business schools (Gordon and Howell 1959; Pierson 1959).

The emphasis on general managers as distinctive competencies was important not only in the field of strategic management, but in closely related fields as well. For example, through the early 1950s, the study of business history was confined largely to the study of individual business people and firms. Traditionally, business historians were reluctant to generalize beyond individual biographies and firm histories to discuss broader trends in the economy that may have led to different forms of business organization, let alone the efficiency characteristics of these different organizational forms. For business history, like strategic management, explanations of the growth and success of firms were no more than the biographies of those who created and managed those firms (Chandler 1984).

Indeed, there is little doubt that general managers can have a very significant impact on firm performance (Mackey 2006). There continues to be a tradition of leadership research that examines the skills and abilities of leaders and documents their impact on the performance of firms (Finkelstein and Hambrick 1996). Some of the best of this work focuses on general managers as change agents and emphasizes the impact that these 'transformational leaders' can have on a firm's performance (Tichy and Devanna 1986). Most observers can point to specific general managers who have been instrumental in improving the performance of the firms within which they work. The continuing popularity of books, articles, and seminars (e.g. Bennis 1989, 2003; Covey 1989; Kanter, Stein, and Jick 1992; Pfeffer 1994; Kotter 1996; Ulrich 1997; Kotter and Cohen 2002; Zenger and Folkman 2002; Finkelstein 2003) that describe the attributes of individuals that enable them to become leaders in their firms is a testament to the popularity of the belief that leaders, and in particular, general managers, are the most important determinant of a firm's performance.

Unfortunately, there are some very important limitations of this general management approach to explaining persistent performance differences among firms. First, even if one accepts the notion that general management decisions are the most important determinants of firm performance, the qualities and characteristics that make up a high-quality general manager are ambiguous and difficult to specify. In fact, the qualities of a 'good' general manager are just as ambiguous as the qualities of good leaders (Yukl 1989). In the case literature, general managers with widely different styles are shown to be quite effective. For example, John Connelly, former president of Crown Cork & Seal, was intensely involved in every aspect of his organization (Hamermesh and Rosenbloom 1989). Other successful chief executive officers (CEOs) tend to delegate much of the day-to-day management of their firms (Stogdill 1974). Yet both types of general managers can be very effective.

Second, general managers are an important possible distinctive competence for an organization, but they are not the only such competence.

An exclusive emphasis on general managers as an explanation of superior performance ignores a wide variety of firm attributes that may be important for understanding firm performance. For example, it may be the case that a firm possesses very highly skilled general managers but lacks the other resources it needs to gain performance advantages. Or it may be the case that a firm has other resources that enable it to gain performance advantages, even though it does not have unusual managerial talent. In the end, general managers in organizations are probably similar to baseball managers: they receive too much credit when things go well and too much blame when things go poorly.

A sociologist named Phillip Selznick was among the first scholars to recognize that general management skill was only one of several distinctive competencies that a firm might control. In a series of articles and books, culminating in his book *Leadership and Administration* (Selznick 1957), Selznick examined the relationship between what he called institutional leadership and distinctive competence.

According to Selznick, institutional leaders in organizations do more than carry out the classic general management functions of decision-making and administration. In addition, they create and define an organization's purpose or mission (Selznick 1957). In more contemporary terms, institutional leaders help create a vision for an organization around which its members can rally (Finkelstein and Hambrick 1996; Collins and Porras 1997). Institutional leaders also organize and structure a firm so that it reflects this fundamental purpose and vision. With this organization in place, Selznick suggests, institutional leaders then focus their attention on safeguarding a firm's distinctive values and identity—the distinctive vision of a firm—from internal and external threats. This organizational vision, in combination with organizational structure, helps define a firm's distinctive competencies—those activities that a particular firm does better than any competing firms.

Selznick did not go on to analyze the competitive or performance implications of institutional leadership as a distinctive competence in any detail. However, it is not difficult to see that firms with distinctive competencies have strengths that may enable them to obtain superior performance, and that leaders as visionaries and institution builders, rather than just as decision-makers and administrators, may be an important source of this performance advantage (Selznick 1957).

Selznick's analysis of distinctive competence has much to recommend it, but it has limitations as well. Most important of these is that Selznick's analysis focuses only on senior managers (his institutional leaders) as the ultimate source of competitive advantage for a firm, and on a single tool (the development of an organizational vision) that senior managers can use to create distinctive competencies. Although these are important possible explanations of performance differences across firms, they are not the only possible such explanations.

RICARDO'S ANALYSIS OF LAND RENTS

Research on general managers and institutional leaders as possible explanations of differences in firm performance focuses exclusively on top managers, but the next major influence on the evolution of resource-based theory—Ricardo's analysis of land rents—traditionally included little or no role for managers as possible sources of superior performance. Instead, David Ricardo was interested in the economic consequences of the 'original, unaugmentable, and indestructible gifts of Nature' (Ricardo 1817). Much of this early work focused on the economic consequences of owning land.

Unlike many factors of production, the total supply of land is relatively fixed and cannot be significantly increased in response to higher demand and prices. Such factors of production are perfectly inelastic, since their quantity of supply is fixed and does not respond to price changes. In these settings, it is possible for those that own higher-quality factors of production with inelastic supply to earn an economic rent. As suggested earlier, an economic rent is a payment to an owner of a factor of production in excess of the minimum required to induce that factor into employment.

Ricardo's argument concerning land as a factor of production is summarized in Figure 1.1. Imagine that there are many parcels of land suitable for growing wheat. Also suppose that the fertility of these different parcels of land varies from high fertility (low costs of production) to low fertility (high costs of production). The long-run supply curve for wheat in this market can be derived as follows: at low prices, only the most fertile land will be cultivated; as prices rise, production continues on the very

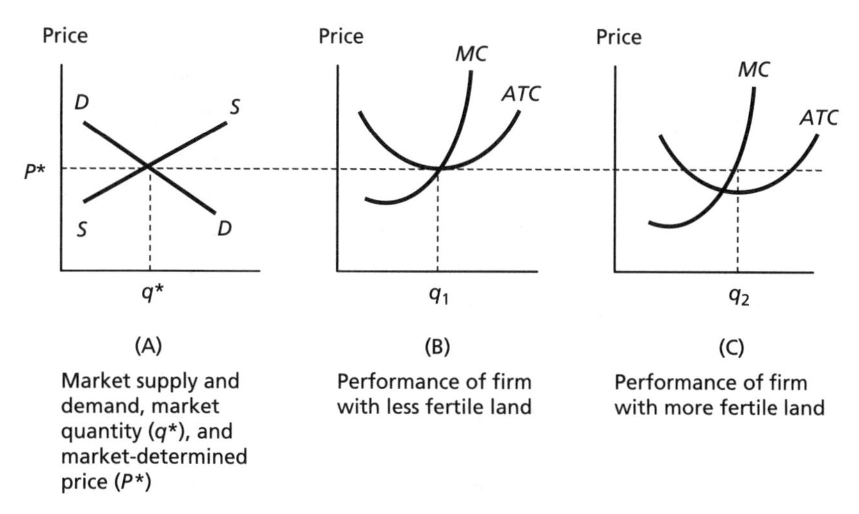

Figure 1.1. Ricardian rents and the economics of land with different levels of fertility

fertile land and additional crops are planted on less fertile land; at still higher prices, even less fertile land will be cultivated. This analysis leads to the simple market supply curve presented in panel A of Figure 1.1. Given market demand, P^* is the market-determined price of wheat in this market.

Now consider the situation facing two different kinds of firms. Both of these firms follow traditional profit-maximizing logic by producing a quantity (q) such that marginal cost equals marginal revenue. However, this profit-maximizing decision for the firm with less fertile land (in panel B of Figure 1.1) generates zero economic profit. On the other hand, the firm with more fertile land (in panel C of Figure 1.1) has average total costs less than the market-determined price and thus is able to earn an economic rent.

In traditional economic analysis, the economic rent earned by the firm with more fertile land should lead other firms to enter into this market, to obtain some land and begin production of wheat. However, all the land that can be used to produce wheat in a way that generates at least zero economic profits given the market price P^* is already in production. In particular, there is no more very fertile land left, and fertile land (by assumption) cannot be created. This is what is meant by land being inelastic in supply. Thus the firm with more fertile land and lower production costs has a higher level of performance than farms with less fertile land, and this performance difference will persist, since fertile land is inelastic in supply.

Of course, at least two events can threaten this sustained performance advantage. First, market demand may shift down and to the left. This would force firms with less fertile land to cease production, and it would also reduce the economic rent of the firm with more fertile land. If demand shifted far enough, this economic rent may disappear altogether.

Second, firms with less fertile land may discover low-cost ways of increasing their land's fertility, thereby reducing the performance advantage of the firm with more fertile land. For example, firms with less fertile land may be able to use inexpensive fertilizers to increase their land's fertility, and they may be able to reduce their production costs to be closer to the costs of the firm that had the more fertile land initially. The existence of such low-cost fertilizers suggests that though *land* may be in fixed supply, *fertility* may not be. If enough firms can increase the fertility of their land, then the rent originally earned by the firm with the more fertile land will disappear, and firms competing in this market can expect to earn only zero economic rents.

Traditionally, most economists have implicitly assumed that relatively few factors of production have inelastic supply. Most economic models presume that if prices for a factor rise, more of that factor will be produced, increasing supply and ensuring that suppliers will earn only normal economic rents. However, resource-based theory suggests that numerous resources used by firms are inelastic in supply and are possible sources of economic rents. Thus although labor per se is probably not inelastic in supply, highly skilled and creative laborers may be. Although individual managers are probably not inelastic in supply, managers who can work effectively in teams may be. And although top managers may not be inelastic in supply, top managers who are also institutional leaders (as suggested by Selznick and others) may be. Firms that own (or control) these kinds of resources may be able to earn economic rents by exploiting them.

One issue that Ricardo did not examine but which becomes very important in resource-based theory is: 'How did farms with more fertile land end up with that land?' Or, more precisely, 'What price did farms with more fertile land pay for that land?' Resource-based theory suggests that if the price that farmers pay to gain access to more fertile land anticipates the economic rents that that land can create, then the value of those rents will be reflected in that price, and even though it may appear that farms with more fertile land are outperforming farms with less fertile land, this is not the case. This argument, originally developed by Barney (1986*a*), is discussed in more detail in Chapter 2.

PENROSE

In 1959, Edith Penrose published a book titled *The Theory of the Growth of the Firm*. Penrose's objective was to understand the process through which firms grow and the limits of growth. Traditional economic models had analyzed firm growth using the assumptions and tools of neoclassical microeconomics (Penrose 1959). Most important of these, for Penrose, was the assumption that firms could be appropriately modeled as if they were relatively simple production functions. In other words, traditional economic models assumed that firms simply observed supply and demand conditions in the market and translated these conditions into levels of production that maximized firm profits (Nelson and Winter 1982).

This abstract notion of what a firm is, had, and continues to have utility in some circumstances. However, in attempting to understand constraints on the growth of firms, Penrose (1959) concluded that this abstraction was not helpful. Instead, she argued that firms should be understood, first, as an administrative framework that links and coordinates activities of numerous individuals and groups, and second, as a bundle of productive resources. The task facing managers was to exploit the bundle of productive resources controlled by a firm through the use of the administrative framework that had been created in a firm. According to Penrose, the growth of a firm is limited (*a*) by the productive opportunities that exist as a function of the bundle of productive resources controlled by a firm, and (*b*) the administrative framework used to coordinate the use of these resources.

Besides looking inside a firm to analyze the ability of firms to grow, Penrose made several other contributions to what became resource-based theory. First, she observed that the bundles of productive resources controlled by firms could vary significantly by firm—that firms, in this sense, are fundamentally heterogeneous even if they are in the same industry.

Second, Penrose adopted a very broad definition of what might be considered a productive resource. Where traditional economists (including Ricardo) focused on just a few resources that might be inelastic in supply (such as land), Penrose began to study the competitive implications of such inelastic productive resources as managerial teams, top management groups, and entrepreneurial skills. Finally, Penrose recognized that, even within this extended typology of productive resources, there might still be additional sources of firm heterogeneity. Thus in her analysis of entrepreneurial skills as a possible productive resource, Penrose observed that some entrepreneurs are more versatile than others, some are more ingenious in fund-raising, some are more ambitious, and some exercise better judgment.

THE ANTITRUST IMPLICATIONS OF ECONOMICS

As a field of study, economics has always been interested in the social policy implications of the theories it develops. One of the most important ways that economics has been used to guide social policy is in the area of antitrust regulation. Based on the conclusion that social welfare is maximized when markets are perfectly competitive, economists have developed various techniques for describing when an industry is less than perfectly competitive, what the social welfare implications of this imperfect competition are, and what remedies, if any, are available to enhance competitiveness and restore social welfare (Scherer 1980).

One of the most obvious ways that an industry may be less than perfectly competitive is if that industry is dominated by only a single firm (the condition of monopoly) or by a small number of cooperating firms (the condition of oligopoly). In both these settings, according to traditional economic analyses, prices will be higher than what would exist in a competitive market, and thus social welfare will be less than what would be the case in that more competitive market.

This approach to analyzing social welfare and antitrust developed into the 'structure-conduct-performance' (SCP) paradigm mentioned earlier in this chapter (Bain 1956). The SCP paradigm suggests that the structure of a firm's industry defines the range of activities that a firm can engage in—so-called conduct—and, in turn, the performance of firms in that industry. Firms that operate in industries with structures that are different from the perfectly competitive ideal in important ways may have conduct options that will enable them to obtain levels of performance that reduce social welfare in significant ways. In the extreme, this view of the determinants of firm performance suggests that any persistent superior performance enjoyed by a firm must, by definition, reflect noncompetitive firm conduct that is antithetical to social welfare.

Beginning in the early 1970s, a small group of antitrust scholars began to question the SCP and related approaches to antitrust regulation. Among the first of these was Harold Demsetz. In 1973, Demsetz published an article in the *Journal of Law and Economics* that argued that industry structure was not the only determinant of a firm's performance. Even more fundamentally, Demsetz (1973) argued that a firm earning persistent superior performance could not be taken as prima facie evidence that that firm was engaging in anticompetitive activities. Indeed, anticipating resource-based theory, Demsetz argued that some firms might enjoy persistent performance advantages either because they are lucky or because they are more competent in addressing customer needs than other firms. Demsetz (1973: 3) argues

> Superior performance can be attributed to the combination of great uncertainty plus luck or atypical insight by the management of a firm . . . Even though the profits that arise from a firm's activities may be eroded by competitive imitation, since information is costly to obtain and techniques are difficult to duplicate, the firm may enjoy growth and a superior rate of return for some time . . .
>
> Superior ability also may be interpreted as a competitive basis for acquiring a measure of monopoly power. In a world in which information is costly and the future is uncertain, a firm that seizes an opportunity to better serve customers does so because it expects to enjoy some protection from its rivals because of their ignorance of this opportunity or because of their inability to imitate quickly.

While developed in the context of discussions of antitrust regulation, Demsetz clearly anticipates some important tenets of resource-based theory. It is interesting that Demsetz develops his arguments as an alternative to SCP-based theories of antitrust. And since Porter (1979, 1980) traces the theoretical roots of his work back to the SCP paradigm, in an important sense, Demsetz also anticipates the theoretical debates that have emerged between resource-based theory and the Porter framework.

Thus we see that resource-based theory, far from emerging out of nowhere to become an important explanation of persistent superior firm performance in the field of strategic management, has deep theoretical roots in both economics and sociology. These theoretical streams have been united and modified to develop what has become resource-based theory.

The development of resource-based theory

EARLY RESOURCE-BASED CONTRIBUTIONS[1]

Perhaps the first resource-based theory publication in the field of strategic management identified as such was by Wernerfelt (1984). Ironically, Wernerfelt's resource-based arguments did not grow directly from any of the four theoretical traditions identified above. Rather, Wernerfelt's argument is an example of dualistic reasoning common in economics. Such reasoning suggests that it is possible to restate a theory originally developed from one perspective with concepts and ideas developed in a complementary (or dual) perspective. For example, in microeconomics, it is possible to develop economic theories of decision-making using either utility theory, revealed preference theory, or state-preference theory; in finance, it is possible to estimate the value of an investment using the Capital Asset Pricing Model or Arbitrage Pricing Theory. Wernerfelt (1984) attempted to develop a theory of competitive advantage based on the resources a firm develops or acquires to implement product market strategy as a complement or dual of Porter's theory (1980) of competitive advantage based on a firm's product market position. This is why Wernerfelt (1984) called his ideas the resource-based 'view'—since he was simply viewing the same competitive problem described by Porter (1980) from the perspective of the resources a firm controls.

This approach to developing a theory of competitive advantage supposes that the portfolio of product market positions that a firm takes is reflected in the portfolio of resources it controls. Competition among product market positions held by firms can thus also be understood as competition among resource positions held by firms. In principle, for every concept that enables the analysis of the competitiveness of a firm's product market (e.g. barriers to entry), there should exist a complementary concept that enables the analysis of the level of competition among resources controlled by different firms (e.g. barriers to imitation).

One of Wernerfelt's primary contributions (1984) was recognizing that competition for resources among firms based on their resource profiles could have important implications for the ability of firms to gain advantages in implementing product market strategies. In this way, Wernerfelt anticipated some of the critical elements of resource-based theory as it developed in the 1990s.

In the same year that Wernerfelt (1984) published his paper, Rumelt (1984) published a second resource-based paper in a book of readings coming out of a conference on strategic management. While these papers addressed similar kinds of issues, they did not refer to each other. Where Wernerfelt (1984) focused on establishing the possibility that a theory of firm performance differences could be developed in terms of the resources that a firm controls, Rumelt began describing a strategic theory of the firm, that is, a theory explaining why firms exist that focused on the ability of firms to more efficiently generate economic rents than other forms of economic organization. At its most general level, such a theory would suggest the conditions under which firms, as an example of hierarchical governance (Williamson 1975, 1985), would be a more efficient way to create and appropriate economic rents than other forms of governance, including markets. Rather than firms existing as efficient ways to minimize the threat of opportunism in transactions—as suggested by the transactions cost theorists (Williamson 1975)—Rumelt (1984) was exploring the rent generating and appropriating characteristics of firms.

This theme of linking rent generation, transactions cost, and governance emerges much later, in the work of Conner and Prahalad (1996), Grant (1996), Liebeskind (1996), Kogut and Zander (1996), and Spender (1996), in efforts to develop a resource-based theory of the firm.[2] It also anticipates a very important issue that may ultimately serve as a theoretical link between resource-based theories of firm performance and transactions cost theories of governance. In particular, both theories point to the importance of transaction-specific investments as independent variables that explain different dependent variables. For resource-based theorists, transaction-specific or firm-specific investments can be thought of as resources that are among the most likely to have the ability to generate economic rents

(Barney 2001*a*). For transactions cost theorists, transaction-specific investments create problems of opportunism that must be resolved through governance choices. Teece (1980) brings these two ideas together explicitly by arguing that the kinds of relations among businesses that are most likely to be a source of economic profits for firms pursuing a corporate diversification strategy are also the kinds of relations that will be difficult to manage through nonhierarchical forms of governance. Thus, for Teece, resource-based theories and transactions cost theories, together, constitute a theory of corporate diversification.

The strategic theory of the firm that Rumelt (1984) develops has many of the attributes that will later be associated with resource-based theory. For example, Rumelt defines firms as a bundle of productive resources and he suggests that the economic value of these resources will vary, depending on the context within which they are applied. He also suggests that the imitability of these resources depends on the extent to which they are protected by 'isolating mechanisms'. He even develops a list of these isolating mechanisms and begins to discuss the attributes of resources that can enhance their inimitability.

The third resource-based article published in the field of strategic management is Barney (1986*a*). Similar to Wernerfelt (1984), Barney (1986*a*) suggests that it is possible to develop a theory of persistent superior firm performance based on the attributes of the resources a firm controls. However, Barney (1986*a*) moves beyond Wernerfelt (1984) by arguing that such a theory can have very different implications than theories of competitive advantage based on the product market positions of firms. Thus, Barney (1986*a*) begins a shift from what might be called the resource-based view toward what is currently called resource-based theory.

Barney (1986*a*) introduces the concept of strategic factor markets as the market where firms acquire or develop the resources they need to implement their product market strategies.[3] He shows that if strategic factor markets are perfectly competitive, the acquisition of resources in those markets will anticipate the performance those resources will create when used to implement product market strategies. This suggests that, if strategic factor markets are perfectly competitive, even if firms are successful in implementing strategies that create imperfectly competitive product markets, those strategies will not be a source of economic rents. Put differently, the fact that strategic factor markets can be perfectly competitive implies that theories of imperfect product market competition are not sufficient for the development of a theory that explains persistent performance differences between firms. This, of course, contradicts one of the central tenants of Porter's theory of industry attractiveness—that the ability of firms to enter and operate in attractive product markets is an explanation of persistent superior firm performance. In the extreme, Barney's argument suggests that if strategic factor markets are always perfectly competitive, it is not possible for firms to earn economic rents.

Of course, strategic factor markets are not always perfectly competitive. Barney (1986*a*) suggests two ways that such markets can be imperfectly competitive: First, in the face of uncertainty, firms can be lucky and, second, it may be the case that a particular firm has unusual insights about the future value of the resources it is acquiring or developing in a strategic factor market. Barney (1986*a*) concludes his paper by suggesting that the resources a firm already controls are more likely to be sources of economic rents for firms than resources that it acquires from external sources.

Dierickx and Cool (1989) extended Barney's argument (1986*a*) by describing what it is about the resources a firm already controls that may make it possible for that resource to generate economic rents. Following Rumelt's discussion (1984) of isolating mechanisms, Dierickx and Cool (1989) suggest that resources that are subject to time compression diseconomies (what others [Arthur 1989] have called path dependence), that are causally ambiguous, that are characterized by interconnected asset stocks, or that are characterized by asset mass efficiencies are less likely to be subject to strategic factor market competition than other kinds of resources. Many of the attributes of a firm's resources that make them not subject to strategic factor market competition identified by Dierickx and Cool (1989) are later discussed and applied by Barney (1991*b*).

Together, these four papers—Wernerfelt (1984), Rumelt (1984), Barney (1986*a*), and Dierickx and Cool (1989)—outline some of the basic principles of resource-based theory. These papers suggest that it is possible to develop a theory of persistent superior firm performance using a firm's resources as a unit of analysis. These papers also describe some of the attributes that resources must possess if they are to be a source of sustained superior firm performance—Rumelt's concepts (1984) of value and isolating mechanisms and Barney's notion (1986*a*) that resources already controlled by a firm are more likely to be a source of economic rents than other kinds of resources. They also suggest that it is the bundle of unique resources possessed by a firm that may enable a firm to gain and sustain superior performance.

Of course, a great deal of work has followed these initial four papers. For example, Barney (1986*b*) developed a resource-based explanation of why an organization's culture can be a source of sustained competitive advantage (to be discussed further in Chapter 4), and Barney (1988) applied the logic developed in Barney (1986*a*) to mergers and acquisitions to show that strategic relatedness, per se, was not sufficient for bidding firms to earn economic rents from acquiring target firms (to be discussed further in Chapter 10). Conner (1991) explored the relationship between resource-based theory and other traditions in microeconomics. Building on Rumelt (1984), she also began to explore some of the theory of the firm implications of resource-based logic. Castanias and Helfat (1991) showed how the creation and appropriation of economic rents aligned the interests of a firm's managers and equityholders and thus how resource-based logic helped address incentives problems identified in agency theory (see Alchian and Demsetz 1972; Jensen and Meckling 1976). Barney (1991*b*) published a paper that outlined the basic assumptions of resource-based logic and how those assumptions could be used to develop testable assertions about the relationship between a firm's resources and its competitive advantages (to be discussed further in Chapter 3).[4] Rumelt (1991) published an empirical paper that showed that firm-level effects explained more variance in firm performance than either corporate or industry level effects, a result consistent with resource-based logic and a result that contradicted earlier published work that showed that industry effects were a more important determinant of firm performance than firm effects (Schmalensee 1985; Wernerfelt and Montgomery 1986). Hansen and Wernerfelt (1989) published a paper that demonstrated that the characteristics of a firm's organizational culture had a more significant impact on its performance than the attributes of the industry within which it operated—results that also were consistent with resource-based expectations. Peteraf (1993) published a paper that thoroughly grounded resource-based logic in microeconomics, and Mahoney (1993) published an article that compared and contrasted resource-based logic with other theories of competitive advantage. Grant (1996) published an article that, among other things, began to explore the managerial implications of resource-based logic.

Together, these and many other papers created the foundation of what has become known as resource-based theory. The major assumptions, assertions, and predictions of this body of theory are examined in detail in subsequent chapters of this book.

Parallel streams of 'resource-based' work

As this resource-based theory was developing, scholars in other research traditions were developing theories of competitive advantage that had numerous similarities to resource-based logic but were developed largely independent of the work cited earlier. Two of the most important of these parallel streams were the theory of invisible assets (Itami 1987), and work on competence-based theories of corporate diversification (e.g. Prahalad and Bettis 1986; Prahalad and Hamel 1990).

ACCUMULATING AND MANAGING INVISIBLE ASSETS

As described by Itami (1987: 12), invisible assets are information-based resources such as technology, customer trust, brand image, and control of distribution, corporate culture, and management skills. For Itami, physical (visible) assets must be present for business operations to take place but invisible assets are necessary for competitive success. Invisible assets are the real sources of competitive power and adaptability because they are hard and time-consuming to accumulate, can be used in multiple ways simultaneously, and are both input and outputs of business activity. People are both accumulators and producers of invisible assets.

Itami classifies information as being environmental, corporate, and internal. Environmental information flows from the environment to the firm, creating invisible assets related to the environment such as production skills and customer information. Corporate information, such as corporate reputation, brand image, corporate image, and marketing know-how, flows from the firm to its environment. Internal information, such as corporate culture, morale of workers, and management capability, originates and terminates within the firm. In each category, the amount of information gathered, its nature, as well as the channels through which it is gathered, are all invisible assets.

Invisible assets are accumulated either directly—where a firm takes explicit actions such as choosing a technology for research and development—or indirectly—where assets are accumulated as by-products of daily operations. According to Itami (1987), the accumulation and maintenance of invisible assets indirectly through operations can take more time than direct efforts, but the results of this process are more reliable. For example, word-of-mouth customer appreciation is much more effective than a television advertisement in convincing potential customers to buy a firm's products. However, this is not to suggest that the direct route has to be completely abandoned, but rather that a balance between these two methods of invisible asset accumulation is necessary.

Given the role of both visible and invisible assets of the firm, firms should choose projects that are within the firm's area of expertise and appropriate to its skills (Itami 1987: 159). However, firms intending to grow have to create deviations from this ideal fit to accumulate new invisible assets. Firms that choose to accumulate new invisible assets need to understand that they usually will not be able to compete in a new business as effectively as they have competed in their original market. However, this temporary loss of effectiveness may be necessary if a firm is to continually develop new invisible assets it can use to grow and prosper.

Of course, Itami's emphasis on the intangible and invisible aspects of a firm directly parallels resource-based theory. However, rather than simply focusing on how resources can explain a firm's current performance, Itami examines the impact of these invisible assets on a firm's diversification efforts. This links Itami's work very closely with the work on the core competence of the organization.

COMPETENCE THEORIES OF CORPORATE DIVERSIFICATION

With respect to competence-based theories of corporate diversification, it has already been suggested that Teece (1980) was among the first scholars to begin to apply resource-based logic to the problem of corporate diversification. In an effort that paralleled Teece's work, Prahalad and his colleagues (Prahalad and Bettis 1986; Prahalad and Hamel 1990) also began developing an approach to understanding corporate diversification that, while never explicitly labeled as a 'resource-based approach' had a great deal in common with resource-based logic as it was developing through the 1990s. Where most previous corporate strategy work had focused on the importance of shared tangible assets across the multiple businesses a diversified firm had begun operating in (see, e.g. Rumelt 1974; Montgomery 1979), Prahalad began emphasizing the potential importance of sharing less tangible assets across businesses and the role that this sharing could play in creating value through diversification.

In Prahalad and Bettis (1986: 491), these shared intangible assets were called a firm's dominant logic. They define a firm's dominant logic as 'a mindset or a worldview or conceptualization of the business and the administrative tools to accomplish goals and make decisions in that business.' Clearly, dominant logic, as an economic justification for corporate diversification, emphasizes intangible, even cognitive, bases for diversification. Certainly, one of the advantages of such bases of diversification compared to more tangible bases is that competing corporations would have more difficulty imitating these intangible bases of diversification.

Prahalad and Hamel (1990) extended the concept of dominant logic in a very influential paper that defined the notion of a corporation's 'core competence'. Prahalad and Hamel (1990: 82) defined a corporation's core competence as 'the collective learning in the organization, especially how to coordinate diverse production skills and integrate multiple streams of technologies.' Here again, Prahalad and his coauthors focus on intangible rather than tangible assets as a basis for competitive advantage in choosing and implementing corporate strategy.

While developed independently of resource-based logic, this emphasis on the economic value of the intangible is common to both Prahalad's work and resource-based theory as it was developing in the 1990s. Indeed, since these early contributions by Prahalad, Bettis, and Hamel, most scholars that have either further developed the ideas of a firm's 'dominant logic' (Grant 1988) or core competence or tested the empirical implications of these ideas have approached this work in ways that are consistent with resource-based logic (e.g. Wernerfelt and Montgomery 1988; Robins and Wiersema 1995). Indeed, resource-based theories of corporate diversification, as is shown in Chapter 11, have been one of the most popular ways to empirically test resource-based logic.[5]

Additional comments about resource-based theory

Before continuing this discussion, a few additional comments about resource-based theory are needed. These concern the confusion about terms describing factors of production controlled by a firm and the definition of competitive advantage in resource-based theory. These clarifications will greatly simplify the discussion in the remainder of this book.

TERMS TO DESCRIBE FACTORS OF PRODUCTION CONTROLLED BY A FIRM

First, there continues to be some ongoing confusion about the terms used to describe factors of production controlled by a firm. Through the 1990s, various authors have tried to develop typologies of these tangible and intangible assets in an effort to suggest that different types of assets can have different competitive effects for firms. For example, Wernerfelt (1984) and Barney (1991*b*) simply called these assets 'resources' and made no effort to divide them into any finer categories. Prahalad and Hamel (1990) developed the concept of 'core competencies' and, building on Selznick (1957) and others, added the term *competence* to the resource-based lexicon. Stalk, Evans, and Shulman (1992) argued that there was a difference between competencies and capabilities, and thus this term (*capabilities*) was added to the terminological fray. Teece, Pisano, and Shuen (1997) emphasized the importance of the ability of firms to develop new capabilities, a perspective emphasized by their choice of the term 'dynamic capabilities'. (Note: these are 'capabilities that are dynamic'.) Several authors have suggested that knowledge *is* 'the' most important resource that can be controlled by a firm and have developed what they call a 'knowledge-based theory' of sustained superior firm performance (see, e.g. Grant 1996; Liebeskind 1996; Spender and Grant 1996).

In principle, distinctions among terms like 'resources', 'competencies', 'capabilities', 'dynamic capabilities', and 'knowledge' can be drawn. For example, in their textbooks, Hill and Jones (1992) and Hitt, Ireland, and Hoskisson (1997) distinguish between resources and capabilities by suggesting that resources are a firm's 'fundamental' financial, physical, individual, and organizational capital attributes, while capabilities are those attributes of a firm that enable it to exploit its resources in implementing strategies. Drawing upon Amit and Schoemaker (1993), Makadok (2001) defines capabilities as special types of resources that are 'organizational embedded non-transferable firm-specific resources whose purpose is to improve the productivity of other resources'. Makadok (2001) notes complementary and substitute effects between 'resource-picking' and 'capability-building'—these are distinct rent-creation mechanisms. Teece, Pisano, and Shuen's concept (1997) of dynamic capabilities tends to focus on the ability of firms to learn and evolve (Lei, Hitt, and Bettis 1996). Among the stream of work exploring this perspective, Eisenhardt and Martin (2000) define dynamic capabilities as 'the antecedent organizational and strategic routines by which managers alter their resource base—acquire and shed resources, integrate them together, and recombine them—to generate value-creating strategies.' General practice suggests that the concept of competencies is most often applied in the context of a firm's corporate diversification strategy. Knowledge is clearly a special case—albeit an important one—of some of these other terms or concepts.

While these distinctions among types of resources can be drawn and can be helpful in understanding the full range of resources a firm may possess, the effort to make these distinctions has had at least one unfortunate side effect: those who have developed new ways to describe a firm's resources have often labeled their work as a 'new' theory of persistent superior performance. Thus, the strategic management literature currently has proponents of 'resource-based theories of superior performance', 'capability theories of superior firm performance', 'dynamic capability theories of superior performance', 'competence theories of superior performance', and 'knowledge-based theories of superior performance'.

While each of these 'theories' has a slightly different way of characterizing firm attributes, they share the same underlying theoretical structure. All focus on similar kinds of firm attributes as critical independent variables, specify about the same conditions under which these firm attributes will generate persistent superior performance, and lead to largely interchangeable empirically testable assertions. Battles over the label of this common theoretical framework are an extreme example of a classic academic 'tempest in a tea pot'—'full of sound and fury but signifying nothing'.

Given this state of affairs, the following conventions have been adopted throughout this book. First, the terms resources and capabilities will be used interchangeably and often in parallel. Second, the term core competence is applied only in discussions of the conception or implementation of corporate diversification strategies (Prahalad and Hamel 1990).

A variety of authors have generated lists of firm resources, capabilities, and competencies that enable firms to conceive and implement value-creating strategies (Thompson and Strickland 1983; Hitt and Ireland 1986; Grant 1991; Hall 1992; Amit and Schoemaker 1993; Collis and Montgomery 1995; Hitt, Ireland, and Hoskisson 1997). For purposes of this discussion, these numerous possible firm resources can be conveniently classified into four categories: physical capital resources (Williamson 1975), financial capital resources, human capital resources (Becker 1964), and organizational capital resources (Tomer 1987). Physical capital resources include the physical technology used in a firm, a firm's plant and equipment, its geographic location, and its access to raw materials. Financial capital resources include all a firm's many revenues, including its debt, equity, and retained earnings. Human capital resources include the training, experience, judgment, intelligence, relationships, and insight of individual managers and workers in a firm. Organizational capital resources include attributes of collections of individuals associated with a firm, such as a firm's culture, its formal reporting structure, its formal and informal planning, controlling, and coordinating systems, its reputation in the marketplace, as well as informal relations among groups within a firm and between a firm and those in its environment.

THE DEFINITION OF COMPETITIVE ADVANTAGE IN RESOURCE-BASED THEORY

Second, there has also been much debate recently about the dependent variable in resource-based theory, variously identified as 'competitive advantage', 'sustained competitive advantage', and 'economic rents'. Competitive advantage can be defined as follows:

> An enterprise has a *Competitive Advantage* if it is able to create more economic value than the marginal (break even) competitor in its product market. (Peteraf and Barney 2003: 314)

This definition is consistent in spirit with the definition of competitive advantage provided by Barney (1986*a*, 1991*a*) and with the usage of this term by Porter (1985). It is consistent, as well with the value-based approach to competitive advantage presented in Peteraf (2001). It resembles the value-creation frameworks of Brandenburger and Stuart (1996) and of Besanko et al. (2000), though it differs in terms of its reference point. Its precise meaning, of course, depends on a clear definition of what it means to 'create economic value'. Thus 'economic value' is defined in concert with the definition of competitive advantage.

> The *Economic Value* created by an enterprise in the course of providing a good or service is the difference between the perceived benefits gained by the purchasers of the good and the economic cost to the enterprise. (Peteraf and Barney 2003: 314)

Several things about this definition are notable. First, it is a *net* benefits approach to value creation. It is the benefits produced by a firm's undertakings, net of their costs. Chapter 2 of this book focuses on identifying precisely what the total costs associated with conceiving and implementing a strategy are.

Second, it is a view of value creation closely aligned with fundamental economic principles. Value is expressed in terms of the difference between perceived benefits, or customer willingness-to-pay, on the one hand, and economic costs on the other. This is, in essence, the same as the economic concept of *total surplus*, which equals the sum of the economic rents (*producer surplus*) and customers' 'value for the money' or *consumer surplus*. The definition supports the notion that the value that an enterprise creates has the potential to enhance the welfare of all of its stakeholders. It is independent of the price of the product, though prices serve to allocate the surplus (see Figure 1.2).

Third, it emphasizes *perceived* benefits, suggesting that the perceptions of consumers, rather than some absolute notion of quality differentials, are what really matter. This is consistent with a marketing view of how value is created.

Finally, greater value implies greater *efficiency*. To create more value than its rivals, an enterprise must either produce greater benefits for the same cost or the same benefits for a lower cost. Thus it supports an efficiency view of resource-based theory.

Taken together, these two definitions (of competitive advantage and of economic value) provide a precise picture of what a competitive advantage consists, as well as how it may be achieved, in the most general terms.

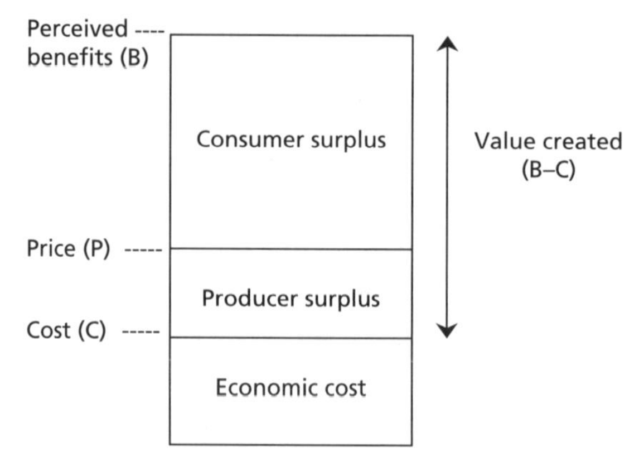

Figure 1.2. Prices allocate the value created

Competitive advantage is expressed in terms of the ability to create relatively more economic value. To create more value than its rivals, an enterprise must produce greater net benefits, through superior differentiation and/or lower costs. The benchmark for comparison is the marginal competitor. This implies that a competitive advantage may be held by several or even many firms in a given industry and suggests that there may be several different routes to competitive advantage. It simply requires an enterprise to be a superior value generator, relative to the least efficient competitor capable of breaking even. An enterprise with competitive advantage need not be the very best performer in all dimensions.

These definitions can also link competitive advantage to economic rents. Begin by comparing the situation of two single-business firms competing in a product market, one of which has a competitive advantage over the other (see Figure 1.3). For illustrative purposes, we assume that the focal firm, firm A, creates $180 of economic value for each unit of output that it provides the market, while its rival, firm B, creates only $150 of value per unit of output. Note that economic value can be expressed in monetary terms, since the level of perceived benefits is reflected in the customers' maximum willingness-to-pay for the good, while economic costs have a corresponding dollar counterpart.

In this scenario, product price determines how much of the economic value created by a firm is distributed to customers, in terms of benefits received over and above their cost to the consumer (price paid). If each

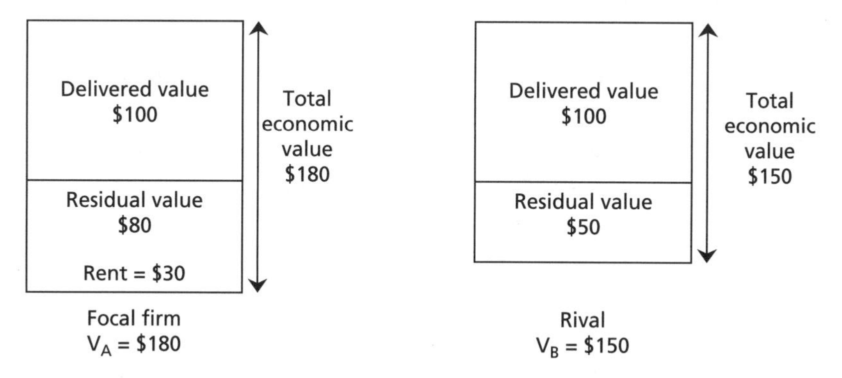

Figure 1.3. Greater economic value supports the generation of rent

firm delivers the same level of benefits to consumers, say $100, firm A will have a pool of *residual value* that exceeds that of firm B by $30 ($80–$50).

What is residual value? It is what is left over after the consumers have been allocated a share of the total value. This is the share of total value that remains to be divided among other claimants, including the firm. In Figure 1.3, the residual value available to firm A is $80, while firm B has only $50 of total value left to allocate. Firm A has a positive differential in residual value of $30 ($80–$50). What does this positive differential in residual value represent? This, of course, is firm A's competitive advantage over firm B, and it provides a protective cushion for A against competition from B.

To illustrate this, imagine that fierce price competition breaks out in this product market. Under such conditions, each firm will continue to lower prices in an effort to attract one another's customers until prices reach that point at which one of the firms is no longer willing to supply. For either firm, that will occur at the point that its residual value dips below zero. (When the residual pool of value is zero, there is nothing left for the firm to claim over and above its economic costs. When the residual value is negative, the firm cannot even recover its costs.) Since B will reach that point first, B will become the marginal, breakeven competitor and prices will stabilize. Firm A can continue to produce profitably, due to its cushion of $30 per unit.

Alternatively, the competition between A and B could take place on the cost side, through, say, greater advertising or auxiliary services. This kind of competition will also whittle away at the residual value. Once again, the limit to this competition occurs when the residual value of the least efficient firm is completely dissipated. That firm again is firm B, leaving A with a residual of $30 per unit.

This pool of excess residual value is equal to the *economic rents* attributable to the more efficient factors of firm A. *Economic rents* are defined as *returns to a factor in excess of its opportunity costs*. To understand why it is possible to view this excess value as a rent, consider a firm that possesses scarce resources and capabilities that enable it to increase the amount of economic value it creates. The greater value that is generated by these resources and capabilities is properly viewed as a *rent* to these scarce critical resources. It is a 'return' to resources in the sense that the production of the rent is dependent on the efficiency differences among the resources in use. Without the more efficient resources, the rent would cease to exist. It is a return above the opportunity costs of resources of this general type, in that it exceeds the opportunity cost of the marginally productive resources. It is greater than the return necessary to draw resources of this general type into production. It is not, however, a return to the resource in the sense that the resource holder necessarily receives the surplus value. How this excess residual value is divided among the firm and other claimants requires further analysis (Peteraf 1993, 2001; Coff 1999). See Figure 1.4 for a summary of the connection between resources, residual value, and rents.

Of course, the rents that are generated in this manner may be fleeting and of limited consequence. What is more interesting is whether the rents can be sustained for some period and whether the firm has any hope of claiming them in the form of superior profits. These questions are also

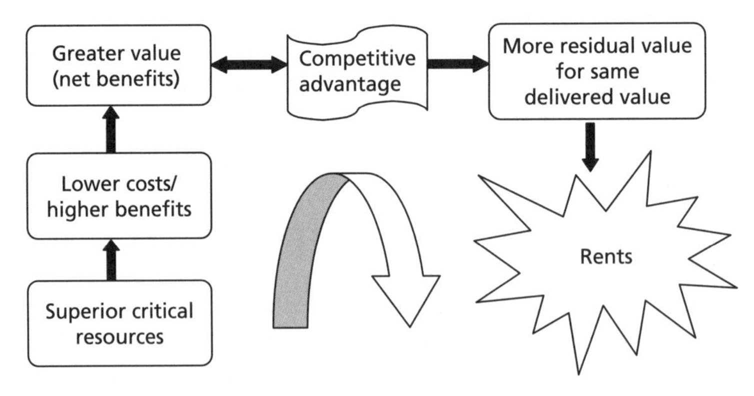

Figure 1.4. The chain of logic from resources to rents

addressed by resource-based theory and are discussed later in this book (Barney 1991*a*; Peteraf 1993).

Because, in general, it is possible to always link competitive advantages and economic rents, these two terms are used interchangeably throughout this book. However, since firms do not necessarily appropriate all the competitive advantage and economic rents they generate, the term *firm profits* will only be applied to that part of the competitive advantage/economic rent a firm is able to appropriate.

Summary and overview book plan

This chapter began by distinguishing between two explanations of sustained superior firm performance—market power explanations and efficiency explanations—and suggesting that the primary topic of this book—resource-based theory—is an example of the second type of explanation. Then, four papers that were central to the development of resource-based theory were introduced, along with a brief discussion of work that evolved largely independent of resource-based theory as it was developing, but is very consistent with that theory. The chapter concluded with some additional remarks—about the different terms used to describe the factors of production controlled by a firm and about definitions of competitive advantage and economic rents.

In Chapter 2, the competitive nature of strategic factor markets is described and discussed. In Chapter 3 the resource-based framework for evaluating resources as potential sources of sustained competitive advantage for a firm is outlined. The VRIO framework is presented and implications of resource-based theory for other business disciplines are considered.

In Part II, applications of resource-based theory for specific organizational capabilities are outlined. The potential of four capabilities to be sources of sustained competitive advantage is considered including: organizational culture (Chapter 4), trust (Chapter 5), human resource (HR) practices (Chapter 6), and information technology (IT) (Chapter 7).

In Part III, applications of the resource-based logic to three key strategies are presented. The business and corporate strategies featured include: vertical integration (Chapter 8), diversification (Chapter 9), and mergers and acquisitions (Chapter 10).

In Part IV, an overview of the current state of resource-based theory is presented. First, a summary of empirical research that has been conducted to date based on the resource-based logic is presented in Chapter 11. Finally, current issues in the development of resource-based theory are discussed and topics for future development of resource-based theory are presented in Chapter 12.

NOTES

1. The contributions of, and relationships among, these early resource-based papers are subject to significant personal interpretation. The history described here is one interpretation, but certainly not the only interpretation, of those contributions and relationships. It is also the case that the history described here is not meant to emphasize some contributions over others. Our view is that, collectively, authors like Barney, Cool, Dierickx, Hamel, Montgomery, Prahalad, Rumelt, Teece, and Wernerfelt were all very important in the creation and development of resource-based theory, broadly interpreted.
2. These ideas were also considered in the economics literature by Richard Langlois (1992, *Industrial and Corporate Change*), and Nicolai Foss (1993, *Journal of Evolutionary Economics*). Contributions by Winter (1987) and Demsetz (1973) are also important.
3. Barney (1986*a*) was inspired by a not very well-known paper by Rumelt and Wensley (1981*b*) published only in the *Proceedings of the Academy of Management*. In that paper, Rumelt and Wensley suggest for the existence of the 'market for market share' and argue that if the market for market share is perfectly competitive, that increases in market share will not lead to increases in firm performance. Rumelt and Wensley also provide some rigorous empirical support for this assertion. If pressed to describe the 'very first' resource-based paper published, a good argument could be made for Rumelt and Wensley (1981*b*).
4. Conner (1991), Castanias and Helfat (1991), and Barney (1991*a*) were all published in a special theory forum in the *Journal of Management* edited by Barney. See Barney (1991*c*). Interestingly, Peteraf (1993) and Teece, Pisano, and Shuen (1997) were both originally submitted to this special theory forum. Later, they were each published in the *Strategic Management Journal*.
5. This said, conversations with Prahalad suggest that he does not see this work as an example of resource-based logic. Some other of Prahalad's work, however, is explicitly cast in resource-based terms, e.g. Conner and Prahalad (1996).

2 Strategic factor markets and competitive advantage*

Historically, strategic management scholars focused on competitive imperfections in product markets to explain persistent differences in firm performance (Porter 1980). This emphasis on product markets is quite reasonable since most economic logic suggests that when product markets are perfectly competitive, firms in these markets will earn a rate of return just large enough to cover their cost of capital (Foss and Knudsen 2003). Logically, it seems to follow that if product markets are competitively imperfect, then at least some firms in these markets will be able to earn superior levels of firm performance.

Work on competitive imperfections in product markets has evolved dramatically over the years. In economics, the number of papers and theories describing the social welfare and other implications of various forms of competitive imperfections in product markets continues to proliferate (Segal 1998; Hsu and Wang 2005; Smythe and Zhao 2006). In strategic management, Porter's 'five forces framework' (Porter 1980) describes competitive imperfections in product markets and how, apparently, these competitive imperfections can be used to create opportunities to earn superior returns.

However, that a firm operating in an imperfectly competitive product market may earn superior levels of performance is not the same thing as asserting that a firm that implements strategies to create an imperfectly competitive product market will earn such performance. Whether implementing strategies that create imperfectly competitive product markets

* This chapter draws from Barney (1986*a*).

generates superior performance depends on both the revenues created by these strategies when implemented in product markets and the total cost of their implementation. This cost includes not just the specific expenses associated with implementing a particular product market strategy, but also the expenses associated with developing the resources necessary to conceive and implement this product market strategy in the first place.

A failure to account for the full costs associated with developing strategic resources can lead firms to overstate the returns generated by implementing their product market strategies. This chapter argues that—except in specific conditions described here—the total cost of these resources will often equal their value in creating imperfect product market competition. In this situation, even if a firm is successful in creating an imperfectly competitive product market, it will still not be able to earn superior levels of performance. This suggests that the historical emphasis in the strategic management literature on competitive imperfections in product markets is mistaken—such competitive imperfections, per se, may or may not be a source of superior performance for a firm depending on the cost of the resources needed to create these imperfections.

The conceptual tool used to discuss the cost of the resources necessary to conceive and implement a strategy designed to create imperfect product market competition is the strategic factor market mentioned briefly in Chapter 1. A strategic factor market is the market where the cost of the resources used to conceive and implement a firm's product market strategies is determined. For example, if a firm decides that an acquisition will help create imperfect competition in a particular product market, it must enter the market for corporate control. The market for corporate control—as a strategic factor market—is the market where the cost of using an acquisition to create an imperfectly competitive product market is determined. If the cost of an acquisition equals the value of the imperfect competition in a product market this acquisition creates, then it will not generate superior performance for a firm, even if it actually creates imperfect product market competition.

All the resources a firm uses to conceive and implement its product market strategies have, or have had, strategic factor markets associated with them. Some of these factor markets have been studied in detail, for example, the market for corporate control. Others have received less theoretical or empirical attention, for example, the market for the creative capability of entrepreneurs. This chapter examines the relationship between the competitiveness of these strategic factor markets, the cost of the resources used by a firm to conceive and implement its product market strategies, and the ability of those strategies to generate superior levels of performance.

This discussion is developed in four parts. First, it is shown that when strategic factor markets are perfectly competitive, the cost of the resources developed in those markets will equal the value they generate when used to conceive and implement product market strategies. In such settings, firms will not obtain competitive advantages, even if they are able to create imperfect product market competition. Second, it is argued that firms that expect to obtain economic rents from conceiving and implementing product market strategies must have more accurate expectations about the value of these resources than other firms competing to develop them.[1] Third, it is also shown that other apparent sources of advantage in developing resources—including the apparent nontradability of some resources (Dierickx and Cool 1989)—are, in reality, just examples of these more accurate expectations or a manifestation of a firm's good luck. Finally, some ways that firms can become better informed about the future value of the resources they are developing, including through the analysis of a firm's competitive environment and through the analysis of resources it already controls, are discussed. It is shown that environmental analysis, by itself, cannot be expected to create the required insights, while in some circumstances, the analysis of a firm's current resources can.

Perfect strategic factor market competition

When firms seeking to develop resources to implement a strategy (strategizers) and those who currently own or control these resources (controllers) have exactly the same, and perfectly accurate, expectations about the future value of product market strategies before they are actually implemented, then the price of the resources needed to conceive and implement these strategies will approximately equal their value once they are actually implemented. This is a conclusion of zero economic rents consistent with all perfect information models of competition where no competitive uncertainty exists (Lippman and Rumelt 1982). Under these perfect expectation conditions, controllers will never make their resources available if the full value of those resources is not reflected in their price, nor will strategizers pay a price for a resource greater than its value in actually implementing a strategy. In such markets, all rents that could have been had when the strategy in question was implemented will be anticipated and competed away.

This conclusion has been examined empirically in several different strategic factor markets. For example, in the market for corporate control, it has been well documented that when several firms compete to acquire the same target to accomplish the same strategic objectives, that the price of this target will rapidly rise to equal its value in realizing this strategic objective (Jensen and Ruback 1983). This is one reason that bidding firms in the market for corporate control usually just break even on their merger and acquisition strategies.

However, this conclusion also applies to some less well-studied strategic factor markets. For example, suppose a firm concludes that, in order to implement its product market strategies, it must enhance the reputation of its products. Enhancing product reputation is likely to require several strategic resources—some of which a firm may already possess and some of which it may need to develop. For example, this firm is likely to have to hire some quality management professionals, consultants, and employees who will then have to change this firm's orientation toward quality. Alternatively, this firm may invest to train some of its current employees in quality processes. Also, this firm is likely to have to hire or train some research and development specialists to develop new extensions of its current products, some marketing people to help position these products in the marketplace, and sales people who can sell this new type of product. It is also likely to have to invest in marketing campaigns to help develop its product market reputation. Of course, to the extent that this firm's competition becomes aware of its strategies, they might also begin to assemble the resources needed to compete in this new way.

The aggregate cost of developing the resources necessary to implement this new product market strategy—whether through hiring new employees, training and reassigning current employees, or making other investments—can be substantial. If those that control each of these resources—be they current or future employees, marketing outlets, and so forth—anticipate their impact on this firm's ability to implement its new strategy, they will each require a payment equal to the value of their resource for the firm.[2] In this setting, the total cost of developing the resources necessary to implement this product market strategy will equal the value this strategy creates in the product market, and even if this firm is successful in creating competitive imperfections in the product market, it will still not generate competitive advantages.

Heterogeneous expectations in strategic factor markets

These perfect competition dynamics, and the zero economic rents from implementing strategies they imply, depend, of course, on the very strong assumption that all strategizers and controllers have the same, and perfectly accurate, expectations concerning the future value of strategies. This is a condition that is not likely to exist very often in real strategic factor markets.

More commonly, different strategizers and controllers in these markets will have different expectations about the future value of a strategy. Because of these differences, some expectations will be more accurate than others, although strategizers and controllers will typically not know, with certainty, ahead of time, how accurate their expectations are. When different strategizers and controllers have different expectations concerning the future value of a strategy, it will often be possible for some strategizers to generate rents from developing or acquiring the resources necessary to conceive and implement a product market strategy and then implementing that strategy.

Consider first the return potential of a strategizer that has more accurate expectations concerning the future value of a particular product market strategy than others—either other strategizers or controllers—who might be interested in this strategy. Two likely possibilities exist. On the one hand, several others might overestimate a strategy's return potential. This overestimation will typically lead to strategic factor market entry, competition, and the setting of a price for the relevant strategic resource *greater* than the actual value of that resource when it is used to implement a strategy.

In this situation, those with more accurate expectations concerning the return potential of a strategy will usually not enter the strategic factor market, for they will believe that in doing so they will probably sustain an economic loss by paying more for a strategic resource than that resource is worth in implementing a strategy. Thus, in the long run, those with more accurate expectations will usually be able to avoid economic losses associated with buying overpriced strategic resources. Those that do pay for these overpriced resources suffer from the 'winner's curse', that is, the fact that they successfully develop the resources in question suggests that they overpaid (Bazerman and Samuelson 1983).

The second possibility facing those with more accurate expectations is that others, rather than overestimating the return potential of a strategy, might underestimate that strategy's true future value. Competition in the strategic factor market would, in this case, typically lead to a strategic resource price less than the actual future value of the strategy. In this situation, those with more accurate expectations about the future value of the strategy in question will enter the strategic factor market and will pay the same for the relevant strategic resource as those with less accurate (i.e. pessimistic) expectations. The cost of these resources will not be any less to those with more accurate expectations because of the inaccurate expectations held by ill-informed controllers and strategizers. And those with more accurate expectations will certainly not want to spend more than necessary for these resources. As strategies are implemented, equal competitive advantages will accrue to all those firms that use the resource in question to implement this strategy, the well-informed and ill-informed alike.

Thus, on the one hand, those with more accurate expectations concerning the future value of a strategy can avoid economic losses due to optimistic expectations. On the other hand, these firms will also be able to anticipate and exploit any opportunities for competitive advantage in strategic factor markets when they exist. Thus, by avoiding losses and exploiting rent generating opportunities, these firms, over the long run, can expect to perform better than firms with less accurate expectations about the future value of strategies.

Despite the advantages of having a superior understanding of a strategy's return potential when acquiring or developing the resources necessary to implement that strategy, firms without this superior insight can still obtain economic rents when implementing strategies. This can occur when several of these firms underestimate the potential of a strategy to create economic value. Because of this underestimation, the cost of the resources necessary to implement a strategy will be less than the actual future value of the strategy. In this sense, these firms are able to buy a strategy generated cash flow for less than the value of that cash flow. However, this competitive advantage must be a manifestation of these firms' good fortune and luck, for the price of the strategic resource developed was based on expectations about the value-creating potential of that strategy. Value greater than what was expected is, by definition, unexpected. Unexpected superior economic returns are just that, unexpected, a surprise, and a manifestation of a firm's good luck, not of its ability to accurately anticipate the future value of a strategy.

Even well-informed firms can be lucky in this manner. Whenever the actual value created by a strategy is greater than *expected* returns, the resulting difference is a manifestation of a firm's unexpected good fortune. The more accurate a firm's expectations about a strategy's potential, the less a role luck will play in generating competitive advantages. In the extreme, though probably very rare case, where a firm knows with certainty the value potential of a strategy before that strategy is implemented, there can be no unexpected value created by implementing strategies and thus no financial surprises. However, to the extent that a firm has less than perfect expectations, luck can play a role in determining a firm's competitive advantage from implementing its strategies.

Other apparent competitive imperfections: the question of tradability

Firms with consistently more accurate expectations concerning the value-creating potential of strategies they are implementing can expect to enjoy competitive advantages from implementing their strategies over the long run. In this sense, differences in firm expectations constitute a strategic factor market competitive imperfection.

Some have suggested that other differences between firms, besides differences in firm expectations, can create competitive imperfections in strategic factor markets. These firm differences, it is thought, can prevent certain firms from implementing strategies that other firms can implement. However, close analysis of these other differences between firms suggests that, to the extent that they constitute competitive imperfections in strategic factor markets, they are actually a manifestation of different expectations firms hold about the future value of strategies being implemented. In this sense, differences in firm expectations are the central source of competitive advantages from developing or acquiring resources to implement product market strategies.

LACK OF SEPARATION

It has been suggested that a competitive imperfection in a strategic factor market exists when a small number of firms seeking to implement a strategy already control all the resources necessary to implement it. In this setting, these firms do not need to develop the resources necessary to implement a strategy, and thus apparently stand in some competitive advantage. An example of this lack of separation might include a uniquely well-managed firm seeking to implement a low-cost manufacturing strategy. Such a firm already controls most, if not all, the resources necessary to implement such a strategy and thus is apparently at an advantage compared to firms that would have to improve their efficiency in order to implement such a strategy (Porter 1980).

Indeed, Dierickx and Cool's argument (1989) about the limitations of strategic factor market theory is a special case of this lack of separation argument. These authors suggest that many resources that are relevant in creating imperfect product market competition are not tradable, and thus not subject to the competitive pressures that exist in strategic factor markets. Dierickx and Cool (1989) argue that it is this lack of tradability, not imperfectly competitive factor markets, that enables firms to gain competitive advantages from exploiting their resources in creating imperfectly competitive product markets.

Of course, there is little doubt that some of the specific resources controlled by a firm are not tradable. For example, one firm cannot sell its culture to another firm; one firm cannot sell the teamwork among its managers to another firm. However, that these resources, individually, are not currently tradable does not mean that they are, and always have been, immune to the competitive pressures of strategic factor markets. This is true for several reasons.

First, the nontradable assets that a firm currently possesses are, according to Dierickx and Cool (1989) and Barney (1986*b*), developed over long periods. Indeed, the path-dependent nature of these resources is what creates the asset interconnectedness that Dierickx and Cool (1989) cite as one of the major reasons resources may not be tradable. However, over this period, these resources require investment and commitment in order to develop. The sum of these costs is what must be balanced against the revenues that any strategies exploiting these resources may create. If these costs are greater than this value, then even when firms use these resources to generate imperfect product market competition, no competitive advantages are generated.

While understanding these costs is important in understanding the full value created by a strategy, it is not unreasonable to believe that when these investments in an emerging resource are made, both those controlling these resources and those looking to invest in these resources will not have the same and perfectly accurate expectations about their future value. These resources evolve in ways that are difficult to predict and may enable the implementation of product market strategies that cannot yet be anticipated. That is, the strategic factor markets within which these resources are developed are clearly imperfect. If strategizers have more accurate expectations about the future value of the resources they are investing in than controllers and other strategizers, these 'internally evolved' resources can be expected to be sources of competitive advantage. If both strategizers and controllers underestimate the future value of these resources, competitive advantages can still be generated, but they will be a manifestation of a firm's good luck.

Put differently, that resources are not tradable is not, by itself, the reason resources can be sources of competitive advantage. Rather, it is the imperfectly competitive factor markets through which these resources are developed that enable some of these resources to be sources of economic rents when they are used to implement product market strategies. Thus, rather than suggesting that strategic factor markets are irrelevant in understanding the rent generating potential of resources, Dierickx and Cool's argument (1989) identifies several different reasons that a particular strategic factor market may be imperfectly competitive.

UNIQUENESS

Others have argued that when only one firm can implement a strategy, then a strategic factor market competitive imperfection exists (Arthur 1984). Such a firm may have a unique history or constellation of other assets, and thus may uniquely be able to pursue a strategy. In such settings, competitive dynamics cannot unfold, and uniquely strategizing firms could obtain competitive advantages from acquiring strategic resources and implementing strategies.

However, as before, a firm's uniqueness is actually a manifestation of the expectational attributes of previous strategic factor markets. The key issues become: 'How did the strategizing firm obtain the unique assets that allow it to develop the unique strategy it is implementing?', 'What price did this firm have to pay for these assets?', 'What price must potential strategizers pay in order to reproduce this set of organizational assets so that they can enter and create a competitive strategic factor market?', and 'What are the opportunity costs associated with using these resources to implement a strategy?' If the current value of 'unique' resources in implementing a strategy was anticipated at the time those resources were acquired or developed, then competitive advantages would not exist.

LACK OF ENTRY

Another source of an apparent competitive imperfection in a strategic factor market exists when firms that could enter such a market by becoming strategizers do not do so. This lack of entry, however, like separation and uniqueness is actually a special case of the expectations firms hold about the future value of strategies. Lack of entry might occur for one of at least three reasons. First, firms that, in principle, could enter might not because they are not attempting to act in a profit-maximizing manner. Second, potential strategizers may not have sufficient financial strength to enter a strategic factor market and compete for strategic resource. Finally, firms that, in principle, could enter, may not know how to, for they may not understand the return generating characteristics of the strategies that current strategizers are implementing. Each of these possibilities is considered in order.

Profit maximizing

Firms may abandon profit-maximizing behavior for several reasons. For example, managers may engage in activities that improve their situation in a firm, even if those activities do not maximize firm performance (Jensen and Meckling 1976). Also managers may be subject to a variety of systematic biases in their decision-making, biases that lead to decisions that are inconsistent with profit maximization (Busenitz and Barney 1997; Hirshleifer and Hirshleifer 1998). For these and other reasons, it would not be surprising to see firms fail to engage in profit-maximizing behavior some of the time.

However, over the long term, failure to maximize profits can put a firm's survival at risk. Moreover, markets typically react whenever a firm veers from profit maximizing in some significant ways: additional corporate governance is put into place to reign in agency problems (Jensen 1986) and unfriendly takeovers replace managers engaging in grossly biased decision-making (Jensen 1988). In the long run, as these reasons for not engaging in profit-maximizing become less relevant, one possible reason why a firm may not enter into a strategic factor market remains: Differences in expectations about the future value of these resources. In this setting, it is not that firms are abandoning a profit-maximizing motive. Rather, firms may legitimately disagree how to realize this profit (Alchian 1950). This disagreement about the value of resources in implementing a product market strategy is what leads to the lack of entry, not abandoning profit-maximizing behavior (Shleifer 2000).

Financial strength

Another apparent strategic factor market competitive imperfection exists when only a few firms have enough financial backing to enter a strategic factor market and attempt to acquire or develop the resources needed to implement a product market strategy. Because only a few firms are competing for the relevant strategic resources, perfect competition dynamics are less likely to unfold, and it may be possible to obtain competitive advantages from using the acquired resources to implement a strategy.

However, even large differences in financial strength typically reflect expectational differences in strategic factor markets rather than differences between the financial strengths of firms, per se. Two ways in which differences in financial strength represent these differences in firm expectations are considered below.

First, in some circumstances, the actual future value of a given strategy may be the same for whatever firm implements it. In this case, if capital markets are efficient and well informed concerning the actual future value of a strategy, then funds will flow to firms wishing to enter a strategic factor market with anticipated positive economic rents. Sources of capital will recognize the possibility of these rents and will provide whatever funds are necessary to ensure that potential strategizers will enter and become actual strategizers (Copeland and Weston 1979). The same holds true for controllers. In this way, competition within a strategic factor market will grow, and any anticipated rents will approach zero. This entry will only *not* occur if capital sources are under-informed about the possibility that firms can obtain competitive advantage from acquiring resources to implement a strategy. In this situation, potential strategizers and controllers would not be able to obtain adequate financial backing from under-informed sources of capital to enter into the strategic factor market. This lack of entry creates the possibility of competitive advantages for firms that do enter.

However, when are capital sources likely to be under-informed concerning the anticipated returns from implementing a strategy? If potential strategizers and controllers are as well informed as actual strategizers and controllers, then it seems likely that the relevant information needed to generate return expectations falls into the general category of 'publicly available information', and thus would be taken into consideration by capital sources in making funding decisions (Fama 1970; Copeland and Weston 1979). Thus, only when actual strategizers and controllers have expectational advantages over potential strategizers and controllers is it likely that sources of capital will be under-informed. Thus, in this case, the lack of entry into a strategic factor market due to insufficient financial backing is, once again, a reflection of the expectational advantages enjoyed by some firms in a strategic factor market.

In an efficient capital market, when the actual future value of strategies does not depend on which firm implements them, then the inability of firms to attract sufficient financial support to enter and compete for strategic resources must reflect differences in expectations among current and potentially competing firms. However, sometimes a strategy implemented by one firm will have a greater future value than that same strategy implemented by other firms. In this situation, and under the assumption of efficient and well-informed capital markets, capital will flow to high-profit potential firms, while low-profit potential firms may not receive such financial backing (Copeland and Weston 1979). This lack of financial backing may prevent entry and thus constitute a competitive imperfection in a strategic factor market.

However, when can one firm implementing a strategy obtain competitive advantages from doing so compared to other firms implementing this strategy? The answer must be that this firm already controls other strategically relevant assets not controlled by other firms (Barney 1991*a*). Thus, this firm's ability to attract financial backing is a reflection of its unique portfolio of strategically valuable assets and resources, resources not controlled by other firms. In this sense, lack of entry is simply a special case of a firm implementing a unique strategy, and the previous discussion of expectations in strategic factor markets applies here as well. In short, firms with unique resources that give them the opportunity to gain competitive advantages are either exploiting special insights they had into the future value of those resources when those resources were acquired, or, if they enjoyed no such insights, they are simply enjoying their good fortune.

Lack of understanding

A final reason entry might not occur is that entrants may not understand the value generating processes underlying a strategy. Firms form their return expectations about specific strategies based on their understanding of the processes by which strategies generate economic value, that is, on their understanding of the cause and effect relations between organizational actions and economic value (Lippman and Rumelt 1982). Some of this understanding may be of the 'learning-by-doing' variety (Williamson 1975), and thus not available to potential strategizers and controllers. When potential entrants do not understand the relationship between organizational actions and economic value as well as current actors in a strategic factor market, potential entrants are likely to incorrectly estimate the true value of strategies. If they underestimate this value, then these firms will not enter the strategic factor market, even when expectations set with a more complete understanding of a strategy's value generating processes would suggest that entry was appropriate. Again this lack of entry, and the competitive imperfection that it might create, reflects the different expectations firms have about the potential of strategies to be implemented to generate economic value.

Developing insights into strategic value

Thus far, it has been argued that, in perfectly competitive strategic factor markets, the cost of the resources necessary to implement a strategy will approximately equal the discounted present value of that strategy once it is implemented. It has also been argued that competitive imperfections in this market can give firms opportunities for obtaining economic rents when implementing strategies, but that the existence of these imperfections depends on different firms having different expectations concerning the future value of a strategy. Other apparent competitive imperfections in strategic factor markets, including lack of separation, uniqueness, lack of entry, and different financial resources, in fact, reflect the expectational characteristics of either current or previous strategic factor markets.

In imperfectly competitive strategic factor markets, firms can obtain competitive advantages from acquiring the resources necessary to implement strategies in one or a combination of two ways. First, firms with consistently more accurate expectations about the future value of a strategy than other firms can use these insights to avoid economic losses and obtain economic rents when acquiring or developing resources to implement strategies. Second, firms can obtain competitive advantages through luck when they underestimate the true future value of a strategy. Thus, because luck is, by definition, out of a firm's control, an important question for managers becomes, 'How can firms become consistently better informed about the value of strategies they are implementing than any other firms?' Firms that are successful at doing this can, over time, expect to obtain higher returns from implementing strategies than less well-informed firms, although, as always, firms can be lucky.

There are fundamentally two possible sources of the informational advantages necessary to develop consistently more accurate insights into the value of strategies: the analysis of a firm's competitive environment and the analysis of organizational skills and capabilities already controlled by a firm (Stevenson 1976; Lenz 1980; Porter 1980; Barney 1985*a*, 1985*b*). Each of these possibilities is considered below.

ENVIRONMENTAL ANALYSIS

Of these two sources of insights into the future value of strategies, environmental analysis seems less likely to systematically generate the expectational advantages needed to obtain competitive advantage. This is because both the methodologies for collecting this information (Porter 1980; Thompson and Strickland 1980) and the conceptual models for analyzing it (e.g. Henderson 1979; Porter 1980) are in the public domain. It will normally be the case that firms applying approximately the same publicly available methodology to the analysis of the same environment will collect about the same information. And these same firms applying publicly available conceptual frameworks to analyze this information will typically come to similar conclusions about the potential of strategies. Thus, analyzing a firm's competitive environment cannot, on average, be expected to generate the expectational advantages that can lead to expected competitive advantages in strategic factor markets.

Some would suggest that it is not the availability of these environmental methods of data collection and analysis that is important, but rather the skill with which these methods are applied. More skilled firms can thus generate the required expectational advantages through an analysis of the competitive environment. However, the skills of environmental analysis can be 'rented' from various investment banking and consulting firms, and thus skill advantages in analyzing competitive environments will typically only be temporary.

It may be the case that, in the collection of information concerning the value of a strategy from a firm's competitive environment, a firm might 'stumble' onto some information that gives it an expectational advantage over other firms. However, if such information was obtained through the systematic application of environmental analysis techniques, then other firms besides the firm that has this information would have obtained it and it would no longer give an advantage. Thus, only if the information was obtained through nonsystematic means can it give a firm expectational advantage. However, such information, because it does not result from the systematic application of environmental analysis methodologies, must be stochastic in origin. Any informational advantages obtained in this manner must reflect a firm's good fortune and luck, not their skill in evaluating the return potential of strategies.

ORGANIZATIONAL ANALYSIS

While firms cannot obtain systematic expectational advantages from an analysis of the competitive characteristics of their environment, it may be possible, under certain conditions, to obtain such advantages by turning inwardly and analyzing information about the assets a firm already controls. Firms will usually enjoy access to this type of information that is not available to other firms. If these assets also have the potential to be used to implement valuable product market strategies, and if similar assets are not controlled by large numbers of competing firms, then they can be a source of competitive advantage. Examples of the types of organizational assets that might generate such expectations include special manufacturing know-how (Williamson 1975), unique combinations of business experience in a firm (Chamberlin 1933), and the teamwork of managers in a firm (Alchian and Demsetz 1972). Firms endowed with such organizational skills and abilities can be consistently better informed concerning the true future value of strategies they implement than other firms by exploiting these assets when choosing strategies to implement.

Conclusion

In summary, firms seeking to obtain competitive advantages from implementing product market strategies must have consistently more accurate expectations about the future value of those strategies when developing or acquiring the resources necessary to implement them, although firms can be lucky. Moreover, while it is usually not possible to obtain these advantages through the analysis of a firm's competitive environment, firms can sometimes obtain them when choosing to implement strategies that exploit resources already under their control.

These conclusions have important implications for the practice and theory of strategy. For example, firms that do not look inwardly to exploit resources they already control in choosing strategies cannot expect to obtain competitive advantages from their strategizing efforts. For a strategy of diversification through acquisition, this implies that firms that fail to discover unique synergies between themselves and potential acquisitions, but rather rely only on publicly available information when pricing an acquisition, cannot expect competitive advantages from their acquisition strategies, though these firms might be lucky and acquire a firm with an unanticipated synergy. For a low-cost manufacturing strategy, these arguments suggest that firms without any special skills at low-cost manufacturing cannot expect competitive advantages from imitating the low-cost manufacturing strategies of other firms, while firms with cultural or other advantages in low-cost manufacturing, if few other firms have these same advantages, can exploit them to obtain such advantages (Ouchi 1981; Peters and Waterman 1982, 2004). Also firms that currently enjoy competitive advantages may do so because of unique insights and abilities they controlled when their strategies were chosen. On the other hand, these firms might also have been lucky. Thus, competitive advantage is not always a sign of strategizing and managerial excellence (Peters and Waterman 1982, 2004).

This emphasis on the nature of the competition for the resources needed to implement strategies differs from previous work in the field of strategy. Much of this research was based on the observation that firms which compete in imperfectly competitive *product* markets enjoy competitive advantages (Porter 1980). As a description of the correlation between imperfect product market competition and economic rents, this research has significant theoretical and empirical support (Hirshleifer 1980). Its implications for managers are less clear. Simply because firms that compete in imperfectly competitive product markets earn economic rents does not necessarily imply that firms that adopt strategies to *create* these product market imperfections will enjoy such performance. As suggested here, this will depend on the competitive characteristics of the markets through which the resources necessary to implement these strategies are developed or acquired, that is, on the competitive characteristics of strategic factor markets.

Perhaps the central conclusion of the arguments developed here is that the search for competitive advantage and superior firm performance must begin with an analysis of the resources and capabilities a firm currently controls. But of all the assets currently controlled by a firm, which are most likely to be a source of sustained competitive advantage? This question is addressed in more detail in Chapter 3.

NOTES

1. As suggested in Barney (1986*a*), economic rents can also be unexpected. However, these will be a manifestation of a firm's good luck rather than its strategic choices. This possibility is also discussed briefly below.
2. How this total cost is allocated across these different, but interrelated, strategic factor markets depends on the relative contribution of each of these factors of production to a firm's ability to conceive and implement successful product market strategies. See Coff (1999).

3 Firm resources and sustained competitive advantage*

Chapter 1 of this book defined and developed the strategic management question—Why do some firms outperform other firms?—and described the evolution of resource-based theory as one approach to answering this question. Chapter 2 introduced the concept of a strategic factor market to demonstrate that whether a firm gains competitive advantages does not depend just on strategies that create competitive imperfections in product markets, but on the total cost of implementing these strategies. This total cost is determined by the competitiveness of strategic factor markets. One of the central conclusions of this argument is that firms that exploit resources and capabilities they already control in choosing and implementing strategies are more likely to gain competitive advantages than firms that acquire the resources and capabilities they need to implement a strategy in more competitive factor markets.

Of course, this conclusion is hardly unique to resource-based theory. Indeed, identifying and exploiting a firm's strengths while avoiding its weaknesses has been one of the central features of one of the oldest organizing frameworks in the field of strategic management—the SWOT framework (Ansoff 1965; Andrews 1971; Hofer and Schendel 1978). This framework, summarized in Figure 3.1, suggests that firms obtain competitive advantages by implementing strategies that exploit their internal strengths, through responding to environmental opportunities, while neutralizing external threats and avoiding internal weaknesses. Most research on sources of competitive advantage has focused either on isolating a firm's opportunities and threats (Porter 1980, 1985), describing its strengths and weaknesses (Penrose 1959; Stinchcombe 1965;

* This chapter draws from Barney (1991*a*).

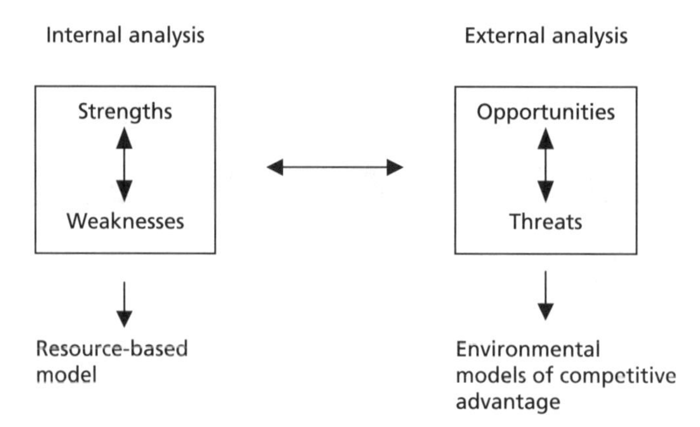

Figure 3.1. The relationship between traditional 'SWOT' analysis, the resource-based model, and models of industry attractiveness

Hofer and Schendel 1978), or analyzing how these are matched to choose strategies.

While SWOT analysis does draw attention to the important role of understanding a firm's internal capabilities in choosing strategies, it has at least one important limitation in this regard: there is, in this framework, no logic provided to identify a firm's strengths or weaknesses. That is, the framework suggests that, for example, firms should choose strategies that exploit their strengths, but no mechanism is described through which these strengths can be identified.

In practice, applications of SWOT analysis often devolve into generating lists of 'things' a firm is 'good' at, together with lists of 'things' a firm is 'not so good' at. This can lead to what has sometimes been called 'decision-making by list length'—whatever strategic option gets the most strengths listed for it is the best strategy. Sometimes, the results of this list making are almost comical. For example, if you ask successful entrepreneurs why they are successful, they will routinely identify three central strengths—they worked hard, they took risks, and they surrounded themselves by good people. Ask failed entrepreneurs what happened, and they will often shrug their shoulders: 'I don't know, I worked hard, took risks, and surrounded myself by good people.' You ask CEOs what their firm's core strengths are; they almost always identify their top management team. When asked to evaluate their competition's top management teams, CEOs instantly acknowledge, 'They are really good, too.'

Perhaps the most extreme example of listing as strategic analysis was shared at a meeting of the Strategic Management Society.[1] A consultant described an unnamed company whose CEO decided that the firm would only keep any of its diversified operations if those operations 'contributed to the core competence of the corporation'. Division managers were given several months to develop ways that their business units helped define the 'strengths' of the corporation. The average division identified over 500 ways it contributed to the core competence of this corporation!

One way to help resolve this problem might be to turn to the literature that helps firms identify environmental opportunities and threats. However, this literature—exemplified in Porter's five forces framework (1980)—has implicitly adopted two simplifying assumptions. First, these environmental tools have assumed that firms within an industry (or firms within a strategic group) are, except for firm size, essentially the same in terms of the strategically relevant resources they control and the strategies they pursue (Scherer 1980; Porter 1981; Rumelt 1984). Second, these models assume that should resource heterogeneity develop in an industry or group (perhaps through new entry), this heterogeneity will be very short lived because the resources that firms use to implement their strategies are highly mobile (i.e. they can be bought and sold in factor markets, see Chapter 2).[2]

The link between a firm's internal characteristics and performance obviously cannot build on these same assumptions. These assumptions effectively eliminate firm resource heterogeneity and immobility as possible sources of competitive advantage (Penrose 1959; Rumelt 1984; Wernerfelt 1984, 1989). Resource-based theory substitutes two alternate assumptions in analyzing sources of competitive advantage. First, this model assumes that firms within an industry (or group) may be heterogeneous with respect to the strategic resources they control. Second, this model assumes that these resources may not be perfectly mobile across firms, and thus heterogeneity can be long lasting. The resource-based model of the firm examines the implications of these two assumptions for the analysis of sources of sustained competitive advantage.

Of course, not all of a firm's resources are likely to be economically valuable. Indeed, some of these firm attributes may actually make it more difficult for a firm to conceive and implement valuable strategies (Barney 1986*b*). Others may have no impact on a firm's strategizing efforts.

However, those attributes of a firm's physical, financial, human, and organizational capital that do enable a firm to conceive and implement strategies that improve its efficiency and effectiveness are, for purposes of this discussion, valuable firm resources (Wernerfelt 1984). The purpose of this chapter is to specify the conditions under which such firm resources can be a source of sustained competitive advantage for a firm.

Competitive advantage and sustained competitive advantage

The concept of competitive advantage was defined in Chapter 1. There, it was suggested that a firm has a competitive advantage when it is able to create more economic value than the marginal firm in its industry. However, as important as it is to explain the existence of competitive advantages among firms, the sustainability of these advantages is also important. Some competitive advantages are fleeting, others can be long lasting. In resource-based logic, a firm is said to have a *sustained competitive advantage* when it is creating more economic value than the marginal firm in its industry and when other firms are unable to duplicate the benefits of this strategy. A couple of comments about sustained competitive advantage are in order.

First, unlike the concept of competitive advantage, sustained competitive advantage does not focus exclusively on a firm's competitive position vis-à-vis firms that are already operating in its industry. Rather, following Baumol, Panzar, and Willig (1982), a firm's competition is assumed to include not only all of its current competitors, but also potential competitors poised to enter an industry at some future date.

Second, the definition of *sustained* competitive advantage adopted here does not necessarily depend on the period of calendar time during which a firm enjoys a competitive advantage. One indicator that a firm may have a sustained competitive advantage is that it has a competitive advantage that lasts a long time (Porter 1985; Jacobsen 1988). However, in some industry settings, a sustained competitive advantage may not last a long period of calendar time. In such settings, it may be possible for a firm to have a competitive advantage that lasts for a relatively short period. But if that advantage is not competed away through other firms duplicating the strategy of the firm with a competitive advantage, then that advantage may still have been sustained.

The imperfect link between the calendar time a firm enjoys a competitive advantage and the concept of a sustained competitive advantage reflects the fact that the sustainability of a competitive advantage ultimately depends on what might be called the 'condition of duplication'. If current and potential firms are unable to duplicate the competitive advantage of a successful firm, that firm's competitive advantage is sustained. In this sense, the 'condition of duplication' is analogous to the 'condition of entry' in many SCP-based models of firm performance (Bain 1968) and, following Lippman and Rumelt (1982) and Rumelt (1984), the resulting definition of sustained competitive advantage can be thought of as an equilibrium definition.

However, that a firm has a sustained competitive advantage does not mean that its competitive advantage will last forever. Changes in technology, demand, and the broader institutional context within which a firm operates can all make what used to be a source of sustained competitive advantage no longer valuable.

These kinds of changes have been called 'Schumpeterian Shocks' by several authors (Schumpeter 1934, 1950; Rumelt and Wensley 1981*a*; Barney 1986*c*). Such shocks redefine which of a firm's resources are valuable and which are not. Some of these resources, in turn, may be sources of sustained competitive advantage in the newly defined industry structure (Barney 1986*c*). However, what were resources in a previous industry setting may be weaknesses, or simply irrelevant, in a new industry setting. A firm enjoying a sustained competitive advantage may experience these major shifts in the structure of competition and may see its competitive advantages nullified by such changes. Just as being the world's best buggy whip manufacturer is not a source of sustained competitive advantage in a world dominated by automobiles, so too can political connections that were a source of sustained competitive advantages in one political regime no longer be a source of sustained competitive advantage if that regime is overthrown. In all these cases, however, a sustained competitive advantage is not lost through the efforts of other firms to duplicate the bases of these advantages. Rather, this sustained competitive advantage is replaced when alternative technologies, changes in demand, or other changes take place.

Competition with homogeneous and perfectly mobile resources

Armed with a definition of sustained competitive advantage, it is now possible to explore the impact of resource heterogeneity and immobility on this concept. This is done by first examining the possibility of sustained competitive advantage when firm resources are *perfectly* homogeneous and mobile. Then, the possibility of sustained competitive advantage under heterogeneity and immobility is examined.

Of course, the analysis of sustained competitive advantage under perfect firm homogeneity and mobility does not suggest that there are industries where the attributes of perfect homogeneity and mobility actually exist. Although this is ultimately an empirical question, it seems reasonable to expect that most industries will be characterized by at least some degree of resource heterogeneity and immobility (Barney and Hoskisson 1989). Thus, rather than making an assertion that firm resources are homogeneous and mobile, the purpose of this analysis is to examine the possibility of discovering sources of sustained competitive advantage under these conditions. Not surprisingly, it is argued that firms, in general, *cannot* expect to obtain sustained competitive advantage when strategic resources are evenly distributed across all competing firms and highly mobile. This conclusion suggests that the search for sources of sustained competitive advantage must focus on firm resource heterogeneity and immobility.

Imagine an industry where firms possess exactly the same resources. This condition suggests that firms all have the same amount and kinds of strategically relevant physical, financial, human, and organizational capital. Is there a strategy that could be conceived and implemented by any one of these firms that could not also be conceived and implemented by all other firms in this industry? The answer to this question must be no. The conception and implementation of strategies employs various firm resources (Wernerfelt 1984; Barney 1986*a*; Hatten and Hatten 1987). That one firm in an industry populated by identical firms has the resources to conceive and implement a strategy means that these other firms, because they possess the same resources, can also conceive and implement this strategy. Because these firms all implement the same strategies, they all will improve their efficiency and effectiveness in the same way and to the same extent. Thus, in this kind of industry, it is not possible for firms to enjoy a competitive advantage.

One objection to this conclusion concerns so-called 'first-mover advantages' (Lieberman and Montgomery 1988). In some circumstances, the first firm in an industry to implement a strategy can obtain a sustained competitive advantage over other firms. These firms may gain access to distribution channels, develop goodwill with customers, or develop a positive reputation, all before firms that implement their strategies later. Thus, first-moving firms may obtain a competitive advantage which might also be sustained.

However, upon reflection, it seems clear that if competing firms are *identical* in the resources they control, it is not possible for any one firm to obtain a competitive advantage from first moving. To be a first mover by implementing a strategy before any competing firms, a particular firm must have insights about the opportunities associated with implementing a strategy that are not possessed by other firms in the industry, or by potentially entering firms (Lieberman and Montgomery 1988). This unique firm resource (information about an opportunity) makes it possible for the better-informed firm to implement its strategy before others. However, by definition, there are no unique firm resources in this kind of industry. If one firm in this type of industry is able to conceive and implement a strategy, then all other firms will also be able to conceive and implement that strategy, and these strategies will be conceived and implemented in parallel, as identical firms become aware of the same opportunities and exploit that opportunity in the same way.

It is not being suggested that there can never be first-mover advantages in industries. It is being suggested that in order for there to be a first-mover advantage, firms in an industry must be heterogeneous in terms of the resources they control.

A second objection to the conclusion that sustained competitive advantages cannot exist when firm resources in an industry are perfectly homogeneous and mobile concerns the existence of 'barriers to entry' (Bain 1956) or more generally, 'mobility barriers' (Caves and Porter 1977). The argument here is that even if firms within an industry (group) are perfectly homogeneous, if there are strong entry or mobility barriers, these firms may be able to obtain a sustained competitive advantage vis-à-vis firms that are not in their industry (group).

However, from another point of view, barriers to entry or mobility are only possible if current and potentially competing firms are heterogeneous in terms of the resources they control and if these resources are not perfectly mobile (Barney, McWilliams, and Turk 1989). The heterogeneity requirement is self-evident. For a barrier to entry or mobility to exist, firms protected by these barriers must be implementing different strategies than firms seeking to enter these protected areas of competition. Firms restricted from entry are unable to implement the same strategies as firms within the industry or group. Because the implementation of strategy requires the application of firm resources, the inability of firms seeking to enter an industry or group to implement the same strategies as firms within that industry or group suggests that firms seeking to enter must not have the same strategically relevant resources as firms within the industry or group. Thus, barriers to entry and mobility only exist when competing firms are heterogeneous in terms of the strategically relevant resources they control. Indeed, this is the definition of strategic groups suggested by McGee and Thomas (1986).

The requirement that firm resources be immobile in order for barriers to entry or mobility to exist is also clear. If firm resources are perfectly mobile, then any resource that allows some firms to implement a strategy protected by entry or mobility barriers can easily be acquired by firms seeking to enter into this industry or group. Once these resources are acquired, the strategy in question can be conceived and implemented in the same way that other firms have conceived and implemented their strategies. These strategies are thus not a source of sustained competitive advantage.

Again, it is not being suggested that entry or mobility barriers do not exist. However, it is being suggested that these barriers only become sources of sustained competitive advantage when firm resources are not homogeneously distributed across competing firms and when these resources are not perfectly mobile.

Research that has focused on the impact of opportunities and threats in a firm's environment on competitive advantage has recognized the limitations inherent in analyzing competitive advantage with the assumption that firm resources are homogeneously distributed and highly mobile. In his work, Porter (1985) introduced the concept of the value chain to assist managers in isolating potential resource-based advantages for their firms. The resource-based theory developed here simply pushes this value chain logic further, by examining the attributes that resources isolated by value chain analyses must possess in order to be sources of sustained competitive advantage (Porter 1990).

Firm resources and sustained competitive advantage

Thus far, it has been suggested that in order to understand sources of sustained competitive advantage, it is necessary to build a theoretical model that begins with the assumption that firm resources may be heterogeneous and immobile. Of course, not all firm resources hold the potential of sustained competitive advantages. To have this potential, a firm resource must have four attributes: (*a*) it must be valuable, in the sense that it exploits opportunities and/or neutralizes threats in a firm's environment, (*b*) it must be rare among a firm's current and potential competition, (*c*) it must be imperfectly imitable, and (*d*) it must be able to be exploited by a firm's organizational processes. These attributes of firm resources can be thought of as indicators of how heterogeneous and immobile a firm's resources are, and thus how useful these resources are for generating sustained competitive advantages. Each of these attributes of a firm's resources is discussed in more detail below.

VALUABLE RESOURCES

Firm resources can only be a source of competitive advantage or sustained competitive advantage when they are valuable. As suggested earlier, resources are valuable when they enable a firm to conceive or implement strategies that improve its efficiency and effectiveness. The traditional 'strengths–weaknesses–opportunities–threats' model of firm performance suggests that firms are able to improve their performance only when their strategies exploit opportunities or neutralize threats. Firm attributes may have the other characteristics that could qualify them as sources of competitive advantage (e.g. rarity, inimitability, and organizational abilities/processes), but these attributes only become valuable resources when they exploit opportunities or neutralize threats in a firm's environment.

This analysis perfectly correlates with the definition of competitive advantage presented in Chapter 1. A valuable resource enables a firm to increase the economic value it creates by increasing the willingness of customers to pay, decreasing its costs, or both.

That firm attributes must be valuable in order to be considered as possible sources of sustained competitive advantage points to an important complementarity between environmental models of competitive advantage and the resource-based model. These environmental models help isolate those firm attributes that exploit opportunities and/or neutralize threats. The resource-based model then suggests what additional characteristics these resources must possess if they are to generate sustained competitive advantage. Note, this means that the value of a firm's resources needs to be evaluated within the context of the firm's strategy and the specific market environment.

RARE RESOURCES

Valuable firm resources possessed by large numbers of competing or potentially competing firms cannot be sources of either a competitive advantage or a sustained competitive advantage. A firm enjoys a competitive advantage when it creates more economic value than the marginal firm in an industry. If a particular valuable firm resource is possessed by large numbers of firms, then each of these firms has the capability of exploiting that resource in the same way, thereby implementing a common strategy that gives no one firm a competitive advantage.

The same analysis applies to bundles of valuable firm resources used to conceive and implement strategies. Some strategies require a particular mix of physical, financial, human, and organizational capital resources for implementation. One firm resource required in the implementation of almost all strategies is managerial talent (Hambrick 1987). If this particular bundle of firm resources is not rare, then large numbers of firms will be able to conceive and implement the strategies in question, and these strategies will not be a source of competitive advantage, even though the resources in question may be valuable.

To observe that competitive advantages (sustained or otherwise) only accrue to firms that have valuable and rare resources is not to dismiss common (i.e. not rare) firm resources as unimportant. Instead, these valuable but common firm resources can help ensure a firm's survival when they are exploited to create competitive parity in an industry (Barney 1989). Under conditions of competitive parity, though no one firm obtains a competitive advantage, firms do increase their probability of economic survival (Porter 1980; McKelvey 1982).

How rare a valuable firm resource must be in order to have the potential for generating a competitive advantage is a difficult question. It is not difficult to see that if a firm's valuable resources are absolutely unique among a set of competing and potentially competing firms, those resources will generate at least a competitive advantage and may have the potential of generating a sustained competitive advantage. However, it may be possible for a small number of firms in an industry to possess a particular valuable resource and still generate a competitive advantage. In general, as long as the number of firms that possess a particular valuable resource (or a bundle of valuable resources) is less than the number of firms needed to generate perfect competition dynamics in an industry, that resource has the potential of generating a competitive advantage.

IMPERFECTLY IMITABLE RESOURCES

It is not difficult to see that valuable and rare organizational resources may be a source of competitive advantage. Indeed, firms with such resources will often be strategic innovators, for they will be able to conceive and engage in strategies that other firms could either not conceive, or not implement, or both, because these other firms lacked the relevant firm resources. The observation that valuable and rare organizational resources can be a source of competitive advantage is another way of describing first-mover advantages accruing to firms with resource advantages.

However, valuable and rare organizational resources can only be sources of *sustained* competitive advantage if firms that do not possess these resources cannot obtain them by direct duplication or substitution. In language developed in Lippman and Rumelt (1982) and Barney (1986*a*, 1986*b*), these firm resources are imperfectly imitable. Why might a competing firm face a cost disadvantage in imitating a firm's resources?

Firm resources can be imperfectly imitable (or costly to imitate) for one or a combination of three reasons: (*a*) the ability of a firm to obtain a resource is dependent on *unique historical conditions*, (*b*) the link between the resources possessed by a firm and a firm's sustained competitive advantage is *causally ambiguous*, or (*c*) the resource generating a firm's advantage is *socially complex* (Dierickx and Cool 1989). Each of these sources of the imperfect imitability of firm resources is examined below.

Unique historical conditions

Another assumption of most environmental models of firm competitive advantage, besides resource homogeneity and mobility, is that the performance of firms can be understood independent of the particular history and other idiosyncratic attributes of firms (Scherer 1980; Porter 1981). These researchers seldom argue that firms do not vary in terms of their unique histories, but rather that these unique histories are not relevant to understanding a firm's performance (Porter 1980).

The resource-based theory of competitive advantage developed here relaxes this assumption. Indeed, this approach asserts that not only are firms intrinsically historical and social entities, but that their ability to acquire and exploit some resources depends on their place in time and space. Once this particular unique time in history passes, firms that do not have space- and time-dependent resources cannot obtain them and thus these resources are imperfectly imitable.

Resource-based theorists are not alone in recognizing the importance of history as a determinant of firm performance and competitive advantage. Traditional strategy researchers (e.g. Ansoff 1965; Stinchcombe 1965; Learned et al. 1969) often cited the unique historical circumstances of a firm's founding, or the unique circumstances under which a new management team takes over a firm, as important determinants of a firm's long-term performance. In addition, several economists (e.g. David 1985; Arthur, Ermoliev, and Kaniovsky 1987) have developed models of firm performance that rely heavily on unique historical events as determinants of subsequent actions. Employing path-dependent models of economic performance (Arthur 1983, 1984*a*, 1984*b*; Arthur, Ermoliev, and Kaniovski 1994), these authors suggest that the performance of a firm does not depend simply on the industry structure within which a firm finds itself at a particular point in time, but also on the path a firm followed through history to arrive where it is. If a firm obtains valuable and rare resources because of its unique path through history, it will be able to exploit those resources in implementing value-creating strategies that cannot be duplicated by other firms, for firms without that particular path through history cannot obtain the resources necessary to implement the strategy.

The acquisition of all the types of firm resources examined in this chapter can depend on the unique historical position of a firm. A firm that locates its facilities on what turns out to be a much more valuable location than was anticipated when the location was chosen possesses an imperfectly imitable physical capital resource (Ricardo 1966). A firm with scientists who are uniquely positioned to create or exploit a significant scientific breakthrough may obtain an imperfectly imitable resource from the history-dependent nature of the scientist's individual human capital (Winter 1987; Burgelman and Maidique 1988). Finally, a firm with a unique and valuable organizational culture that emerged in the early stages of a firm's history may have an imperfectly imitable advantage over firms founded in another historical period, where different (and perhaps less valuable) organizational values and beliefs come to dominate (Zucker 1977; Barney 1986*b*).

The literature in strategic management is infused with examples of firms whose unique historical position endowed them with resources that are not controlled by competing firms and that cannot be imitated (e.g. Caterpillar—Rukstad and Horn 1989; Lucent Technologies—Kupfer 1997). These examples are the case analyses that have dominated teaching and research for so long in the field of strategic management (Learned et al. 1969; Miles and Cameron 1982). In addition, the impact of history on firm performance has been studied systematically (Collins and Porras 1997). There are at least two ways that unique historical conditions can give a firm a sustained competitive advantage. First, it may be that a particular firm is the first in an industry to recognize and exploit an opportunity, and being first gives the firm a first-mover advantage. Second, when events early in the evolution of a process have significant effects on subsequent events, path dependence allows a firm to gain a competitive advantage in the current period based on the acquisition and development of resources in earlier periods.

Causal ambiguity

Unlike the relationship between a firm's unique history and the imitability of its resources, the relationship between the causal ambiguity of a firm's resources and imperfect imitability has received systematic attention in the strategic management and related literatures (Alchian 1950; Mancke 1974; Lippman and Rumelt 1982; Rumelt 1984; Barney 1986*b*; Reed and DeFillippi 1990). In this context, causal ambiguity exists when the link between the resources controlled by a firm and a firm's sustained competitive advantage is not understood or understood only very imperfectly.

When the link between a firm's resources and its sustained competitive advantage is poorly understood, it is difficult for firms that are attempting to duplicate a successful firm's strategies through imitation of its resources to know which resources it should imitate. Imitating firms may be able to describe some of the resources controlled by a successful firm. However, under conditions of causal ambiguity, it is not clear that the resources that can be described are the same resources that generate a sustained competitive advantage, or whether that advantage reflects some other nondescribed firm resource. As suggested by Demsetz (1973), sometimes it is difficult to understand why one firm consistently outperforms other firms. Causal ambiguity is at the heart of this difficulty. In the face of such causal ambiguity, imitating firms cannot know the actions they should take in order to duplicate the strategies of firms with a sustained competitive advantage.

To be a source of sustained competitive advantage, both the firms that possess resources that generate a competitive advantage and the firms that do not possess these resources but seek to imitate them, must be faced with the same level of causal ambiguity (Lippman and Rumelt 1982). If firms that control these resources have a better understanding of their impact on competitive advantage than firms without these resources, then firms without these resources can engage in activities to reduce their knowledge disadvantage. They can do this, for example, by hiring away well-placed knowledgeable managers in a firm with a competitive advantage or by engaging in a careful systematic study of the other firm's success. Although acquiring this knowledge may take some time and effort, once knowledge of the link between a firm's resources and its ability to implement certain strategies is diffused throughout competing firms, causal ambiguity no longer exists and thus cannot be a source of imperfect imitability. In other words, if a firm with a competitive advantage understands the link between the resources it controls and its advantages, then other firms can also learn about that link, acquire the necessary resources (assuming they are not imperfectly imitable for other reasons), and implement the relevant strategies. In such a setting, a firm's competitive advantages are not sustained because they can be duplicated.

On the other hand, when a firm with a competitive advantage does not understand the source of its competitive advantage any better than firms without this advantage, that competitive advantage may be sustained because it is not subject to imitation (Lippman and Rumelt 1982). Ironically, in order for causal ambiguity to be a source of sustained competitive advantage, all competing firms must have an imperfect understanding of the link between the resources controlled by a firm and a firm's competitive advantages. If one competing firm understands this link and no others do, in the long run this information will be diffused through all competitors, thus eliminating causal ambiguity and imperfect imitability based on causal ambiguity.

At first, it may seem unlikely that a firm with a sustained competitive advantage will not fully understand the source of that advantage. However, given the very complex relationship between firm resources and competitive advantage, such an incomplete understanding is not implausible. The resources controlled by a firm are very complex and interdependent. Often, they are implicit, taken for granted by managers, rather than being subject to explicit analysis (Polanyi 1962; Nelson and Winter 1982; Winter 1988). Numerous resources, taken by themselves or in combination with other resources, may yield sustained competitive advantage. Although managers may have numerous hypotheses about which resources generate their firm's advantages, it is rarely possible to rigorously test these hypotheses. As long as numerous plausible explanations of the sources of sustained competitive advantage exist within a firm, the link between the resources controlled by a firm and sustained competitive advantage remains somewhat ambiguous, and thus which of a firm's resources to imitate remains uncertain.

Three situations in which managers may not fully understand their sources of competitive advantage include: (*a*) when the resources and capabilities are taken-for-granted organizational characteristics or invisible assets (Itami 1987) such as teamwork among top mangers, organizational culture, relationships with suppliers and customers; (*b*) when managers are unable to evaluate which of their resources and capabilities, alone or in combination, actually create the competitive advantage; and (*c*) when the resources and capabilities are complex networks of relationships between individuals, groups, and technology, identified by Dierickx and Cool (1989) as interconnectedness of asset stocks and asset mass efficiencies. Whenever the sources of competitive advantage are widely diffused across people, locations, and processes in a firm, those sources of competitive advantage will be difficult to identify and costly to imitate.

Social complexity

A third reason that a firm's resources may be imperfectly imitable is that they may be very complex social phenomena, beyond the ability of firms to systematically manage and influence. When competitive advantages are based in such complex social phenomena, the ability of other firms to imitate these resources is significantly constrained.

A wide variety of firm resources may be socially complex. Examples include the interpersonal relations among managers in a firm (Hambrick 1987), a firm's culture (Barney 1986*b*), a firm's reputation among suppliers (Porter 1980), and customers (Klein, Crawford, and Alchian 1978; Klein and Lefler 1981). Note that in most of these cases it is possible to specify how these socially complex resources add value to a firm. Thus, there is little or no causal ambiguity surrounding the link between these firm resources and competitive advantage. However, understanding that, say, an organizational culture with certain attributes or quality relations among managers can improve a firm's efficiency and effectiveness does not necessarily imply that firms without these attributes can engage in systematic efforts to create them (Barney 1986*b*; Dierickx and Cool 1989). Such social engineering may be, for the time being at least, beyond the capabilities of most firms (Porras and Berg 1978*b*; Barney 1986*b*). To the extent that socially complex firm resources are not subject to such direct management, these resources are imperfectly imitable.

Note that complex physical technology is not included in this category of sources of imperfectly imitable resources. In general, physical technology, whether it takes the form of machine tools or robots in factories (Hayes and Wheelwright 1984) or complex information management systems

(Howell and Fleishman 1982), is *by itself* typically imitable. If one firm can purchase these physical tools of production and thereby implement some strategies, then other firms should also be able to purchase these physical tools, and thus such tools should not be a source of sustained competitive advantage.

On the other hand, the exploitation of physical technology in a firm often involves the use of socially complex firm resources. Several firms may all possess the same physical technology, but only one of these firms may possess the social relations, culture, traditions, etc. to fully exploit this technology in implementing strategies (Wilkins 1989). If these complex social resources are not subject to imitation (and assuming they are valuable and rare and no substitutes exist), these firms may obtain a sustained competitive advantage from exploiting their physical technology more completely than other firms, even though competing firms do not vary in terms of the physical technology they possess. These issues are examined further in Chapter 7.

Substitutability

History, causal ambiguity, and social complexity can all increase the cost of another firm duplicating the resources of a particular firm. However, if substitutes for these resources exist, and if these substitutes are themselves not costly to duplicate, then firms without these resources can imitate their effects by substituting resources they can duplicate at low cost. Two valuable firm resources (or two bundles of firm resources) are substitutes when they are strategically equivalent, that is, when they each can be exploited separately to implement the same strategies.

Suppose that one of these valuable firm resources is rare and imperfectly imitable, but the other is not. Firms with this first resource will be able to conceive and implement certain strategies. If there were no strategically equivalent firm resources, these strategies would generate a sustained competitive advantage (because the resources used to conceive and implement them are valuable, rare, and imperfectly imitable). However, that there are strategically equivalent resources suggests that other current or potentially competing firms can implement the same strategies, but in a different way, using different resources. If these alternative resources are either not rare or imitable, then numerous firms will be able to conceive and implement the strategies in question and those strategies will not generate a sustained competitive advantage. This will be the case even though one approach to implementing these strategies exploits valuable, rare, and imperfectly imitable firm resources.

Substitutability can take at least two forms. First, though it may not be possible for a firm to imitate another firm's resources exactly, it may be able to substitute a similar resource that enables it to conceive and implement the same strategies. For example, a firm seeking to duplicate the competitive advantages of another firm by imitating that other firm's high-quality top management team will often be unable to copy that team exactly (Hambrick 1987). However, it may be possible for this firm to develop its own unique top management team. Although these two teams will be different (different people, different operating practices, a different history, etc.), they may likely be strategically equivalent and thus be substitutes for one another. If different top management teams are strategically equivalent and if these substitute teams are common or highly imitable, then a high-quality top management team is not a source of sustained competitive advantage even though a particular management team of a particular firm is valuable, rare, and imperfectly imitable.

Second, very *different* firm resources can also be strategic substitutes. For example, managers in one firm may have a very clear vision of the future of their company because of a charismatic leader in their firm (Zucker 1977). Managers in competing firms may also have a very clear vision of the future of their companies, but this common vision may reflect these firms' systematic, companywide strategic planning process (Pearce, Freeman, and Robinson 1987). From the point of view of managers having a clear vision of the future of their company, the firm resource of a charismatic leader and the firm resource of a formal planning system may be strategically equivalent and thus substitutes for one another. If large numbers of competing firms have a formal planning system that generates this common vision (or if such a formal planning is highly imitable), then firms with such a vision derived from a charismatic leader will not have a sustained competitive advantage even though the firm resource of a charismatic leader is probably rare and imperfectly imitable.

Of course, the strategic substitutability of firm resources is always a matter of degree. It is the case, however, that substitute firm resources need not have exactly the same implications for an organization in order for those resources to be equivalent from the point of view of the strategies that firms can conceive and implement. If enough firms have these valuable substitute resources (i.e. they are not rare), or if enough firms can acquire them (i.e. they are imitable), then none of these firms (including firms whose resources are being substituted for) can expect to obtain a sustained competitive advantage.

ORGANIZATION

Valuable, rare, and imitable resources can only be a source of sustained competitive advantage if the firm is organized to exploit the potential offered by these resources. Organizational processes provide the fourth condition necessary for realization of sustainable competitive advantage. Numerous components of a firm's organization influence its ability to exploit the full competitive potential of its resources and capabilities, including its formal reporting structure, its explicit management control systems, and its compensation policies. These components are often called complementary resources and capabilities as they have limited ability to generate competitive advantage in isolation. However, in combination with other resources and capabilities they can enable a firm to realize its full potential for competitive advantage.

For example, much of Caterpillar's sustained competitive advantage in the heavy-construction industry can be traced to its becoming the primary supplier of this equipment to the Allied forces in World War II. However, if Caterpillar's management had not taken advantage of this opportunity by implementing a global formal reporting structure, global inventory and other control systems, and compensation policies that created incentives for employees to work around the world, then Caterpillar's potential for competitive advantage would not have been fully realized. By themselves, these attributes of Caterpillar's organization could not be a source of competitive advantage—that is, adopting a global organizational form was relevant for Caterpillar only because it was pursuing a global opportunity. However, this organization was essential for Caterpillar to realize its full competitive advantage potential.

In a similar way, much of Wal-Mart's continuing competitive advantage in the discount retailing industry can be attributed to its early entry into rural markets in the southern United States. However, to fully exploit this geographic advantage, Wal-Mart needed to implement appropriate reporting structures, control systems, and compensation policies. One component of Wal-Mart's organization—its point-of-purchase inventory control system—is being imitated by K-Mart, and thus, by itself, is not likely to be a source of sustained competitive advantage. However, this inventory control system has enabled Wal-Mart to take full advantage of its rural locations by decreasing the probability of stock outs in those locations.

Having an appropriate organization in place has enabled Caterpillar and Wal-Mart to realize the full competitive advantage potential of their resources and capabilities. Having an inappropriate organization in place prevented Xerox from taking full advantage of some of its most critical valuable, rare, and costly to imitate resources and capabilities.

Through the 1960s and early 1970s, Xerox invested in a series of very innovative technology development research efforts. Xerox managed this research effort by creating a stand-alone research center in Palo Alto (Palo Alto Research Center—PARC) and assembling a large group of highly creative and innovative scientists and engineers to work there. Left to their own devices, these scientists and engineers at Xerox PARC developed an amazing array of technological innovations—the personal computer, the 'mouse', Windows-type software, the laser printer, the 'paperless office', Ethernet, and so forth. In retrospect, it is clear that the market potential of these technologies was enormous. Moreover, because they were developed at Xerox PARC, they were rare. Xerox may have been able to gain some important first-mover advantages if the organization had been able to translate these technologies into products, thereby increasing the cost to other firms of imitating these technologies.

Xerox possessed very valuable, rare, and costly to imitate resources and capabilities in the technologies developed at Xerox PARC, but did not have the organization in place to take advantage of these resources. No structure existed whereby Xerox PARC innovations could become known to managers at Xerox. Indeed most Xerox managers—even many senior managers—were unaware of these technological developments through the mid-1970s. Once they did become aware of them, very few of the technologies survived Xerox's highly bureaucratic product development process, a process where product development projects were divided into hundreds of minute tasks and progress in each task was reviewed by dozens of large committees. Even innovations that survived the product development process were not exploited by Xerox managers because management compensation at Xerox depended exclusively on maximizing current revenue. Short-term profitability was relatively less important in compensation calculations and the development of markets for future sales and profitability was essentially irrelevant. Xerox's formal reporting structure, its explicit management control systems, and its compensation policies were all inconsistent with exploiting the valuable, rare, and costly to imitate resources developed at Xerox PARC. Not surprisingly, Xerox failed to exploit any of the potential sources of sustained competitive advantage.[3]

A framework for resource-based analysis: VRIO

The relationship between resource heterogeneity and immobility; value, rarity, imitability, and organization; and sustained competitive advantage is summarized in Figure 3.2. This has been developed into a framework that can be applied in analyzing the potential of a broad range of firm resources to be sources of sustained competitive advantage. These analyses not only specify the theoretical conditions under which sustained competitive advantage might exist, they also suggest specific empirical questions that need to be addressed before the relationship between a particular firm resource and sustained competitive advantage can be understood.

The *VRIO framework* expresses the four key parameters for resource-based analysis as a series of questions about the business activities of the firm:

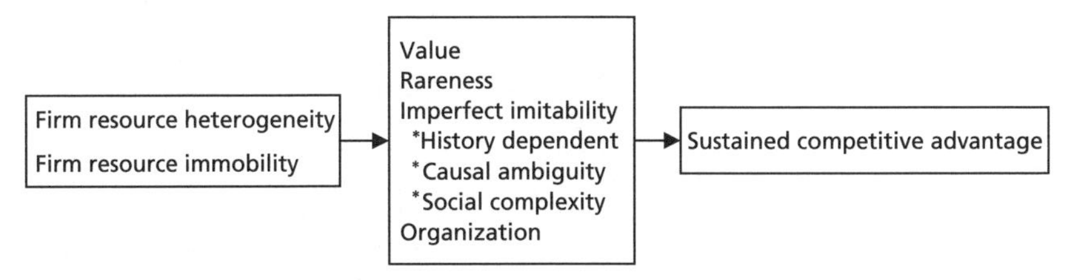

Figure 3.2. The relationship between resource heterogeneity and immobility, value, rareness, imperfect imitability, and organization, and sustained competitive advantage

1. The question of *Value*: Do a firm's resources and capabilities enable the firm to respond to environmental threats or opportunities?
2. The question of *Rarity*: Is a resource currently controlled by only a small number of competing firms?
3. The question of *Imitability*: Do firms without a resource face a cost disadvantage in obtaining or developing it?
4. The question of *Organization*: Are a firm's other policies and procedures organized to support the exploitation of its valuable, rare, and costly to imitate resources?

Bringing these questions of value, rarity, imitability, and organization together provides a single framework to understand the return potential associated with exploiting any of a firm's resources or capabilities. This framework is summarized in Table 3.1.

If a resource or capability controlled by a firm is not valuable, then that resource will not enable a firm to choose or implement strategies that exploit environmental opportunities or neutralize threats. Organizing to exploit this resource will increase a firm's costs or decrease its revenues. These types of resources are weaknesses. Firms will either have to fix these weaknesses or avoid using them when choosing and implementing strategies. If firms do exploit these kinds of resources or capabilities, they can expect to put themselves at a competitive disadvantage compared to firms

Table 3.1. The VRIO framework

Is a resource or capability . . .					
Valuable?	Rare?	Costly to imitate?	Exploited by organization?	Competitive implications	Economic performance
No	—	—	No	Competitive disadvantage	Below normal
Yes	No	—	↑	Competitive parity	Normal
Yes	Yes	No	↓	Temporary competitive advantage	Above normal
Yes	Yes	Yes	Yes	Sustained competitive advantage	Above normal

that either do not possess these nonvaluable resources or do not use them in conceiving and implementing strategies.

If a resource or capability is valuable but not rare, exploiting this resource in conceiving and implementing strategies will generate competitive parity. Exploiting these valuable but not rare resources will generally not create competitive advantages for a firm, but failure to exploit them can put a firm at a competitive disadvantage. In this sense, valuable-but-not-rare resources can be thought of as organizational strengths.

If a resource or capability is valuable and rare but not costly to imitate, exploiting this resource will generate a temporary competitive advantage for a firm. A firm that exploits this kind of resource is, in an important sense, gaining a first-mover advantage, because it is the first firm that is able to exploit a particular resource. However, once competing firms observe this competitive advantage, they will be able to acquire or develop the resources needed to implement this strategy through direct duplication or substitution at no cost disadvantage compared to the first-moving firm. Over time, any competitive advantage that the first mover obtained would be competed away as other firms imitate the resources needed to compete. However, between the time a firm gains a competitive advantage by exploiting a valuable and rare but imitable resource or capability and the time that competitive advantage is competed away through imitation, the first-moving firm can earn above-normal economic performance. Consequently, this type of resource or capability can be thought of as an organizational strength and distinctive competence.

If a resource or capability is valuable, rare, and costly to imitate, exploiting this resource will generate a sustained competitive advantage. In this case, competing firms face a significant cost disadvantage in directly duplicating a successful firm's resources and capabilities and no easy to duplicate substitutes for these resources exist. As suggested earlier in this chapter, this disadvantage may reflect the unique history of the successful firm, causal ambiguity about which resources to imitate, or the socially complex nature of these resources and capabilities. In any case, attempts to compete away the advantages of firms that exploit these resources will not generate competitive advantages for imitating firms. Even if these firms were able to acquire or develop the resources or capabilities in question, the very high costs of doing so would put them at a competitive disadvantage compared to the firm that already possessed the valuable, rare, and costly to imitate resources. These kinds of resources and capabilities are organizational strengths and sustainable distinctive competencies.

The question of organization operates as an adjustment factor in the VRIO framework. For example, if a firm has a valuable, rare, and costly to imitate resource and capability but fails to organize itself to take full advantage of this resource, some of its potential competitive advantage could be lost (as in the Xerox example). Extremely poor organization, in this case, could actually lead a firm that has the potential for competitive advantage to obtain only competitive parity or even competitive disadvantages.

Discussion

This VRIO framework suggests the kinds of questions that need to be addressed in order to understand whether a particular firm resource is a source of sustained competitive advantage: Is that resource valuable?, Is it rare?, Is it imperfectly imitable?, and Is the firm organized to exploit this resource? This framework is applied to understand the competitive implications of a variety of firm resources—in Part II of this book—and specific strategies—in Part III of this book. However, before examining these applications of the theory, it is appropriate to note some of the broader implications of resource-based logic and the VRIO framework.

SUSTAINED COMPETITIVE ADVANTAGE AND SOCIAL WELFARE

The resource-based model presented here addresses important social welfare issues linked with strategic management research. Most authors agree that the original purpose of the structure-conduct-performance paradigm in industrial organization economics was to isolate violations of the perfectly competitive model and to address these violations in order to restore the social welfare benefits of perfectly competitive industries (Porter 1981; Barney 1986*c*). As applied by strategy theorists focusing on environmental determinants of firm performance, social welfare concerns were abandoned in favor of the creation of imperfectly competitive industries within which a particular firm could gain a competitive advantage (Porter 1980). At best, this approach to strategic analysis ignores social welfare concerns. At worst, this approach focuses on activities that firms can engage in that will almost certainly reduce social welfare.

The resource-based model developed here suggests that, in fact, strategic management research can be perfectly consistent with traditional social welfare concerns of economists. Beginning with the assumptions that firm resources are heterogeneous and immobile, it follows that a firm that exploits its resource advantages is simply behaving in an efficient and effective manner (Demsetz 1973). To fail to exploit these resource advantages is inefficient and does not maximize social welfare. In this sense, the higher levels of performance that accrue to a firm with resource advantages are due to the efficiency of these firms in exploiting those advantages, rather than to the efforts of firms to create imperfectly competitive conditions in a way that fails to maximize social welfare. These profits, in a sense, can be thought of as 'efficiency rents' (Demsetz 1973) as opposed to 'monopoly rents' (Scherer 1980).

SUSTAINED COMPETITIVE ADVANTAGE AND ORGANIZATION THEORY AND BEHAVIOR

A variety of authors have suggested that economic models of organizational phenomena fundamentally contradict models of organizations based in organization theory or organizational behavior (Perrow 1986; Donaldson 1990*a*, 1990*b*). This assertion is fundamentally contradicted by the resource-based model of sustained competitive advantage (Barney 1990). This model suggests that sources of sustained competitive advantage are firm resources that are valuable, rare, imperfectly imitable, and exploited by the organization. These resources include a broad range of organizational, social, and individual phenomena within firms that are the subject of a great deal of research in organization theory and organizational behavior (Daft 1983). Rather than being contradictory, the resource-based model of strategic management suggests that organization theory and organizational behavior may be a rich source of findings and theories concerning rare, nonimitable, and exploitable resources in firms. Indeed, a resource-based model of sustained competitive advantage anticipates a more intimate integration of the organizational and the economic factors as a way to study sustained competitive advantage.

FIRM ENDOWMENTS AND SUSTAINED COMPETITIVE ADVANTAGE

Finally, the model presented here emphasizes the importance of what might be called firm resource endowments in creating sustained competitive advantages. Implicit in this model is the assumption that managers are limited in their ability to manipulate all the attributes and characteristics of their firms (Barney and Tyler 1991). It is this limitation that makes some firm resources imperfectly imitable, and thus potentially sources of sustained competitive advantage. Thus, the study of sustained competitive advantage depends, in a critical way, on the resource endowments controlled by a firm.

That the study of sources of sustained competitive advantage focuses on valuable, rare, imperfectly imitable, and exploitable resource endowments does not suggest—as some population ecologists would have it (e.g. Hannan and Freeman 1977)—that managers are irrelevant in the study of such advantages. In fact, managers are important in this model, for it is managers that are able to understand and describe the economic performance potential of a firm's endowments. Without such managerial analyses, sustained competitive advantage is not likely. This is the case even though the skills needed to describe the rare, imperfectly imitable, and exploitable resources of a firm may themselves not be rare, imperfectly imitable, or exploitable.

Indeed, it may be the case that a manager or a managerial team is a firm resource that has the potential for generating sustained competitive advantages. The conditions under which this will be the case can be outlined using the VRIO framework. However, in the end, what becomes clear is that firms cannot expect to 'purchase' sustained competitive advantages on open markets (Barney 1986*a*, 1988; Wernerfelt 1989). Rather, such advantages must be found in the rare, imperfectly imitable, and exploitable resources already controlled by a firm (Dierickx and Cool 1989).

NOTES

1. This meeting was held in 1995 in Mexico City. The substance of this story comes from personal communication.
2. Thus, e.g. Porter (1980) suggests that *firms* should analyze their competitive environment, choose their strategies, and then acquire the resources needed to implement their strategies. Firms are assumed to have the same resources to implement these strategies or to have the same access to these resources. More recently, Porter (1985) has introduced a language for discussing possible internal organizational attributes that may affect competitive advantage. The relationship between this 'value chain' logic and the resource-based theory of the firm is examined below.
3. See Kearns, D. T. and Nadler, D. A. (1992). *Prophets in the Dark*. New York: HarperCollins; and Smith, D. K. and Alexander, R. C. (1988). *Fumbling the Future*. New York: William Morrow.

Part II

RBT and Organizational Capabilities

4 Culture as a source of sustained competitive advantage*

Many attempts to explain the sustained superior financial performance of firms like Dell, McDonald's, and Southwest Airlines have focused on the managerial values and beliefs embodied in these firms' organizational cultures (Corporate Culture 1980; Deal and Kennedy 1982; Peters and Waterman 1982; Tichy 1983; Kotter and Heskett 1992; Quick 1992; Freiberg and Freiberg 1996; Collins and Porras 1997). These explanations suggest that firms with sustained competitive advantages typically are characterized by a strong set of core managerial values that define the ways they conduct business. It is these core values (about how to treat employees, customers, suppliers, and others) that foster innovativeness and flexibility in firms; when they are linked with management control, they are thought to lead to sustained competitive advantage.

Many of these explanations have a strong normative orientation. Firms with strong cultures are pointed out as examples of excellent management (Peters and Waterman 1982); mechanisms for modifying the cultures of other firms to approximate closely the cultures of successful firms have been widely discussed and applied (Corporate Culture 1980; Quinn 1980; Tichy 1983). These efforts are seen not only as ways of improving employee morale or quality of work life, but also as vital for improving a firm's performance. Recall that Peters and Waterman (1982) and Collins and Porras (1997) chose firms for their samples that not only had an excellent reputation for management, but also were superior financial performers over long periods.

This chapter examines the relationship between organizational culture and sustained competitive advantage. The conditions under which a firm's

* This chapter draws from Barney (1986*b*).

culture can be a source of sustained competitive advantage. It is concluded that, under a relatively narrow set of conditions, a firm's culture can be the source of such sustained advantages. However, arguments suggest that the normative implications of studies on organizational cultures are limited significantly. While some firms may obtain sustained competitive advantages from their organizational cultures, firms without such cultures cannot expect to engage in managerial activities that will develop cultures that, in turn, will generate such activities. Thus, the normative implications of studies on organizational cultures are limited to describing how firms enjoying sustained competitive advantages can maintain their success, and how less successful firms can obtain competitive parity. Studies of cultures cannot be used to describe how less successful firms, by modifying their cultures, can come to enjoy sustained competitive advantages.

First, some of the key concepts used in this analysis are defined. Second, the attributes that a firm's culture must have in order to be a source of sustained competitive advantage are discussed. Third, the organizational cultures of at least some firms are examined to see if they meet these criteria. Finally, whether firms that do not currently have organizational cultures that are a source of advantage can engage in managerial actions to develop such cultures is considered.

Defining culture and competitive advantage

Few concepts in organizational theory have as many different and competing definitions as 'organizational culture'. Smircich (1983), for example, has cited five classes of such definitions in her literature review. Rather than attempt to resolve these numerous and subtle definitional conflicts, a definition that is consistent with most of the research about organizational culture and a firm's performance is used here (e.g. Deal and Kennedy 1982; Peters and Waterman 1982). In this work, organizational culture typically is defined as a complex set of values, beliefs, assumptions, and symbols that define the way in which a firm conducts its business. In this sense, culture has pervasive effects on a firm because a firm's culture not only defines who its relevant employees, customers, suppliers, and competitors are, but it also defines how a firm will interact with these key actors

(Louis 1983; Schein 1999). This conception of organizational culture blurs classical distinctions between an organization's culture and its structure and strategy (Tichy 1983) because these attributes of a firm are direct manifestations of cultural assumptions about what business a firm is in and how it conducts that business.

While it is difficult to identify a single definition of organizational culture that incorporates all the facets of this concept, the dependent variable in this analysis—sustained competitive advantage—is defined as described in Chapters 1 and 3. A firm has a competitive advantage when it is creating more economic value than the marginal firm in its industry; it has a sustained competitive advantage when efforts to duplicate the bases of that advantage have ended. Sustained competitive advantages tend to last longer than other kinds of competitive advantages.

Culture and sustained superior financial performance

In order for a firm's culture to provide sustained competitive advantages, three conditions must be met (Barney 1991*a*). First, the culture must be valuable; it must enable a firm to do things and behave in ways that lead to high sales, low costs, high margins, or in other ways create economic value to the firm. Because sustained competitive advantage is an economic concept, culture, to generate such performance, must have positive economic consequences. Second, the culture must be rare; it must have attributes and characteristics that are not common to the cultures of a large number of other firms. Finally, such a culture must be imperfectly imitable; firms without these cultures cannot engage in activities that will change their cultures to include the required characteristics, and if they try to imitate these cultures, they will be at some disadvantage (reputational, experience, etc.) compared to the firm they are trying to imitate.

These three characteristics are all derived from the VRIO framework presented in Chapter 3. The first requirement that a firm's culture must enable it to do things and behave in ways that add economic value to the firm is clearly a prerequisite for generating even competitive parity. If a firm's culture enables it to behave in ways that are inconsistent with a firm's competitive situation, then that culture cannot be a source of superior performance, sustained, or otherwise.

The requirement that valuable cultures must be rare to generate sustained competitive advantages reflects the dynamics of competition created by a competitive advantage. If many firms have similar cultures that allow them to behave and compete in approximately the same way, then none will possess a culturally based competitive advantage.

Finally, even if the above conditions are met, it is still necessary for a firm's culture to be imperfectly imitable for it to generate sustained superior financial performance. Perfectly imitable cultures, even if they are valuable, and even if they are currently rare, are subject to imitation that dissipates any competitive advantages they may provide. The culture-driven success of one firm creates an incentive for other firms to modify their cultures to duplicate that success. If the culture is perfectly imitable, it cannot give any one firm a sustained competitive advantage. Thus, for example, if the cultural attributes isolated by Peters and Waterman (1982) are, in fact, easily transferable, as is suggested on the cover of one of the paperback editions of their book, then these cultural attributes cannot be a source of sustained competitive advantage.

A firm that has a valuable, rare, and imperfectly imitable culture enjoys a sustained competitive advantage that reflects that culture. Such a firm will enjoy the positive economic consequences of its culture. Relatively few other firms will be able to obtain these same benefits, and those firms that currently do not enjoy them cannot engage in activities that will make it possible to obtain them. However, the overall performance of a firm with such advantages can be reduced if a firm fails to manage other strategically relevant functions successfully (Peters and Waterman 1982). These other functions might include both the financial and analytical characteristics of a firm's business. In addition, while a firm with a valuable, rare, and imperfectly imitable culture can obtain sustained advantages, other attributes of a firm, including, perhaps, unique geographic advantages and luck, also can lead to such performance (Barney 1985*b*).

This analysis does not imply that firms currently enjoying culturally based advantages will always enjoy these advantages, because a valuable culture today could, in different economic or competitive conditions, become an economic liability. Moreover, because other attributes of a firm also can generate sustained advantages, it is possible that several firms in an industry all can obtain sustained superior financial performance based on different competitive advantages (Lippman and Rumelt 1982). However, it will not be possible for a large number of firms to obtain such performance on the basis of a single type of organizational culture.

Competitive advantage from organizational culture

If a firm's culture, in order to be the source of sustained competitive advantages, must be valuable, rare, and imperfectly imitable, then the possibility that organizational cultures with these characteristics exist must be evaluated. Previous research on organizational cultures suggests that at least some cultures of some firms have these characteristics, and thus can be a source of sustained competitive advantage. This research also suggests that not all firms have cultures with these three attributes (Martin et al. 1983; Tichy 1983), and thus organizational culture is not a source of competitive advantage for all firms.

THE ECONOMIC VALUE OF CULTURE

Much of the literature on organizational culture and the performance of a firm can be interpreted as suggesting that culture can have significant positive economic value for a firm. Certain organizational cultures apparently enable firms to do and be things for employees, customers, suppliers, and others that could not be done, or could not be done as well, by firms without these cultures (Ouchi 1981; Deal and Kennedy 1982). Many of these activities have shown a positive economic impact on firms.

Peters and Waterman (1982) provided a broad description of the economic value of certain organizational cultures. Each of their eight characteristics of an excellent company reflects strong values and beliefs in organizational cultures. Thus, for example, firms that are simultaneously loosely and tightly coupled typically have an organizational culture with a strong set of core values—one of which encourages creativity and innovativeness (Peters and Waterman 1982: 319). Firms without such a culture may attempt to develop the attributes of a tight–loose system, but such attempts generally are not as successful because the culture of the organization neither supports nor values such behavior. In a similar vein, firms that are successful at obtaining productivity through their people generally have an organizational culture that supports and values the worth of the employee. Firms without such a supportive culture generally do not succeed in maximizing their productivity through their people. Firms that stay close to their customers typically are obsessed with customer service and satisfaction. This obsession, once again, reflects some of the core values of an organization's culture.

Each of these cultural traits can result in positive economic gains for firms. Both Peters and Waterman (1982) and Porter (1980) note that staying close to one's customer can result in timely market information, joint product development activities, and intense brand loyalties. These benefits result in high sales and increased margins, and thus have a direct positive financial impact on a firm. Innovativeness, productivity through people, and the other cultural factors cited by Peters and Waterman (1982) also have positive economic consequences.

Simply because the cultures of certain firms enable them to engage in activities with positive economic impact does not imply that all organizational cultures have such effects. Indeed, implicit in much of the organization cultures literature is the notion that an organization's culture can significantly reduce a firm's effectiveness, disabling the firm from perceiving all its competitive/operational options and preventing it from choosing options consistent with competitive/operational necessities (Crozier 1964; Porter 1980; Riley 1983; Tichy 1983).

VALUABLE AND RARE CULTURES

That a firm's culture may enable it to behave in ways with positive economic impact does not necessarily imply that a firm can obtain sustained competitive advantages from its culture. In addition, these cultural attributes must be rare.

The frequency with which valuable organizational cultures occur among firms is ultimately an empirical question. Previous research has indicated that some organizational cultures, far from being rare, are likely to be quite common among any given set of firms (DiMaggio and Powell 1983; Spender 1983). Indeed, some have argued that though cultures may appear to be unique or specific to a given firm, they sometimes actually reflect an underlying commonality and function, and thus are not rare at all (Martin et al. 1983).

Despite these findings, it must be admitted that some organizational cultures might exist in a relatively small number of firms, and thus hold the potential for generating sustained superior financial performance. Numerous authors have noted that firms are idiosyncratic social inventions, reflecting the unique personalities and experiences of those who work there (Polanyi 1958; Barley 1983). Firms are also historically bound, partially reflecting the unique circumstances of their founding (Selznick 1957; Pettigrew 1979), the unique personalities of their founders (Zucker 1977; Schein 1983), and the unique circumstances of their growth (Chamberlin 1933; Clark 1970, 1972). Often, these unique experiences of a firm are reflected in a firm's culture. Rare experiences can lead to a rare culture. If these cultures are also valuable, then they hold the potential for generating sustained competitive advantages.

The assertion that the unique personalities and history of a firm can lead to rare cultures is consistent with the contingency view of culture discussed by Smircich (1983). However, this does not *necessarily* imply that the cultures of these firms will be unique as well (Martin et al. 1983). Different organizational experiences may lead to similar cultural outcomes. Even among firms with unique histories, cultures may not be rare, and thus without potential for generating sustained superior financial performance.

THE IMITABILITY OF CULTURE

For a firm's culture to be a source of sustained competitive advantage, it must not only be valuable and rare, it also must be imperfectly imitable. Without imperfect imitability, any competitive advantage that a valuable and rare culture might give will create strong incentives for imitation.

There is significant evidence which suggests that valuable and rare organizational cultures often may be very difficult, if not impossible, to imitate. First, it may not be possible for individuals observing a culture (let alone those experiencing a culture) to describe what about a particular organization's culture adds value to a firm (Lippman and Rumelt 1982). Values, symbols, beliefs, and the like are notoriously difficult to describe and categorize (Barley 1983; Gregory 1983). Moreover, the relationship between these highly subjective organizational characteristics and a firm's competitive advantages also defies rigorous description and inspection. The valuable and rare aspects of an organization's culture often become part of the unspoken, unperceived common sense of the firm. Many have argued that culture is a powerful force in explaining the behavior of individuals and groups within organizations precisely because it is unspoken and taken for granted (Polanyi 1958; Goffman 1959; Berger and Luckman 1967). If those attempting to observe a culture to imitate it cannot describe what it is about it that is valuable, those aspects of that culture cannot be consciously imitated—though firms might accidentally successfully imitate a culture they cannot describe (Lippman and Rumelt 1982; McKelvey 1982).

Even if valuable and rare organizational cultures can be described by potential imitators, as is apparently sometimes possible (e.g. Ouchi 1981; Peters and Waterman 1982), it still may not be possible to imitate these cultures. The characteristics of organizational culture may make it rare and may also make it difficult to imitate. Valuable organizational cultures may be intrinsically bound up with a firm's unique history and heritage—and history defies easy imitation. This conception of culture is explored in Clark's notion (1970, 1972) of an organizational saga, that is, the embodiment of the values, symbols, and beliefs of a firm as expressed through its unique history. Selznick (1957), Stinchcombe (1965), and Zucker (1977) observed that the constellation of persistent symbols, beliefs, and values that characterize a firm's culture at least partially reflects the unique early history of the firm, including the pattern-setting influence of company founders. A firm with a history significantly different from that of a firm whose culture it would like to imitate may find an unbridgeable barrier to imitation. If this firm's culture is also valuable and rare, then it may enjoy a sustainable competitive advantage.

Finally, even if the economically relevant aspects of a firm's culture can be described, and even if they are not historically specific in character, conscious and successful cultural imitation may still be imperfect. The components of organizational culture (including values, symbols, and beliefs) are as difficult to purposefully change as they are to describe (Smircich 1983). The existence of multiple, possibly contradictory cultures within the same firm makes the management of culture all the more problematic (Gregory 1983). Indeed, the data show that attempts to modify such subtle and interdependent aspects of organizations through organizational development methods have met with mixed results at best (Porras and Berg 1978*a*, 1978*b*). While numerous authors have described ways in which an organization's culture can be managed (Peters 1978; Quinn 1980; Tichy 1983; Schein 1999; Cameron and Quinn 1999), it must be admitted that at least some organizational cultures resist planned change. If a potential imitator cannot manage the change of its own culture to approximate the culture of a firm with a culturally based strategic advantage, then the latter may be safe from imitation and its strategic advantage may be sustained.

It has been argued that the cultures of some firms may be immune from planned imitation. If these cultures are valuable and rare, then they can be a source of sustained competitive advantage. This is not to suggest that a firm's culture stays the same since it certainly does evolve over time (Selznick 1957; Zucker 1977). This also does not suggest that all attributes of all organizational cultures are imperfectly imitable. Rather, previous findings indicate that *some organizational* cultures may be valuable, rare, and imperfectly imitable, and thus the source of sustained competitive advantage.

Normative implications of culture research

These arguments have a variety of normative implications, both for managers in firms without valuable cultures and for managers in firms with valuable cultures.

FIRMS WITHOUT VALUABLE CULTURES

For firms without valuable cultures, the normative implications of these analyses are somewhat limiting. Such firms cannot expect to obtain even temporary competitive advantages on the basis of their organizational culture. However, because a firm's culture can have such a significant impact on the ways a firm conducts its business, these firms are often forced to engage in activities that modify their culture to include at least some economically valuable attributes. Thus, a firm facing a competitive environment that requires low-cost production strategies with a culture that does not emphasize managerial efficiency often will engage in actions to try to develop the value of efficiency among its managers.

Suppose, through significant managerial efforts expended over time, a firm is able to modify its culture. Could this modified culture, then, be a source of sustained competitive advantage? Given our previous analysis, this seems unlikely for at least two reasons. First, if this firm is imitating the valuable culture of a competing firm, then even if this firm is successful at modifying its culture, that modified culture will only enable it to do the things that the firm it is imitating already does. Such successful imitation does not give a firm a competitive advantage, sustained or otherwise, in the area of organizational culture. Rather, it suggests that the valuable culture in question is less rare than it was before imitation, which in turn implies the likely development of reduced margins due to competitive entry. Thus, the best return that a firm can expect from imitating the valuable culture of a competing firm is competitive parity.

The second reason is that if one firm can consciously manage its culture to modify it to enhance its value, then other firms also are likely to modify their cultures in this manner. Returns to culture modifications depend not only on improving the economic value of a firm's culture, but also on the ability of other firms to make modifications in their cultures that result in similar cultures. If a large number of firms can successfully manage this change, then these culture changes will not result in any one firm enjoying a culture-based competitive advantage. But if only a few firms are able to modify their cultures appropriately, then these firms can enjoy a sustained competitive advantage.

There are at least two reasons why modifying a firm's culture in this manner might be possible for only a small number of firms. On the one hand, firms that are able to successfully modify the economic value of their cultures may enjoy a superior understanding of the skills necessary to accomplish this change. That is, they may have superior culture management skills. Such skills, if they are understood by only a few firms (i.e. if they are rare) and if those firms that do not have these skills cannot obtain them (i.e. if they are imperfectly imitable), can enable some firms to make culture changes while other firms cannot. On the other hand, some organizational cultures may be more susceptible to change than others. Young and small firms, for example, often have more flexible organizational cultures than older and larger firms (Tichy 1983). If these changeable cultures are characteristic of only a small number of competing firms (i.e. rare), and if firms without changeable cultures cannot develop change-facilitating attributes (i.e. these changeable cultures are imperfectly imitable), then firms with these types of cultures can obtain sustainable advantages. However, if a large number of competing firms have equally flexible cultures, or if firms without such cultures can engage in activities to increase the changeability of their cultures, then these cultural traits cannot be a source of sustained competitive advantage.

There is a paradox central to this discussion. For an organization's culture to be the source of sustained competitive advantage, it must be valuable, rare, and imperfectly imitable. To obtain sustained advantages from modifying its culture, a firm must have either valuable, rare, and imperfectly imitable culture management skills or it must have a valuable, that is, flexible, rare, and imperfectly imitable culture. Firms either have these attributes, in which case they endow a firm with at least the potential of sustained advantages, or they do not have them. If they do not have these attributes, but are successful in acquiring them, then these attributes are not imperfectly imitable, and thus cannot be the source of sustained competitive advantages. If it was possible to tell a large number of firms how to modify their cultures to include economically valuable attributes, then culture would cease to give any one firm a competitive advantage. Thus, the normative implications of culture research are limited to assisting firms that already possess valuable, rare, and imperfectly imitable cultures and culture management skills in recognizing and nurturing these organizational characteristics to obtain sustained advantages. Such research, and the consulting it implies, cannot be used to help firms without valuable, rare, or imperfectly imitable cultures or culture management skills to obtain such performance, for such efforts are, in principle, imitable.

FIRMS WITH VALUABLE CULTURES

From this brief review of findings on organizational culture, it is possible to conclude that at least some firms have valuable, rare, and imperfectly imitable cultures. For such firms, the normative implications of these arguments are clear. These firms should attempt to understand what it is about their cultures that gives them competitive advantages, and then to nurture and develop these cultural attributes, thereby increasing the likelihood that their competitive advantage will not be dissipated through mismanagement (Stevenson 1976; Lenz 1980).

From another point of view, the injunction that firms should study their culture to nurture its strengths is a reaffirmation of the now popular notion that firms should 'stick to their knitting' (Peters and Waterman 1982). The analysis suggests that this recommendation only applies to those firms that have valuable, rare, and imperfectly imitable cultures. For firms without valuable cultures, sticking to what they know best cannot generate even competitive parity. Such activities will jeopardize a firm's survival in thc long run. Even if firms have valuable cultures, if those cultures are not rare or imperfectly imitable, they cannot be expected to lead to sustained competitive advantages. Only if a firm's culture is valuable, rare, and imperfectly imitable will 'sticking to one's knitting' generate sustained superior financial performance.

Conclusion

A firm's culture can be a source of sustained competitive advantage if that culture is valuable, rare, and imperfectly imitable. The sustained superior performance of firms like Dell, IBM, McDonald's, and Southwest Airlines may be, at least partly, a reflection of their organizational cultures (Peters and Waterman 1982; Quick 1992). Firms with valuable, rare, and imperfectly imitable cultures should nurture these cultures. Firms without valuable, rare, or imperfectly imitable cultures cannot expect their cultures to be the source of sustained competitive advantages. Nor can such firms expect that efforts to change their cultures, although they may successfully incorporate new valuable attributes, will generate sustained superior performance. Such efforts are typically imitable, and thus, at best, only the source of temporary competitive advantages. These firms must look elsewhere if they are to find ways to generate expected sustained competitive advantages.

The analysis presented here has important implications for debates concerning the ability to manage a firm's culture to improve financial performance (Smircich 1983; Tichy 1983). This reasoning suggests that if firms can modify their cultures to improve their financial performance, then such modifications can, in the long run, only generate competitive parity. For if one firm is able to modify its culture, then it is likely that others can as well. In this case, the advantages associated with this culture are imitable, and thus only a source of competitive parity. Only when it is not possible to manage a firm's culture in a planned way does that culture have the potential of generating expected sustained advantages. Thus, those who argue that culture is simply another in a series of manipulatable tools available to managers for the implementation of business strategies (Schwartz and Davis 1981; Tichy 1983) deny the possibility that culture can be a source of sustained advantage, while those who argue that culture is not readily manipulatable (Smircich 1983) uphold the possibility that culture can be a source of such sustained advantages.

A firm's culture is one of several attributes that differentiate firms one from another (Alchian 1950; Alchian and Demsetz 1972). It is in these sustainable differences between firms that explanations of sustained competitive advantage must be sought (Demsetz 1973: 2). It is often not easy to describe what it is about some firms that makes them more successful than others. Precisely because an organization's culture is hard to describe, socially complex and causally ambiguous; because the common sense of managers is taken for granted; and because even if a culture can be described, it is difficult to change; a firm's culture can hold promise for sustained competitive advantages for some firms.

5 Trust as a source of sustained competitive advantage*

Significant differences in assumption and method exist between behaviorally oriented and economically oriented organizational scholars (Barney 1990; Donaldson 1990). While these differences manifest themselves in a wide variety of research contexts, nowhere are they more obvious than in research on the role of trust in economic exchanges.

On the one hand, behaviorally oriented researchers often criticize economic models that assume exchange partners are inherently untrustworthy (Mahoney, Huff, and Huff 1993) and constantly tempted to behave in opportunistic ways (Donaldson 1990). These scholars are dissatisfied with economic analyses that suggest trust will only emerge in an exchange when parties to that exchange erect legal and contractual protections (called governance mechanisms) which make it in their self-interest to behave in a trustworthy manner (Williamson 1975). This rational, calculative, economic approach to trust, many behavioral scholars argue, is empirically incorrect (since most exchange partners are, in fact, trustworthy), socially inefficient (since it leads to an overinvestment in unnecessary governance), and morally bankrupt (Etzioni 1988). A more reasonable approach, it is argued, would adopt the assumption that most exchange partners are trustworthy, that they behave as stewards over the resources they have under their control (Donaldson and Davis 1991), and thus that trust in exchange relationships—even without legal and contractual governance protections—will be common.

* This chapter draws from Barney and Hansen (1994).

On the other hand, more economically oriented scholars respond by observing that, at the very least, it is difficult to distinguish between exchange partners that are actually trustworthy and those that only claim to be trustworthy (Arrow 1974, 1985; Williamson 1985). Since one cannot reliably distinguish between these types of exchange partners, legal and contractual protections are a rational and effective means of assuring efficient exchange. Trust, many economists would argue, is in fact common in exchange relationships, precisely because of the constant threat of opportunistic behavior, linked with governance (Hill 1990). Behavioral assertions that most exchange partners are inherently trustworthy and that legal or contractual governance is thus unnecessary, are at best naive, and at worst, foolish.

These debates about the role of trust in exchange relationships are interesting, in their own right, but they are not terribly relevant for strategic management research. Much of this research focuses on understanding sources of competitive advantage for firms (Bowman 1974; Rumelt, Schendel, and Teece 1991). The effort to understand sources of competitive advantage leads strategy researchers to study differences between firms that enable some firms to conceive of and implement valuable strategies that other firms either cannot conceive of or cannot implement (Barney 1991*b*). Debates between behavioral and economically oriented researchers about how trustworthy individuals or firms are fail to point to these kinds of differences. Moreover, while the behavioral and economic approaches suggest very different processes through which trust emerges in economic exchanges, both these approaches assert that trust in economic exchanges will be very common. Such common attributes of exchange relationships cannot be sources of competitive advantage for individual firms (Barney 1991*b*). To be a source of competitive advantage, trust must be available to only a *few* firms in their exchange relationships, not to most firms in most exchange relationships (Peteraf 1993).

The purpose of this chapter is to understand the conditions under which trust and trustworthiness in exchange relationships can, in fact, be a source of competitive advantage for firms. First, trust, trustworthiness, and the closely related concept of opportunism are defined. Next three types of trust in exchange relationships are described: weak form trust, semi-strong form trust, and strong form trust.[1] Then, the conditions under which these different types of trust will, and will not, be sources of competitive advantage for firms are discussed. This chapter concludes by discussing some of the empirical and theoretical implications of the analysis.

Defining trust and trustworthiness

Numerous definitions of trust and trustworthiness have been presented in the literature (Gambetta 1988; Bradach and Eccles 1989; Lewicki and Bunker 1994). For purposes of this chapter, Sabel's definition of trust (1993: 1133) has been adopted: *trust is the mutual confidence that no party to an exchange will exploit another's vulnerabilities.*

Parties to an exchange can be vulnerable in several different ways. For example, when parties to an exchange find it very costly to accurately evaluate the quality of the resources or assets others assert they will bring to an exchange, these economic actors are subject to adverse selection vulnerabilities (Akerlof 1970). When parties to an exchange find it very costly to accurately evaluate the quality of the resources or assets others are actually offering in an exchange, these economic actors are subject to moral hazard vulnerabilities (Holmstrom 1979). Also, when parties to an exchange make large, asymmetric transaction-specific investments in an exchange, they are subject to holdup vulnerabilities (Klein, Crawford, and Alchian 1978). According to Sabel, when parties to an exchange trust each other, they share a mutual confidence that others will not exploit any adverse selection, moral hazard, holdup, or any other vulnerabilities that might exist in a particular exchange.

A definition of trustworthiness follows directly from Sabel's definition of trust. As the word itself implies, an exchange partner is trustworthy when it is worthy of the trust of others. An exchange partner worthy of trust is one that will not exploit other's exchange vulnerabilities. Note that while trust is an attribute of a relationship between exchange partners, trustworthiness is an attribute of individual exchange partners.

In many ways opportunism is the opposite of trust. A firm's actions are opportunistic to the extent that they take advantage of another's exchange vulnerabilities. Williamson (1979) emphasizes firms exploiting holdup vulnerabilities of exchange partners, caused by asymmetric transaction-specific investment. However, the exploitation of other exchange vulnerabilities, including adverse selection and moral hazard vulnerabilities, can also be opportunistic in nature.

Types of trust

While trust is the mutual confidence that one's vulnerabilities will not be exploited in an exchange, different types of trust can exist in different economic exchanges. These different types of trust depend on different reasons parties to an exchange can have the confidence that their vulnerabilities will not be exploited. At least three types of trust can be identified: weak form trust, semi-strong form trust, and strong form trust.

WEAK FORM TRUST: LIMITED OPPORTUNITIES FOR OPPORTUNISM

One reason that exchange partners can have the mutual confidence that others will not exploit their vulnerabilities is that they have no significant vulnerabilities, at least in a particular exchange. If there are no vulnerabilities, from adverse selection, moral hazard, holdup, or other sources, then the trustworthiness of exchange partners will be high, and trust will be the norm in the exchange.

This type of trust can be called weak form trust because its existence does not depend on the creation of contractual or other forms of exchange governance. Nor does its existence depend on commitments by parties to an exchange to trustworthy standards of behavior. Rather, trust emerges in this type of exchange because there are limited opportunities for opportunism. Parties to an exchange, in this weak form context, will gain all the benefits of being able to trust their exchange partners without substantial governance or other costs.

Of course, weak form trust is likely to emerge in only very specific kinds of exchanges, that is, exchanges where there are limited vulnerabilities. In general, whenever the quality of goods or services that are being exchanged can be evaluated at low cost, and whenever exchange partners do not need to make transaction-specific investments to obtain gains from an exchange, vulnerabilities in that exchange will be limited, and weak form trust will be common. Easy-to-evaluate quality effectively eliminates adverse selection and moral hazard vulnerabilities; no transaction-specific investments effectively eliminate holdup vulnerabilities. Without vulnerabilities, opportunistic behavior is unlikely, and weak form trustworthiness will exist.

In this sense, weak form trust is clearly endogenous, that is, it emerges out of a very specific exchange structure. Of course, this exchange structure can change and evolve over time. If an exchange evolves such that the cost of evaluating the quality of the goods or services in an exchange increases, then adverse selection and/or moral hazard vulnerabilities may emerge, making weak form trust no longer possible. Also, if transaction-specific investments develop over time in an exchange, then holdup vulnerabilities may emerge, and weak form trust will no longer exist.

Given this analysis, an important question becomes: how often will weak form trustworthiness exist? While, ultimately, this is an empirical question, it seems likely that weak form trust will be the norm in highly competitive commodity markets (Williamson 1975). Examples of such markets include the market for crude oil and the market for soybeans. In all these markets, it is relatively easy for buyers and sellers to evaluate the quality of the goods or services they are receiving. Moreover, in all these markets, there are large numbers of equally qualified buyers and sellers. Thus, firms do not have to make transaction-specific investments to trade with any one firm. Since parties to exchanges in these kinds of markets are not subject to significant exchange vulnerabilities, weak form trustworthiness is usually the norm.

Of course, that a market was once a highly competitive commodity market does not mean that it will always be a highly competitive commodity market. The cost of evaluating the quality of goods or services can increase, the number of buyers or suppliers can fall, and significant exchange vulnerabilities can develop. In this new exchange context, exchange partners cannot rely on the emergence of weak form trust, though other types of trust may develop.

SEMI-STRONG TRUST: TRUST THROUGH GOVERNANCE

When significant exchange vulnerabilities exist (due to adverse selection, moral hazard, holdup, or other sources), trust can still emerge, if parties to an exchange are protected through various governance devices. Governance devices impose costs of various kinds on parties to an exchange that behave opportunistically. If the appropriate governance devices are in place, the cost of opportunistic behavior will be greater than its benefit, and it will be in the rational self-interest of exchange partners to behave in a trustworthy way (Hill 1990). In this context, parties to an exchange will have the mutual confidence that their vulnerabilities will not be exploited because it would be irrational to do so. This type of trust can be called semi-strong trust, and is the type of trust emphasized in most economic models of exchange (Hill 1990).

A wide range of governance devices have been described in the literature. Economists have tended to focus on market-based and contractual governance devices. One market-based governance device is the market for reputations (Klein, Crawford, and Alchian 1978). Firms or individuals that develop a reputation for behaving opportunistically will often be excluded from future economic exchanges where exchange vulnerabilities are significant. The cost of these opportunities forgone can be substantial, and the avoidance of these costs can lead exchange partners to be trustworthy in current exchanges, albeit in a semi-strong way. Examples of more contractual forms of governance include complete contingent claims contracts, sequential contracting, strategic alliances, and hierarchical governance (Williamson 1985; Hennart 1988; Kogut 1988). Contractual governance devices explicitly define what constitutes opportunistic behavior in a particular exchange, and specify the economic costs that will be imposed on offending parties (Williamson 1979).

This economic focus on market-based and contractual governance devices has been criticized as being badly under-socialized (Granovetter 1985). Several authors have suggested that a variety of social costs can also be imposed on exchange partners that behave in opportunistic ways. For example, a firm that gains a reputation as a 'cheater' may bear substantial economic opportunity costs (Klein, Crawford, and Alchian 1978), but it may also lose its social legitimacy (DiMaggio and Powell 1983). Also, Granovetter (1985) has argued that exchange partners, be they individuals or firms, that are deeply embedded in social networks put those networks of relations at risk when they engage in opportunistic behavior. The imposition of these social costs also acts to reduce the threat of opportunistic behavior.

One implication of including governance devices that impose social costs on opportunistic exchange partners, instead of just economic costs, is the expectation that opportunistic behavior will be unusual, even in settings where few market-based or contractual governance devices are in place, as long as these more social forms of governance exist (Granovetter 1985). Even some economists are beginning to recognize the importance of these more socially-oriented forms of governance. However, while this more social approach to governance broadens the range of governance devices that should be studied, the trust that emerges among parties to an exchange with these social governance mechanisms in place is of the same type as the trust that emerges with only economic governance devices in place. In both cases, trust emerges because rational actors find it in their self-interest, for both economic and social reasons, to not behave opportunistically. Put another way, neither economic nor behavioral scholars would generally predict the emergence of trust in exchanges where significant vulnerabilities exist, and in which there are no market-based, contractual, or social forms of governance.[2] With governance in place, however, trust—of the semi-strong variety—may emerge, despite the existence of significant exchange vulnerabilities.

Like weak form trust, semi-strong trust is endogenous, that is, it emerges out of the structure of a particular exchange. However, unlike weak form trust, the structure of that exchange is modified, in the semi-strong case, through the use of governance devices of various types. If parties to an exchange create and/or exploit the correct governance devices, then opportunistic behavior in that exchange will be unlikely, and trust—albeit of the semi-strong variety—will exist.

Of course, the creation and exploitation of different forms of governance are not costless. The costs of market-based and contractual forms of governance are well documented (Williamson 1985). While social forms of governance have fewer direct costs associated with them, they are nevertheless costly, in the sense that the use of these forms of governance requires one to only engage in exchanges where potential partners are embedded in specific broader social networks of relations. This limitation on potential exchange partners is an opportunity cost of using social forms of governance.

Traditional transactions cost logic suggests that rational economic actors will insist on just that level of governance necessary to ensure the semi-strong trustworthiness of exchange partners. If existing social forms of governance cannot assure the emergence of semi-strong trustworthiness, then additional, and costly, legalistic and contractual forms of governance (including, perhaps, contingent claims contracts and sequential contacting) will need to be created. If this level of governance is not sufficient, then even more costly hierarchical forms of governance may be erected (Williamson 1975, 1979). There may even be some exchanges where hierarchical governance is not sufficient to create semi-strong form trust (Grossman and Hart 1986).

One implication of this form of analysis is that there may be some potentially valuable exchanges that cannot be pursued. Whenever the cost of governance needed to generate semi-strong trust is greater than the expected gains from trade, an exchange with semi-strong trustworthy partners will not be pursued. This can happen in at least two ways. First, the expected gains from trade may be relatively small, in which case even modest investments in governance mechanisms may not pay off. Second, the expected gains from trade may be very large, but so may be the exchange vulnerabilities in that trade. In this type of exchange, the high cost of governance may still be greater than the expected value of exchange, even if that expected value is large. Indeed, as Grossman and Hart (1986) suggest, there may be some exchanges where no governance devices will create semi-strong trust (i.e. where the cost of governance is infinitely high). If the only types of trust that can exist in economic exchanges are of the weak and semi-strong types, then these valuable, but costly to govern, exchanges may have to remain unexploited.

STRONG FORM TRUST: HARD-CORE TRUSTWORTHINESS

In weak form trust, trust is possible because exchange vulnerabilities do not exist. In the semi-strong case, trust is possible, despite exchange vulnerabilities, because of the significant social and economic governance mechanisms on the opportunistic behavior of exchange partners. In strong form trust, trust emerges in the face of significant exchange vulnerabilities, independent of whether elaborate social and economic governance mechanisms exist, because opportunistic behavior would violate values, principles, and standards of behavior that have been internalized by parties to an exchange.

Strong form trust could also be called principled trust, since trustworthy behavior emerges in response to sets of principles and standards that guide the behavior of exchange partners. Frank (1988) might call strong form trust 'hard-core trust'. Hard-core trustworthy exchange partners are trustworthy, independent of whether exchange vulnerabilities exist and independent of whether governance mechanisms exist. Rather, hard-core trustworthy exchange partners are trustworthy because that is who, or what, they are. This type of trust is, perhaps, closest to the type of trust emphasized by behavioral scholars (Mahoney, Huff, and Huff 1993).[3]

In this sense, strong form trustworthiness is clearly exogenous to a particular exchange structure. Strong form trust does not emerge from the structure of an exchange, but rather, reflects the values, principles, and standards that partners bring to an exchange. Those values, principles, and standards may reflect an exchange partner's unique history, its culture, or the personal beliefs and values of critical individuals associated with it (Barney 1986*b*; Arthur 1989; Dierickx and Cool 1989).

The strong form trustworthiness of individuals

While the existence of strong form trustworthiness is, ultimately, an empirical question, research from a variety of disciplines can be helpful in answering the existence question. If exchange partners are individuals, then research in developmental psychology suggests that strong form trustworthiness can exist in at least some people.

Developmental psychologists have studied the stages of moral development in children and young adults (Kohlberg 1969, 1971). These stages are summarized in Table 5.1.[4] When children are very young (small babies), they are able to make very few, if any, moral choices. In this stage, decision-making and behavior is essentially amoral. However, as children mature, they often have to decide whether to conform their choices and behaviors to a set of values, principles, and standards.[5] In the conventional morality stage (Kohlberg 1969), children conform their choices and behaviors to a set of values, principles, and standards in order to avoid the costs imposed on them by others for failing to do so. In this stage, children are moral because the costs of being caught violating principles and standards (i.e. punishment) are too high. In the postconventional morality stage, choices

Table 5.1. Parallels between stages of moral development and types of trust

Stages in moral development	Types of trust and trustworthiness
Amoral stage When there are no moral choices to be made	*Weak form trust* Limited opportunities for opportunism
Conventional morality Decisions and behaviors conform to standards in order to avoid the cost of being caught violating standards	*Semi-strong form trust* Trust emerges in response to social and economic governance mechanisms that impose costs on opportunistic behavior
Postconventional morality Decisions and behaviors conform to standards because they have been internalized as principles and values	*Strong form trust* An exchange partner behaves in a trustworthy manner because to do otherwise would be to violate values, standards, and principles of behavior

and behaviors conform to a set of values, principles, and standards because they are internalized by individuals. While external costs could still be imposed on choices and behaviors that do not conform to these principles and standards, avoiding these costs is not the primary motivation for moral behavior. Rather, the primary motivation for such behavior is to avoid internally imposed costs, including a sense of personal failure, guilt, and so forth.

Some obvious parallels exist between the types of trust and trustworthiness identified here, and the stages of moral development identified in developmental psychology. These parallels are identified in Table 5.1. The amoral stage in the moral development literature is analogous to weak form trustworthiness. Just as young children cannot violate moral standards when they are unable to make moral choices, individuals in exchange relationships cannot act opportunistically when there are no opportunities to do so. Conventional morality is analogous to semi-strong trustworthiness. In conventional morality, individuals make choices to conform their behavior to a set of principles and standards in order to avoid the cost of failing to do so; in semi-strong trust, opportunistic behavior is avoided because of the economic and social costs imposed on such behavior by governance mechanisms. Finally, postconventional morality is analogous to strong form trustworthiness. In both cases, choices and behavior conform to a set of principles and standards because those principles and standards have been internalized. While external costs may be imposed on individuals who violate these principles and standards, avoiding these external costs is not the primary reason choices and behavior conform to them. Rather, the avoidance of internally imposed costs—including a sense of personal failure and guilt—provide the primary motivation for this type of principled behavior.

Psychologists have shown that postconventional morality is not uncommon (Kohlberg 1971). While some people never mature beyond the amoral or conventional morality stages, many have sets of values, principles, and standards that they use to guide their choices and behaviors. In order for postconventional morality to lead to strong form trustworthiness, all that is additionally required is that some of these values, principles, and standards suggest that exploiting an exchange partner's vulnerabilities is inappropriate.

The strong form trustworthiness of firms

At the individual level, the existence of strong form trustworthiness in at least some people seems plausible. However, that individuals—as exchange partners—can be strong form trustworthy does not necessarily imply that firms—as exchange partners—can be strong form trustworthy. Firms, as exchange partners, can be strong form trustworthy for at least two reasons. Either a firm may possess a culture and associated control systems that reward strong form trustworthy behavior, or the specific individuals involved in a particular exchange may, themselves, be strong form trustworthy.

Zucker (1987) has shown that firm founders can have a very strong impact on the culture and other institutional attributes of firms. This impact can continue, even if these individuals have been dead for many years. Others, besides founders can also have strong cultural and institutional effects. For example, transformational leaders (Tichy and Devanna 1986) can have the effect of recreating a firm's culture and fundamentally changing other of its attributes.

If these and other influential individuals were themselves strong form trustworthy, they may have created an organizational culture characterized by strong form trustworthy values and beliefs. These strong form trustworthy values and beliefs may also be supported and reinforced by internal reward and compensation systems, together with decision-making mechanisms that reflect strong form trustworthy standards. A firm with these cultural and institutional mechanisms in place will often behave in a strong form trustworthy manner in exchange relationships.

Note that if a firm has a strong form trustworthy culture and associated control mechanisms, it is not necessary for each individual in a firm to be strong form trustworthy. Rather, all that is required is that individuals in a firm be at least self-interested in their behavior. In this situation, individuals in a firm will find it in their self-interest to behave in a strong form trustworthy way when representing the firm, for failure to do so would lead them to be subject to a variety of social and economic sanctions. Individuals who are unable to conform themselves to a firm's strong form trustworthy standards have several options, including, for example, finding positions in the firm where trustworthiness issues are not likely to arise or changing firms.

Of course, that a firm once had a culture, and associated internal control mechanisms, that encouraged strong form trustworthiness does not mean that it will always have these attributes. Cultures can evolve, control mechanisms can change, and a firm may no longer have the attributes to qualify for strong form trustworthiness. However, even when firms do not have strong form trustworthiness cultures, it may still be possible for some of the exchanges in which a firm engages to be characterized by strong form trust.

Exchanges between firms are, more often than not, actually exchanges between small groups of individuals in different firms. For example, when an automobile company signs a supply agreement with a supplier, the two groups of individuals most directly involved in this agreement are the purchasing people, in the automobile company, and the sales people, in the supply company. When two firms agree to form an equity joint venture, several groups of people are directly involved, including those in each parent firm that are assigned the responsibility to interact with the joint venture, and those that work in the joint venture itself.

While the firms in these exchanges may not have strong form trustworthy cultures, the specific individuals who are most directly involved in these exchanges may, themselves, be strong form trustworthy. Exchanges between strong form trustworthy individuals in different firms can lead to strong form trust, even though the firms, themselves, may not be strong form trustworthy.[6]

Trust and competitive advantage

Trust can emerge in economic exchanges in any of the three ways discussed. However, these three types of trust are not equally likely to be sources of competitive advantage. A strategic analysis of trust and trustworthiness focuses on the conditions under which a particular type of trust will be a source of competitive advantage.

WEAK FORM TRUST AND COMPETITIVE ADVANTAGE

The exchange attributes that make weak form trust possible suggest that weak form trust will usually not be a source of competitive advantage. As suggested earlier, weak form trust is most likely to emerge in highly competitive commodity markets. It is well known that exchange partners in highly competitive commodity markets can expect to gain few, if any, competitive advantages (Porter 1980). In particular, while those participating in these markets will be able to rely on the existence of weak form trust in their exchange relationships, the advantages of weak form trust will accrue to all exchange partners in these markets equally, thereby giving no one of them a competitive advantage.

Indeed one of the few ways those trading in these markets can expect to gain advantages from weak form trust is if some competitors fail to rely on weak form trust and, indeed, invest in unnecessary and costly governance devices to create semi-strong form trust. Both those that rely on weak form and semi-strong form trust, in these highly competitive commodity markets, can expect trust to exist in their exchange relationships. However, those that invest in governance to generate semi-strong form trust will have higher costs compared to those that rely on weak form trust. Over time, those that have invested in unnecessary (and costly) governance will either abandon those governance devices or suffer from competitive disadvantages.

Put differently, the cost advantage of those that rely on weak form trust over those that rely on semi-strong form trust, in these highly competitive conditions, is a measure of the economic value of weak form trust. However, if numerous competitors are all able to obtain this value at the same low cost, then it will not be a source of competitive advantage to any one of them (Barney 1991*b*).

SEMI-STRONG FORM TRUST AND COMPETITIVE ADVANTAGE

Semi-strong trust in exchange relationships is economically valuable, in the sense that its creation assures parties to an exchange that their vulnerabilities will not be exploited. However, the ability to create semi-strong trust in economic exchanges depends on several important governance skills and abilities that parties to an exchange must possess. For example, for semi-strong trust to emerge, exchange partners must be able to accurately anticipate sources and levels of opportunistic threat in the exchanges in which they may participate. Also, to create semi-strong trust, exchange partners must be able to rely on existing social governance mechanisms, and/or to conceive of, implement, and manage the appropriate market-based and contractual governance mechanisms. Only if exchange partners can accomplish these tasks will the 'right' types of governance be chosen to create semi-strong trust, and will the value of semi-strong trust be realized.

However, for semi-strong trust to be a source of competitive advantage, there must be heterogeneity in the exchange governance skills and abilities of competing firms (Barney 1991*b*). If most competing firms or individuals have similar governance skills and abilities, they will all be equally able to create the conditions under which semi-strong trust will emerge in their exchange relationships. Moreover, the cost of creating semi-strong trust will also not vary dramatically across these equally skilled competitors. Since these competitors do not vary in their exchange governance skills, no one of them will be able to gain a competitive advantage based on the semi-strong trust that they are able to create with these skills.[7]

Of course, there is no reason to believe, a priori, that competing exchange partners will be equally skilled or able in creating the conditions necessary for semi-strong trust. For example, some exchange partners may have developed a high degree of skill in managing, say, intermediate market forms of governance (e.g. equity joint ventures). These highly skilled actors may be able to create semi-strong trust using these intermediate market forms of governance in economic exchanges where less skilled actors may be forced to use hierarchical forms of governance. If intermediate market forms of governance are, in fact, less costly than hierarchical forms of governance, those that obtain semi-strong trust through intermediate market forms will have a competitive advantage over those that must obtain trust in that exchange through hierarchical forms of governance. Similar reasoning could apply to those that are highly skilled in managing contractual forms of governance (e.g. contingent claims contracts) compared to those that are only able to use more costly intermediate market forms of governance or hierarchical forms of governance.

Heterogeneity in the skills and ability to create semi-strong form trust in an exchange may also reflect important social differences among exchange partners. For example, if a particular firm is contemplating an exchange with another firm, where that relationship is deeply embedded in a large complex network of social relations, these firms may be able to rely on (relatively inexpensive) social governance mechanisms to develop semi-strong form trust. On the other hand, if a competing firm is anticipating a similar exchange that is not deeply embedded in this broader social network of relations, parties to this exchange may have to rely on (more costly) economic forms of governance to ensure semi-strong form trust. The firm that can rely on social governance to generate semi-strong form trust will have a cost-based competitive advantage over the firm that must rely on economic governance to generate semi-strong form trust.

Heterogeneity in governance skills and abilities is an important explanation of variance in a wide variety of different economic exchanges. Compare, for example, the exchanges between Toyota and its suppliers, on the one hand, and General Motors (GM) and its suppliers (Womack, Jones, and Roos 1990; Dyer and Ouchi 1993), on the other. Toyota's supply relationships are deeply embedded in long-standing networks of social and economic relationships. These social governance mechanisms have enabled both Toyota and its suppliers to engage in very vulnerable exchanges (due to high transaction-specific investments that lead to a high risk of holdup) with substantially less contractual or other forms of governance than is the case at GM. Without the ability to rely on social embeddedness to constrain the opportunistic behavior of its suppliers, GM has had to reduce the threat of opportunism by reducing the level of transaction-specific investment in its suppliers (i.e. by having multiple competing suppliers), by insisting on elaborate contractual protections, or by vertically integrating the supply relationship (Womack, Jones, and Roos 1990; Dyer and Ouchi 1993). Overall, the cost of creating semi-strong form trust at Toyota has been substantially lower than the cost of creating semi-strong trust at GM.[8]

Of course, if several competitors all possess these special governance skills and abilities to approximately the same level, then they will not be a source of competitive advantage for any of them, even if there are some competitors who do not possess these skills. However, as long as the number of competitors that have these special governance skills and abilities is less than what is required to generate perfect competition dynamics, then they can be a source of competitive advantage for those that possess them (Barney 1991*b*).

Moreover, if these skills and abilities can rapidly diffuse among competitors, they will be the source of only temporary competitive advantages. However, it seems likely that these skills and abilities will not diffuse through most populations. For example, the ability to rely on social governance mechanisms in different exchanges depends on the structure of the network of relations within which an exchange is embedded. Those networks of relations, in turn, are developed over long periods, and are unique to a particular point in history. Such path-dependent (Arthur 1989) phenomena are subject to time decompression diseconomies (Dierickx and Cool 1989), and thus costly to imitate. The development of special governance skills is also path-dependent. Moreover, these skills are often socially complex, and thus costly to imitate (Barney 1991*b*).

Whenever exchange partners possess rare and costly-to-imitate governance skills and abilities, they may be able to use those abilities to gain competitive advantages in creating semi-strong trust. On the other hand, when competing exchange partners possess similar governance skills and abilities, the creation of semi-strong trust will generate only competitive parity.

STRONG FORM TRUST AND COMPETITIVE ADVANTAGE

For strong form trustworthiness to be economically valuable, all those with a significant stake in an exchange must be strong form trustworthy. If one or more parties to an exchange may behave opportunistically in that exchange, then all parties to that exchange will need to invest in a variety of social and economic governance mechanisms to ensure semi-strong trust. Any potential economic advantages of being strong form trustworthy are irrelevant when semi-strong governance protections are erected and exploited, since strong form trustworthy parties are forced to behave as if they were only semi-strong trustworthy.

Economic opportunities in strong form trust exchanges

On the other hand, if all those with a significant stake in an exchange are strong form trustworthy, some important and valuable economic opportunities may exist. These opportunities reflect either the governance cost advantages that strong form trust exchanges may enjoy over semi-strong form trust exchanges, or the ability that strong form trustworthy exchange partners may have to explore exchange options not available to semi-strong form trustworthy exchange partners.

When two or more strong form trustworthy individuals or firms engage in an exchange, they can all be assured that any vulnerabilities that might exist in this exchange will not be exploited by their partners. Moreover, this assurance comes with no additional investment in social or economic forms of governance. As long as the cost of developing and maintaining strong form trustworthiness in an individual or firm, plus the cost of discovering strong form trustworthy partners, is less than the cost of exploiting or creating semi-strong form governance devices, those engaging in a strong form trustworthy context will gain a cost advantage over those exchanging in a semi-strong trustworthy context.

Consider, for example, several competing firms looking to purchase raw materials from a set of suppliers. Suppose that a small number of these buyers and sellers are strong form trustworthy, and that there are some significant exchange vulnerabilities in this raw materials purchase. In order to complete this purchase, those purchasing from semi-strong suppliers will need to rely on or erect a variety of social and economic governance devices. While these governance devices are costly, their existence will enable firms to purchase the raw material in question. On the other hand, strong form trustworthy buyers purchasing from strong form trustworthy suppliers will not have to rely on or erect social or economic forms of governance in order to complete their purchase of the raw material. As long as the cost of developing and maintaining strong form trustworthiness, plus the cost of discovering strong form trustworthy exchange partners, is less than the cost of relying on or erecting social or economic governance devices, the firms purchasing raw materials in a strong form trust exchange will have a cost advantage over those firms purchasing raw materials in a semi-strong trust exchange.[9]

Perhaps even more important than this governance cost advantage, those engaging in strong form trust exchanges may be able to exploit exchange opportunities that are not available to those who are only able to engage in semi-strong trust exchanges. It has already been suggested that valuable semi-strong exchanges will not be pursued when the cost of governance needed to generate semi-strong trust is greater than the expected gains from trade. This can happen when the expected gains from trade are small (but modest vulnerabilities in this exchange require modest levels of expensive governance) or when the expected gains from trade are substantial (but very large vulnerabilities in this exchange require very substantial levels of costly governance). While semi-strong trust exchanges will not be pursued in these situations, it may be possible to pursue strong form trust exchanges. In this sense, strong form trustworthiness may increase the set of exchange opportunities available to an individual or firm, compared to those who are only semi-strong trustworthy (Zajac and Olsen 1993; Ring and Van de Ven 1994).

Consider, for example, several competing firms looking to cooperate with one or more of several other firms in the development and exploitation of a new, and sophisticated, technology. Suppose that only a small number of these two sets of firms are strong form trustworthy, that the technology in question has significant economic potential, but that there are enormous exchange vulnerabilities in the technology development process. Semi-strong trustworthy firms, in this setting, will need to invest in substantial amounts of costly governance to try to create semi-strong trust. It may even be the case that no form of governance will create semi-strong trust (Grossman and Hart 1986). The potential economic return that could be obtained from this exchange will need to be reduced by an amount equal to the present value of the cost of governing this exchange. Moreover, the present value of this exchange will also have to be discounted by any residual threat of opportunism. The reduced value of this exchange could lead semi-strong trustworthy firms to decide not to pursue it, even though substantial economic value may exist.

On the other hand, exchanges of this sort between strong form trustworthy firms are burdened neither by the high cost of governance nor any residual threat of opportunism. Strong form trustworthy firms will be able to pursue these valuable, but highly vulnerable exchanges, while semi-strong form trustworthy firms will be unable to pursue them. This may represent a substantial opportunity cost for semi-strong trustworthy exchange partners, and a source of competitive advantage for strong form trustworthy exchange partners.[10]

Traditional transactions cost logic suggests that when faced with these valuable but highly vulnerable exchanges, exchange partners will opt for hierarchical forms of governance and use managerial fiat as a way to manage trustworthiness problems (Williamson 1985). However, hierarchical governance is not always a solution to these problems. First, there may be important legal and political restrictions on the use of hierarchical governance. For example, one cannot acquire a direct competitor if such actions lead to unacceptably high levels of industry concentration. Also, firms may be required, for political reasons, to maintain market or intermediate market relationships with an exchange partner (e.g. when entering into a new country market).

Second, as Grossman and Hart (1986) suggest, hierarchical governance does not necessarily 'solve' opportunism problems. Rather, it simply shifts those problems from a market or intermediate market context to inside the boundaries of the firm. Where, in market-based exchanges, firms face the threat of opportunism in exchanges with other firms, bringing these transactions within the boundaries of a firm can simply lead to division facing the threat of opportunism in exchanges with other divisions. Put differently, hierarchical governance does not automatically create strong form trust exchanges (Ouchi 1980). These issues are discussed in more detail in section the 'Discussion' section of Chapter 8 which provides a resource-based analysis of vertical integration.

Where hierarchical governance may not always be a solution to the threat of opportunism, exchanges between strong form trustworthy exchange partners—whether those exchanges are within the boundary of a single firm or not—will, in general, create strong form trust. Strong form trustworthy individuals or firms will often be able to gain governance cost advantages over semi-strong trustworthy individuals or firms. Moreover, strong form trustworthy individuals or firms will often be able to engage in economic exchanges that cannot be pursued by semi-strong trustworthy exchange partners. Put differently, the level of vulnerability in some economic exchanges may be greater than the ability of any standard governance devices to protect against the threat of opportunism. The only way to pursue these exchanges is through strong form trustworthiness.

Of course, if most competitors are strong form trustworthy, and engage in exchanges with others that are also strong form trustworthy, then the advantages of strong form trustworthiness would only be a source of competitive parity, and not competitive advantage. However, while the number of strong form trustworthy exchange partners in a particular segment of the economy is ultimately an empirical question, it seems like a reasonable guess that strong form trustworthiness in at least some segments of the economy is probably rare, and thus (assuming exchanges with other strong form trustworthy exchange partners are developed) at least a source of temporary competitive advantage for strong form trustworthy individuals and firms.

Locating strong form trustworthy exchange partners

Given the important competitive advantages that may attend exchanges between strong form trustworthy exchange partners, an important question becomes: how can strong form trustworthy exchange partners recognize each other? This process is problematic, since exchange partners that are not strong form trustworthy have a strong incentive to assert that they are. If a strong form trustworthy individual or firm believes that an exchange partner is strong form trustworthy, even though this partner is not, then that strong form trustworthy individual or firm will be willing to engage in a highly vulnerable exchange without social or economic devices. Without these devices in place, the untrustworthy exchange partner could exploit the strong form trustworthy partner's exchange vulnerabilities with impunity. Thus, simple assertions that one is strong form trustworthy are not sufficient for assuming that an exchange partner is, in fact, strong form trustworthy.

Of course, a simple solution to this adverse selection problem would be to directly observe whether a potential exchange partner is strong form trustworthy, and respond appropriately. Unfortunately, the individual and organizational attributes that create strong form trustworthiness are difficult to directly observe. At an individual level, the values, principles, and standards around which strong form trustworthy individuals organize their lives are clearly not directly observable. At the firm level, an organization's culture, and associated control systems, may be difficult to observe, and their implications for individual behavior ambiguous—at least to those not deeply embedded in this culture and control system. Moreover, if the development of strong form trust depends on the strong form trustworthiness of small groups of people in a larger organization, evaluating the individual values, principles, and standards of these people remains difficult.

Even with these challenges, strong form trustworthy exchange partners can still be found. It will often be the case, for example, that exchange partners will begin a relationship assuming that others are at least semi-strong trustworthy. As this relationship evolves over time, parties to an exchange may be able to gain sufficient information to accurately judge whether others are strong form trustworthy. If two or more parties to an exchange discover that they are strong form trustworthy, any subsequent exchanges between these parties can generate strong form trust, and these exchange partners will subsequently obtain all the advantages of strong form trustworthiness. On the other hand, if experience shows that an exchange partner is only semi-strong form trustworthy, then future exchanges with this partner will continue with semi-strong form trust generating governance mechanism in place.

Note that this process of discovering strong form trustworthy exchange partners assumes that one's trustworthiness type does not automatically change as a result of experience in a semi-strong trust relationship. If the creation of semi-strong trust exchanges inevitably led exchange partners to become strong form trustworthy, then all exchanges would inevitably be characterized by strong form trust, and strong form trustworthiness would not be a source of competitive advantage to any individual or firm. Rather than changing an exchange partner's trustworthiness type, the creation of a semi-strong trust exchange creates an opportunity for exchange partners to more directly observe another's trustworthiness type. While it is certainly true that an exchange partner's trustworthiness type may evolve over the long run, the historical, path-dependent, socially complex, and causally ambiguous nature of strong form trustworthiness makes it unlikely that semi-strong form trustworthy firms will be able to become strong form trustworthy in the short or medium term.

This search for potential strong form trustworthy exchange partners can be shortened through the use of signals of strong form trustworthiness

(Spence 1973). Signals of strong form trustworthiness must have two properties: (*a*) they must be correlated with the underlying (but costly to observe) actual level of strong form trustworthiness in a potential exchange partner, and (*b*) they must be less costly to exchange partners that are actually strong form trustworthy than they are to exchange partners that only claim they are strong form trustworthy (Spence 1973).

Several behaviors by exchange partners qualify as signals for strong form trustworthiness. For example, a reputation for being strong form trustworthy is a signal of strong form trustworthiness.[11] Gaining a reputation as a strong form trustworthy exchange partner occurs, over time, as an exchange partner confronts situations where opportunistic behavior is possible, but chooses not to engage in opportunistic activities. There are no opportunity costs associated with a strong form trustworthy individual or firm not behaving opportunistically, since such behavior is not in this kind of exchange partner's opportunity set. On the other hand, a non-strong form trustworthy exchange partner will have to absorb opportunity costs each time they decide to not behave in an opportunistic way. These opportunity costs make it more costly for an exchange partner that is not strong form trustworthy to develop a reputation as strong form trustworthy, compared to an exchange partner that is actually strong form trustworthy.

While a reputation for being strong form trustworthy is a signal of strong form trustworthiness, it is noisy. In particular, this reputation cannot distinguish between those exchange partners that are actually strong form trustworthy, and those that are not strong form trustworthy, but have yet to engage in an exchange where returns to opportunistic behavior are large enough to motivate opportunistic behavior. While a reputation for being strong form trustworthy does eliminate those exchange partners who have acted opportunistically, it does not eliminate those exchange partners who might act opportunistically, given the right incentives.

Another signal of strong form trustworthiness is being open to outside auditing of the exchange relationship. This is less costly to strong form trustworthy exchange partners, compared to those that are not strong form trustworthy, since trustworthy exchange partners were not going to behave opportunistically anyway. One would expect to see strong form trustworthy firms and individuals to be very open to outside auditors, perhaps even paying the cost of outside auditors chosen by potential exchange partners.

A third signal of strong form trustworthiness might be to make unilateral transaction-specific investments in an exchange before that exchange is actually in place. Gulati, Khana, and Nohira (1994) have found, for example, that it is not uncommon for firms with a strong track record of successfully engaging in joint ventures to sign long-term, third-party supply contracts that are only valuable if a particular joint venture actually goes forward—before that joint venture agreement is complete. Such unilateral transaction-specific investments are less costly to strong form trustworthy firms, since they were not going to behave in an opportunistic manner in developing this joint venture anyway. These investments foreclose opportunistic opportunities for firms that are not strong form trustworthy, and thus represent significant opportunity costs to these firms. If all those involved in an exchange independently make these kinds of unilateral transaction-specific investments, the others in these exchanges can conclude, with some reliability, that they are strong form trustworthy.

If strong form trustworthiness is relatively rare among a set of competitors, and if two or more strong form trustworthy exchange partners are able to engage in trade, then these strong form trustworthy individuals or firms will gain at least a temporary competitive advantage over individuals or firms that are not strong form trustworthy. For this competitive advantage to remain, however, the individual and organizational attributes that make strong form trustworthiness possible must also be costly to imitate and immune from rapid diffusion. Fortunately, the individual and organizational attributes that make strong form trustworthiness possible (i.e. individual values, principles, and standards; an organization's culture and associated control systems) reflect an exchange partner's unique path through history (path dependence) and are socially complex. As was suggested earlier, these types of individual and organizational attributes are usually immune from imitation and rapid diffusion among competitors (Arthur 1989; Dierickx and Cool 1989; Barney 1991*b*).[12]

Discussion

Trust, in economic exchanges, can be a source of competitive advantage. However, trust in these exchanges is not always a source of competitive advantage. Weak form trust is only a competitive advantage when competitors invest in unnecessary and costly semi-strong governance mechanisms. Semi-strong form trust is only a source of competitive advantage when a small number of competitors have special skills and abilities in conceiving of and implementing social and economic governance devices, and when those skills and abilities are immune from low-cost imitation. Strong form trust is a source of competitive advantage when two or more strong form trustworthy individuals or firms engage in an exchange, when strong form trustworthiness is relatively rare among a set of competitors, and when the individual and organizational attributes that lead to strong form trustworthiness are immune from low-cost imitation.

This analysis has important implications for research in organization theory and strategic management. For example, these ideas can be seen as an extension of transactions cost theory—an extension that makes this form of analysis strategically more relevant. Where transactions cost economics (TCE) implicitly assumes that the skills and abilities needed to conceive of and implement governance mechanisms are constant across individuals and firms (Williamson 1985), this approach suggests that these skills and abilities may vary in some strategically important ways. Also, where transactions cost theory assumes either that all potential exchange partners are equally likely to behave opportunistically or that one cannot distinguish between those that will behave opportunistically and those that will not behave opportunistically (Williamson 1985), this analysis suggests that potential exchange partners opportunistic tendencies may vary and that these differences can be discovered. Discovery of exchange partners that will not engage in opportunistic behavior enables firms to gain all the advantages of trade, without the cost of governance.

Thus, consistent with many of the more behaviorally oriented organizational scholars cited earlier, the approach in this chapter rejects both the assumption that all exchange partners are likely to engage in opportunistic behavior and the assumption that it is not possible to know how opportunistic a particular exchange partner is likely to be. However, these transactions cost assumptions are not replaced by equally extreme, if opposite, assumptions that most exchange partners are trustworthy most of the time. Rather, the approach adopted here is that the trustworthiness of exchange partners can vary, and that how trustworthy an exchange partner is can be discovered. The adoption of this approach leads to the conclusion that, in some circumstances, trust can be a source of competitive advantage—a conclusion that is not possible if it is assumed that most exchange partners are either untrustworthy or trustworthy.

This analysis also points to two important exchange processes that have not received sufficient attention in the organizations and strategy literatures. First, the argument suggests that semi-strong form trust can be a source of competitive advantage if competing exchange partners vary in their skills and abilities in conceiving of and implementing governance mechanisms. What these specific skills and abilities might be, and why they might develop in some economic actors and not others, are unexplored issues in this chapter. However, casual observation suggests that, for example, some firms seem to be better at managing certain kinds of governance devices than others. Corning seems to be able to manage joint ventures more effectively than, say, TRW (Sherman 1992). Toyota seems to be able to manage complex supply relationships more effectively than GM (Womack, Jones, and Roos 1990; Dyer and Ouchi 1993). How these different skills and abilities evolve, and their competitive implications, are important research questions. In this context, comparative research on semi-strong form governance in different industries and different countries is likely to be very important (Dyer and Ouchi 1993).

Second, the argument suggests that strong form trustworthy exchange partners may be able to discover other strong form trustworthy exchange partners. Once discovered, these kinds of exchange partners can gain important competitive advantages from working with each other. However, much more empirical work needs to focus on the process through which strong form trustworthiness evolves in an economic actor. Such empirical work will establish whether strong form trustworthiness is a relatively stable attribute of economic actors, and whether this attribute can be imitated at low cost. Also, empirical research needs to focus on the process of searching for strong form trustworthy exchange partners. In particular, the role of signals of strong form trustworthiness deserves empirical attention. In this context it may be helpful to compare the decisions and behaviors of firms that have been able to develop many strong form trustworthy exchanges (e.g. Corning) with the decisions and behaviors of firms that have been unable to develop these strong form trustworthy exchanges.

By examining the competitive implications of different types of trust in economic exchanges, it becomes clear that extreme assumptions about potential exchange partners—that most are trustworthy and that most are opportunistic—are overly simplistic. Rather, the trustworthiness of exchange partners may vary, and in that variance, the possibility of competitive advantage may exist.

NOTES

1. With apologies to Eugene Fama (1970).
2. Granovetter (1985) would probably argue that relatively few economic exchanges are not embedded in some broader network of social relations. This, of course, is ultimately an empirical question. However, Granovetter's theory suggests that without some mechanism to impose social costs on those that behave opportunistically, social governance will not generate trust in a relationship.
3. In principle, some level of compensation will always exist where strong form trustworthy exchange partners will abandon their values, principles, and standards of behavior, and act in opportunistic ways. This level of compensation might be called the 'Faustian' price. However, this level of compensation is *much* higher for a strong form trustworthy exchange partner compared to a semi-strong trustworthy exchange partner.
4. This is a simplification of the actual typology developed by Kohlberg (1969, 1971). However, it is consistent with Kohlberg's findings.
5. These values, standards, and principles are normally taken from a child's parents or other caregivers (Kohlberg 1969).
6. Conflicts between individual and firm values, in this context, act as a constraint on the ability of strong form trustworthy individuals to engage in strong form trust exchanges. However, strong form trustworthy individuals can be expected to engage in a variety of activities to neutralize the non-strong form trustworthy effects of the firm within which they operate. Moreover, the firm has strong incentives to let the strong form trustworthy individuals continue in strong form trust exchanges, since it gains all the advantages of these exchanges.
7. Competing exchange partners do not have to erect the same governance mechanisms for semi-strong trust to generate competitive parity. Rather, all that is required is that competing exchange partners erect functionally equivalent governance devices (i.e. governance devices that generate the same level of semi-strong form trust) and that these governance devices are about equally costly. These arguments also apply to bundles of governance devices to create semi-strong form trust.
8. Obviously, there may be some strong form trustworthiness attributes to Toyota's relationships with its suppliers that do not exist between GM and its suppliers.
9. While ultimately an empirical question, it seems likely that the cost of creating and maintaining strong form trustworthiness, plus the cost of discovering strong form trustworthy exchange partners, will often be less than the cost of relying on or erecting semi-strong governance devices. The cost of creating and maintaining strong form trustworthiness can be spread across numerous economic exchanges,

thus reducing the per exchange cost. The cost of discovering strong form trustworthy exchange partners can be reduced through the discovery and signaling mechanisms described below.

10. As previously, it seems likely that the cost of creating and maintaining strong form trustworthiness, plus the cost of discovering strong form trustworthy exchange partners, will be less than the opportunity cost of relying only on semi-strong form trust governance devices.
11. Note that a reputation for being strong form trustworthy is not the same as not having a reputation for being opportunistic. A potential exchange partner may not have a reputation for being opportunistic (they may not be known as a cheater), but still not have a reputation for being strong form trustworthy (i.e. they may not be known as 'hard-core' trustworthy).
12. Given the challenge of discovering strong form trustworthy exchange partners, these relationships are likely to be relatively stable over time. Indeed, it may well be the case that exchanges between strong form trustworthy partners may continue, even though they have limited potential for generating current economic value (Ring and Van de Ven 1994). In this setting, the challenge facing exchange partners is to discover new ways to generate economic value with older, stable, relationships. Even when this cannot be done, economically nonviable exchanges may continue for sometime because of the close relationships between partners.

6 Human resources as a source of sustained competitive advantage*

Human resource researchers and managers have long maintained that the HR function plays an important role in firm performance. In fact, most corporate annual reports boldly state that the firm's people are its most important asset. Despite these widely held beliefs and all-too-frequent statements, however, many organizational decisions suggest a relatively low priority on both the human resources of the firm and the HR department. For example, when organizations require cost cutting, they often look first to investments in the firm's people such as training, wages, and headcounts. In addition, even when top managers value the firm's people, they may not value the HR department. For example, when asked how the founder and CEO of one of the most successful high-technology companies in the world viewed the importance of human resources, the director of Strategic Leadership Development replied:

> Which do you mean? If you mean the Human Resource function, or what we call 'big HR', then he doesn't have much value for them at all. If you mean the people of the company, or what we call 'little hr', then he places an extremely high value on them.

If top managers publicly espouse their commitment to the firm's human resources, and the firm's HR function has substantial responsibility for managing this valuable firm resource, then why do many organizational decisions not evidence this stated commitment to people or a respect for the HR function?

* This chapter draws from Barney and Wright (1998).

It may be that the fault lies, in part, with the fact that few HR executives can explain, in economic terms, how a firm's people can provide sustainable competitive advantage and the role that the HR function plays in this process. Furthermore, due to this lack of understanding, many HR executives may fail to direct HR activities toward developing characteristics of the firm's human resources that can be a source of sustainable competitive advantage.

In this chapter, the role of human resources in a firm's competitive advantage is examined. Following numerous HR scholars (e.g. Lado and Wilson 1994; Wright, McMahan, and McWilliams 1994; Jackson and Schuler 1995; Boxall 1996, 1998; Snell, Youndt, and Wright 1996; Huselid, Jackson, and Schuler 1997; Boxall and Steeneveld 1999; Lepak and Snell 1999; McMahan, Virich, and Wright 1999; Wright, Dunford, and Snell 2001; Hatch and Dyer 2004), resource-based theory—as outlined in Part I—is used to accomplish this analysis. Following this previous work, a firm's human resources are defined as all of the knowledge, experience, skill, and commitment of a firm's employees, their relationships with each other, and with those outside the firm. A firm's HR practices are defined as all of the programs, policies, procedures, and activities that firms use to manage their human resources.

Resource-based analysis of human resources

THE ECONOMIC VALUE OF HUMAN RESOURCES

Firms create value by either decreasing product/service costs or differentiating the product/service in a way that allows the firm to charge a premium price. Thus, the ultimate goal of any HR executive is to create value through the HR function. The first question that an HR executive must address is 'How can the HR function aid in either decreasing costs or increasing revenues?'

Alcon Laboratories exemplifies the role of HR practices in directly decreasing costs. Trying to hold down the cost of health insurance, Alcon sought to encourage employees to take part in the less expensive Preferred Provider Organization (PPO) rather than the traditional fee-for-service type plans. Vice-president of HR, Jack Walters, noticed that many doctors who were part of the PPO were not the doctors being used by employees. Thus, in negotiations, he asked MetLife to identify the doctors Alcon employees were using and recruit those doctors into the PPO. MetLife was able to bring most of those doctors into its PPO, and, as a result, Alcon's health insurance costs increased at less than half of the industry average.

Increasing revenues, on the other hand, is a more distant goal to HR managers but one in which they can play an important role. For example, Federal Express (now FedEx) illustrates the value created by human resources. Federal Express managers stress that they are a 'people-first' organization. The corporate philosophy statement sums up their view of the source of competitive advantage: 'People—Service—Profit'. Fred Smith, founder and CEO of the firm, says, 'We discovered a long time ago that customer satisfaction really begins with employee satisfaction' (Waterman 1994). In other words, the FedEx philosophy is that people are the primary link in the value chain, and thus, value is created by focusing first on employees.

How is this operationalized to create value? This emphasis on employee satisfaction is illustrated by FedEx's annual attitude survey. Most organizations administer attitude surveys from time to time, and occasionally use the information gleaned from the surveys to address the most glaring organizational problems. At FedEx, however, the attitude survey forms part of the annual managerial evaluation and reward process. The survey addresses the atmosphere of an individual's immediate work group, the immediate manager, the managers at levels higher in the organization, and the company's atmosphere in general. Scores on the items covering the work group and the immediate manager form 'the leadership index'. This index is used in two ways. If an individual manager receives low scores on the index from the employees reporting to him or her, that manager faces a year-long probation. During that time the manager is expected to improve the scores to an acceptable level or face some type of punitive action. Second, each year a goal is set for the company's score on the leadership index. If the goal is not met, the top 300 managers in the firm do not receive any bonus, which usually is about 40 percent of base salary. By linking rewards and punishment to employee satisfaction levels, the firm ensures that employees are treated well. When they are treated well, they treat customers well—and this creates value.

FedEx's philosophy has gained an increasing base of empirical support. For example, Schneider and Bowen (1985) hypothesized that HR practices would be related to employee attitudes which would consequently be related to customer satisfaction. They found significant relationships between HR practices and customer reports of the quality of service they received in a sample of banks. Schlesinger and Zornitsky (1991) found that job satisfaction predicted employees' perceptions of service quality as well as the discrepancy between employee and customer perceptions of quality. Ulrich et al. (1991) found significant relationships between the tenure of employees and customer satisfaction. Tornow and Wiley (1991) found that employee attitudes such as job satisfaction were related to measures of organizational performance. In addition, Schmit and Allscheid (1995) found that employees' climate perceptions of management, supervisor, monetary, and service support were related to employee affect. Affect was related to service intentions, which was related to customer service. Empirical research thus supports the notions that employee satisfaction is linked to service quality and that HR practices are important determinants of employee satisfaction.

Finally, some HR practices can impact on both costs and revenues. Continental Airlines experienced a tremendous turnaround in which the HR function played a vital role. One of the frequently cited HR practices responsible for this turnaround was the on-time bonus, an incentive system in which each employee was paid a bonus of $65 for every month the airline was at the top of the industry in on-time performance (Boissueau 1995). While this may seem like it comes straight from any introductory textbook (Barlow 1996), its origin was not nearly so simple. In early 1995, after years of pay cuts or no pay raises, top management discovered that it again would be unable to give pay raises to employees. HR executives recognized that taking that message to the employees at a critical phase of the turnaround would destroy morale and greatly impede the cultural shift under way. HR executives along with line executives came up with the idea of the on-time bonus. This bonus resulted in Continental moving from last to first in the industry in on-time performance and consequently both decreased costs and increased revenues. On the cost side, the company paid out $51 million in bonuses in the next year but saved $75 million in lower passenger accommodation costs such as money for meals and hotel rooms associated with missed connections. On the revenue side, the bonus was instrumental in restoring employee morale and, thus, increasing customer satisfaction. In addition, because on-time performance is an important criterion for the higher revenue business traveler, this bonus had a strong impact on the firm's revenues as they increased their share of the business traveler market.

RARITY OF HUMAN RESOURCES

The value of a firm's human resources is a necessary but not sufficient criterion for competitive advantage. If the same characteristic of human resources is found in many competing firms, then that characteristic cannot be a source of competitive advantage for any one of them. Valuable but common characteristics of human resources provide only competitive parity, ensuring that a firm is not at a substantial competitive disadvantage because it does not possess that characteristic. Thus, an HR executive must examine how to develop and exploit rare characteristics of the firm's human resources to gain competitive advantage.

For example, most firms view the labor pool for particular jobs as relatively homogeneous. Within any labor pool, however, differences exist across individuals in terms of their job-related skills and abilities. If the assumption exists across firms that the labor pool is homogeneous, there can be tremendous potential to exploit the rare characteristics of those employees for competitive advantage (Wright, McMahan, and McWilliams 1994).

For example, Nordstrom's exists in the highly competitive retailing industry. This industry is usually characterized as having relatively low-skill requirements and high turnover for sales clerks. Nordstrom's, however, has attempted to focus on individual salespersons as the key to its competitive advantage. It invests in attracting and retaining young, college-educated sales clerks who desire a career in retailing. It provides a highly incentive-based compensation system that allows Nordstrom's salespersons to make as much as twice the industry average in pay. The Nordstrom's culture encourages sales clerks to make heroic efforts to attend to customers' needs, even to the point of changing a customer's flat tire in the parking lot. The recruiting process, compensation practices, and culture at Nordstrom's have helped the organization to maintain the highest sales per square foot of any retailer in the nation. Nordstrom's has taken what is considered to be a relatively homogeneous labor pool and exploited the rare characteristics of its employees to gain a competitive advantage.

IMITABILITY OF HUMAN RESOURCES

Valuable and rare characteristics of a firm's human resources can provide above-normal profits for the firm in the short term; however, if other firms can imitate these characteristics, then over time the characteristics will provide no more than competitive parity. The HR executive must attempt to develop and nurture characteristics of the firm's human resources that *cannot* easily be imitated by competitors. This points to focusing on the importance of socially complex phenomena such as an organization's unique history or culture in providing competitive advantage.

Every firm has a unique history that shapes and defines the present situation. This history often provides a foundation for a competitive advantage which other firms find difficult or impossible to imitate. For example, a high-level executive at one of DuPont's competitors observed that no matter what his firm did (including purchasing DuPont's safety training programs), they were unable to match DuPont's safety record. When asked to explain why, he stated: 'When a firm starts out by making dynamite, something happens that just instils in employees' minds the importance of safety.' Thus, DuPont's superior safety performance stems at least in part from its unique history that competitors would find impossible to imitate.

Southwest Airlines exemplifies the role that socially complex phenomena such as culture play in competitive advantage. According to the company's top management, the firm's success can be attributed to the 'personality' of the company; a culture of fun and trust that provides employees with both the desire and the discretion to do whatever it takes to meet the customers' needs. The 'fun' airline uses an extensive selection process for hiring flight attendants who will project the fun image of the airline. Applicants must go through a casting call type exercise where they are interviewed by a panel that includes current flight attendants, managers, and customers. The applicants tell stories, such as their most embarrassing experience, in front of the panel and other applicants. Those who make it through the panel interview are then examined against a psychological profile that distinguished outstanding past flight attendants from those who were mediocre or worse.

In addition to the extensive selection process, employees are empowered to create an entertaining traveling environment by a strong organizational culture that values customer satisfaction. Says Herb Kelleher, CEO:

> We tell our people that we value inconsistency. By that I mean that we're going to carry 20 million passengers this year and that I can't foresee all of the situations that will arise at the stations across our system. So what we tell our people is, 'Hey, we can't anticipate all of these things, you handle them the best way possible. You make a judgment and use your discretion; we trust you'll do the right thing. If we think you've done some thing erroneous, we'll let you know—without criticism, without backbiting.' (Quick 1992)

This extensive selection process and the strong organizational culture contribute to the differentiated service that has made Southwest Airlines the most financially successful airline over the past twenty years and has enabled it to continually be among the best in the industry for having the fewest customer complaints.

Seeing this financial success, competitors, such as Continental Airlines (Continental Lite) and United Airlines (United Express), attempted to compete with Southwest Airlines by providing low-cost service to a number of destinations. Continental Lite ceased operations within a year, and United, while having survived, is still losing to Southwest in most markets where they compete. Kelleher, who believes that Southwest's superior performance has happened because its culture simply cannot be imitated, stated:

> Maybe someone could equal the cost... possibly they could. And maybe someone could equal the quality of service that goes along with that and constitutes great value,... possibly they could. But the one thing they would find it impossible to equal very easily is the spirit of our people and the attitude they manifest toward our customers. (Quick 1992)

In other words, the human resources of Southwest Airlines serve as a source of sustained competitive advantage because they create value, are rare, and are virtually impossible to imitate.

THE ORGANIZATION OF HUMAN RESOURCES

Finally, in order for any characteristic of a firm's human resources to provide a source of sustained competitive advantage, the firm must be organized to exploit the resource. Organization requires having in place the systems and practices that allow HR characteristics to bear the fruit of their potential advantages.

For example, both General Motors (GM) and Ford historically have recruited assembly line workers from the same basic labor market. There is little evidence that the skill levels of Ford's workers are significantly higher than those of GM workers. Ford, however, has been more successful at developing a cooperative, team-based culture than has GM. Both automakers set out to develop employee involvement programs during the late 1970s and early 1980s. Ford more successfully changed the culture and HR systems to allow for, and even value, employee participation in decision-making, relative to GM. Ford's culture and HR systems allow for employees to participate in decision-making and to utilize cognitive skills that the GM systems have been less able to exploit (Templin 1992). In addition, as Ford moves toward hiring even more highly skilled employees through an extensive assessment process, its participative system will leave it poised to increase its relative advantages over GM (Templin 1994).

The question of organization focuses attention on systems, as opposed to single HR practices. Research on HR practices and firm performance seems to indicate that HR practices are most effective when they exist as a coherent system. Wright and Snell (1991) argued that Strategic Human Resource Management (HRM) required coordinated HR activities across the various subfunctions. Similarly, Wright and McMahan's definition (1992) of Strategic HRM called for 'horizontal integration' of the various HR practices rather than viewing each in isolation. Lado and Wilson (1994) hypothesized that the more complex the HR system, the more likely it would be to serve as a source of sustainable competitive advantage. MacDuffie (1995), in a study of automobile manufacturing firms, found that performance was maximized when 'bundles' of HR practices were linked with participative work systems and flexible production systems. Wright et al. (1996) found that HR practices such as selection, appraisal, and compensation were unrelated to the financial performance of petrochemical refineries alone, but that they were strongly positively related to performance among refineries that had highly participative work systems.

These research studies seem to indicate a need for HR functions to pay attention to the system of HR practices, rather than to focus on each in isolation.

Both quantitative and qualitative data gathered from an ongoing research study indicate that very few companies are spending much time and attention on coordinating each of the various HR subfunctions (e.g. staffing, compensation, training, and so on) with one another.[1] Of thirteen firms in this study, only two have actively attended to achieving integration among the compensation, selection, training, and appraisal systems and processes. It appears that firms that do make such efforts have at least temporary advantages over their competitors.

Human resources and sustainable competitive advantage

The VRIO analysis above illustrates how a variety of firms have attempted to develop their human resources to provide sources of sustainable competitive advantage. The VRIO framework (summarized in Table 3.1) provides a tool to assist managers to evaluate the potential for specific firm resources to be sources of competitive disadvantage, competitive parity, competitive advantage, and sustained competitive advantage. According to this framework, aspects of human resources that do not provide value can only be a source of competitive disadvantage. These resources or activities are ones that HR executives should be discarding from the HR function. Aspects of human resources that provide value, but are not rare, are sources of competitive parity. These resources are not to be dismissed; not to have them is a source of competitive disadvantage, but because other firms possess them, they cannot provide an advantage in the competitive arena. Temporary competitive advantage stems from resources that provide value and are rare, but are easily imitated. If these resources do serve as a source of competitive advantage, then other firms will soon imitate them, resulting in competitive parity. Finally, aspects of human resources that are valuable, rare, and not easily imitated can be sources of sustained competitive advantage, but only if the firm is organized to capitalize on these resources.

Clearly the HR function, through either directly controlling or strongly influencing the characteristics of human resources in organizations, plays an important role in developing and maintaining a firm's competitive advantage. Simply making the case that HR *can* influence a firm's performance, however, is only part of the story. In order for HR to *truly develop and maintain* sources of competitive advantage, HR executives need to focus attention and activities toward those aspects of the firm's resources that will provide such advantages.

Now, the potential of several types of human resources to be sources of sustained competitive advantage is examined: firm-specific versus general skills, teams versus individuals, and HR systems versus single HR practices.

FIRM-SPECIFIC VERSUS GENERAL SKILLS

Human capital theory (Flamholtz and Lacey 1981) distinguished between general skills and firm-specific skills of human resources. General skills are skills possessed by individuals that provide value to a firm and are transferable across a variety of firms. For example, all competitor firms have the potential to accrue equal value from acquiring employees with knowledge of general management, the ability to apply financial ratios, or general cognitive ability. Specific skills, on the other hand, provide value *only* to a particular firm and are of no value to competing firms. For example, the knowledge of how to use a particular technology used only by one firm, or knowledge of a firm's policies and procedures provide value to that firm but usually would not be valuable to other firms.

Because general skills provide equal value to all firms, one would expect that, given even moderately efficient labor markets, these would not be a source of competitive advantage for any one organization; thus, to seek to gain sustained competitive advantage through general skills would be futile. On the other hand, there are two reasons that this does not imply that these skills are not important. *First*, general skills are necessary for maintaining competitive parity. For example, basic reading and writing skills are general skills that will not provide competitive advantage to any one firm; however, a firm that hired many employees who could *not* read and write would be at considerable disadvantage in the marketplace. *Second*, most organizations have defined the 'New Deal' between the firm and its employees. This new psychological contract (Rousseau and Greller 1994) is characterized by employers assuring that they will not guarantee employment but will guarantee employability to people (Kissler 1994). This requires providing employees with the necessary training and development that ensures them marketability to other firms (i.e. general skills). Firms that fail to invest in general skills will be unable to attract and retain competent employees.

In addition, while general skills are applicable across organizations and thus most likely to result in only competitive parity, this does not preclude gaining competitive advantage through obtaining the highest level of general skills. For example, Wright et al. (1994) argued that firms that were able to obtain the highest level of average cognitive ability would have a competitive (and possibly sustainable) advantage. We would not argue for ignoring the importance of general skills; they add value and at the highest level are rare.

Greater potential for sustainable competitive advantage stems from investments in firm-specific skills. One avenue to sustained competitive advantage is to focus on developing a firm-specific skill base within an organization, because these skills cannot be easily duplicated by competitors. These skills provide value to the firm, but they are not easily marketable by the employees who possess them. One can accomplish this through investing in constant training and development of employees to perform work processes and procedures that are specific to the firm (Hatch and Dyer 2004). In fact, central to the concept of organizational learning is the process of developing and disseminating tacit knowledge (i.e. firm-specific knowledge) throughout the firm (Senge 1990; Miller 1996). The firm gathers the rents accruing from these firm-specific skills, while providing employees with the opportunity for growth and development.

The importance of firm-specific skills highlights the potential shortsightedness of outsourcing most, or all, of a firm's training and development activities. Outsourced activities such as these most effectively provide general rather than firm-specific skills. While some training firms may be able to develop tailor-made programs for specific firms, these are not feasible when proprietary technologies and processes exist. In addition, the training firm that develops the tailor-made programs also acquires the skills, and can theoretically (although not ethically and possibly not legally) exploit them with competing firms. For these reasons, while some training activities can and should be outsourced, outsourcing of all training activities is not likely to serve as the lever for gaining sustainable competitive advantage through people.

TEAMS VERSUS INDIVIDUALS

Much of the popular literature on top management seems to point to individual CEOs, such as Lee Iaccoca at Chrysler, Jack Welch at General Electric, or Lawrence Bossidy at AlliedSignal, as sources of sustainable competitive advantage. Similarly, much of the academic work on matching human resources to organizational strategies has focused on top managers and ignored the lower-level employees (Gerstein and Reisman 1983; Gupta and Govindarajan 1984; Guthrie, Grimm, and Smith 1991). The inherent assumption in this research is that the skills of the workforce are all common across firms, but that highly skilled individual managers or top management teams are more rare (Wright et al. 1994). This implies that the firm with the right CEO or president might possess a source of sustained competitive advantage. While these individuals are quite valuable, if labor markets are at all efficient, they are not likely to be a source of sustained competitive advantage.

Individuals who possess valuable and rare skills are usually able to claim most of the rents that are attributable to those skills (Wright et al. 1994). An outstanding chief executive, because of the high visibility of his/her performance, will soon be approached by other organizations with higher compensation. In the bidding process for that individual's services she or he can claim most of the rents, and, therefore, the rents will not accrue to whichever firm ultimately obtains that individual's services.

Numerous shifts of top managers from one firm to another (e.g. Gerstner to IBM), as well as the rapidly rising top executive pay, exemplify the futility of seeking sustainable competitive advantage from the skills of one individual. On the other hand, the exploitation of the synergistic value from a large number of individuals who work together is quite costly, if not impossible, for competitors to imitate. Teams or larger groups, due to causal ambiguity and social complexity, provide greater potential to be a source of sustainable competitive advantage.

Alchian and Demsetz (1972) defined team production as 'production in which (1) several types of resources are used, and (2) the product is not a sum of the separable outputs of each cooperating resource' (p. 779). Because output is more than the sum of the separable outputs of each cooperating resource, it is difficult, if not impossible, to identify the specific source of the competitive advantage. In other words, the competitive advantage stemming from team production is characterized as being causally ambiguous, thus making it difficult for competitors to imitate.

An additional benefit of team production is that individuals become linked in transaction-specific relationships, resulting in transaction-specific human capital. In other words, team members become involved in socially complex relationships that are not transferable across organizations, thus only benefiting the organization in which these relationships develop. This nontransferability requires the development of a team orientation, as has been exemplified among the top managers at Continental Airlines. One part of its turnaround was the replacement of thirty-six of the company's top officers within a twelve-month time frame. CEO Gordon Bethune states, 'Why do you think most of those VPs disappeared? Most of them could not be team players.' This has resulted in a reorientation among the top managers at Continental to focus on team goals, instead of being strictly focused on their own personal goals (Boissueau 1995).

This highlights the importance of the HR function in developing and nurturing the relationships among organizational members. Many traditional organizational development activities, such as team building and conflict resolution, are included in the HR activities of Fortune 500 companies (McMahan and Woodman 1992; Kotter and Cohen 2002; Beitler 2003). In addition, researchers are beginning to explore trust among organization members as one determinant of firm performance (Gambetta 1988; Barney and Hansen 1994; Mishra and Mishra 1994). Clearly trust (see Chapter 5) and good relationships among organizational members are firm-specific assets that provide value, are quite rare, and are extremely difficult for competitors to imitate.

HR SYSTEMS VERSUS SINGLE HR PRACTICES

Much of the writing on Strategic HRM has focused on HR practices as a source of competitive advantage (Schuler and MacMillan 1984). The assumption is that firms that engage in the best HR practices, that is, have the best selection system, or best training program, or best reward system, etc., will have a competitive advantage over firms that fail to use this particular practice. Both the work on utility analysis of HR programs (Cascio 1987; Steffy and Maurer 1988; Boudreau 1991; Jones and Wright 1992) and empirical work on the relationship between HR practices and performance (e.g. Terpstra and Rozzell 1993) have demonstrated that HR practices do provide value to the firm.

While each of these practices provides value, VRIO analysis suggests that they are not likely to be sources of sustained competitive advantage. Given the emphasis on benchmarking to identify the most effective HR practices, any individual effective practice is easily imitated, and thus, can provide an advantage only for a short time—until competitors can copy it.

The fact that these individual practices will not likely lead to sustainable competitive advantage does not imply that these practices are unimportant and HR executives can ignore identifying the best practice for each of the various HR activities. The failure to invest in state-of-the-art selection, training, and reward systems can result in a firm having a competitive *disadvantage* among human resources. In addition, a series of temporary competitive advantages gained through constant innovation is still quite valuable to the firm.

The challenge for HR is to develop systems of HR practices that create a synergistic effect, rather than developing a set of independent best practices of HR (Wright and Snell 1991; Lado and Wilson 1994; Becker and Gerhart 1996). This requires a changing mindset from the traditional subfunctional (selection, training, appraisal, compensation, etc.) view of HR to one where all of these independent subfunctions are viewed as interrelated components of a highly interdependent system. The interrelatedness of the system components makes the advantage difficult, if not impossible, for competitors to identify and copy. It also requires investing time and energy into developing systems and structures for integrating various HR practices such that they complement, rather than conflict with, one another. While this sounds quite commonsensical, conversations with a number of HR executives consistently indicate that very few HR departments have developed any such systems and structures. Firms that have developed highly integrated systems seem to have obtained a source of sustainable competitive advantage. Research on bundles of HR practices supports this notion (MacDuffie 1995; Delery and Doty 1996; Youndt et al. 1996).

The implications of this resource-based analysis using the VRIO framework appear contrary to much of the management thinking that emphasizes the importance of finding the right CEO, outsourcing HR functions, or seeking sustained competitive advantage through finding one best HR practice. The analysis does not imply that these activities are not valuable, but only that they are incomplete, particularly in guiding the decision-making of HR executives. The following section examines implications of resource-based analysis for HR executives.

Implications for HR executives

This resource-based analysis has a number of implications for HR executives. In general, it highlights the fact that HR executives play an important role in managing the firm's human assets, those that possess the greatest potential for being sources of sustained competitive advantage. More specifically, it provides guidance regarding the management of the HR function in organizations in ways that will create competitive advantage. Four of these major implications are outlined below, with questions to help guide the HR executive in managing the function.

1. The value of people and their role in competitive advantage. Knowing the economic value of the firm's human resources is a necessary precondition before any HR executive can begin to manage the function strategically. Reichheld (1996) notes that people contribute to firms in terms of efficiency, customer selection, customer retention, customer referral, and employee referral. People play an important role in the success of any firm, but which people do so, and how they contribute, may vary across firms. This knowledge is a necessary starting point for any HR executive to act as a strategic partner.

For example, research indicates that firms that rely heavily on innovation and product development (e.g. Merck) argue that their research and development (R&D) scientists' ability to develop successful new products is the major thing that distinguishes those companies from competitors. Manufacturing firms such as Dell Computer, on the other hand, emphasize the production efficiency advantages they can gain through harnessing all of their peoples' skills and effort. Finally, service-oriented firms, such as Continental Airlines, note that the planes, routes, gates, and fares are virtually identical within the industry. Their competitive advantage can only come through efficient, friendly service that makes fliers want to make their next flight on Continental.

Similarly, while all of the firm's people are important, some provide greater leverage for competitive advantage. Because of the need for innovation, Merck's R&D scientists provide greater leverage for success than do the hourly manufacturing employees. On the other hand, it is the hourly line employees (ticket agents, flight attendants, gate crews, and baggage handlers) who directly impact the flying experience that have a relatively stronger impact on competitive advantage for Continental Airlines.

Thus, HR executives must first understand the role of the firm's people in competitive advantage before being able to make decisions about how to position the deliverables of the function. This leads to the following questions for these executives:

- On what basis is the firm seeking to distinguish itself from competitors? Production efficiency? Innovation? Customer service?
- Where in the value chain is the greatest leverage for achieving this differentiation?
- Which employees or employee groups provide the greatest potential to differentiate a firm from its competitors?

2. The economic consequences of HR practices. Once an HR executive understands the specific ways in which the firm's people provide value, it is necessary to examine the value that HR provides or can provide. Research has uncovered a relationship between HR practices and the financial performance of firms (Huselid 1995; MacDuffie 1995; Youndt et al. 1996). While this research is promising, more research is needed on how, exactly, this impact is gained. At least two possibilities exist.

First, HR practices may be important levers by which firms develop human capital and employee commitment. It is the HR practices that can directly impact the skills of the workforce that can provide value to the firm. These practices also can help to develop committed employees who are willing to allocate their discretionary behavior toward organizational ends (MacDuffie 1995; Wright et al. 1996). In other words, HR practices play an important role in developing the human assets that provide competitive advantage.

It is also important to understand that HR practices and the HR function incur costs for organizations. HR can impact firm performance through its efficiency in developing the human assets that are a source of competitive advantage (Ulrich 1997). The products and services provided by the HR function can be too many or too few, of high quality or of low quality, directly linked to business needs or unrelated to the business. For example, HR practices developed because they are the latest fad, without a careful analysis of their ability to meet strategic business needs, are both excessive and inefficient. Similarly, the failure to develop practices that will help address business needs results in less than optimal organizational effectiveness. Finally, HR practices designed to meet business needs that are delivered at excessive cost or with low quality negatively impact the firm's financial performance. HR executives need to assess both the menu of HR practices and services offered, as well as the quality and efficiency in their delivery.

As part of Continental Airlines' turnaround, for example, the HR function took a long look at the services it provided and how efficiently those services were provided. The result of this analysis was the elimination and consolidation of a number of training programs that simply were unrelated to the business while keeping some of the remaining training programs internal to the firm, the outsourcing of benefits and some training/development activities, and the development of a variety of variable pay plans (the on-time bonus, management bonus plans, profit sharing, etc.). The firm has continued exploring further outsourcing and strategic partnerships as ways to reduce the costs of the function. Finally, in an effort to remain close to its customers, the HR function surveyed the company's officers regarding the importance of the services provided by HR as well as HR's effectiveness at delivering those services. This effort will identify areas for further improvement.

HR executives seeking to explore the value created by their functions need to ask the following questions:

- Who are your internal customers and how well do you know their part of the business?
- Are there organizational policies and practices that make it difficult for your internal clients to be successful?
- What services do you provide? What services should you provide? What services should you not provide?
- How do those services reduce internal customers' costs or increase their revenues?

- Can those services be provided more efficiently by outside vendors?
- Can you provide those services more efficiently?
- Do managers in the HR function understand the economic consequences of their jobs?

3. Comparison of HR practices with competing firms. The previous two points focus on the HR executive's attention within the organization. In a competitive environment, however, one cannot ignore the actions of competitors, and this is also true of HR. It is necessary to examine the HR functions of competitors to gain an understanding of what HR practices and relationships define the present competition. This information is only valuable insofar as it is used for developing strategies for changing the competitive landscape to a firm's advantage.

Such benchmarking activity has become almost commonplace in industry as firms look both within and outside their industries seeking the 'best practices'. Benchmarking provides information that can be valuable or useless, depending upon how it is used. If the goal of the activity is simply to identify the HR practices of successful firms in order to imitate them, then the costs will likely outweigh the benefits. Benchmarking identifies the rules of competition in an industry and can be particularly valuable in providing information on two issues.

First, it helps firms to identify what superior practices the competition is engaged in which might provide them with a competitive advantage until other firms are able to imitate it. For example, Nieman Marcus, the upscale retailer, implemented a sophisticated applicant tracking system that significantly reduced its recruiting costs. Because the system was purchased from an outside vendor, it did not take long for competitors to imitate the advantage through implementing similar systems. Had competitors not identified the system as an advantage, however, their financial performance might have suffered needlessly.

Second, benchmarking should be used to identify ways to leapfrog competitors. This is accomplished through developing innovative HR practices and is especially successful if they are ones that competitors will find it costly or difficult to imitate. For example, one of Merck's manufacturing plants shifted to a variable pay system resembling a gain-sharing type plan. This plan has been hugely successful even while other plants in the industry and geographic area have been disbanding such plans. Why did it work at

Merck? Merck's manufacturing managers attribute the success to the fact that the company has traditionally had a culture that is characterized by high levels of trust between employees and management. The compensation system, while imitable in formulas, structures, and procedures, was not imitable in practice since its success was contingent on Merck's unique history and culture.

HR executives need to understand their functions in relationship to competitors as a means of identifying which practices should be copied to maintain competitive parity, which practices can be innovatively delivered to provide temporary advantage, or which practices can be linked to the unique situation (culture, history, other management systems, etc.) of the firm in order to gain sustainable competitive advantage. This understanding leads to the following questions for HR executives:

- How do the workforce skills of your competitors (particularly in key jobs) compare to those in your firm?
- How does the commitment level of your workforce compare to that of competitors?
- What are your competitors' HR functions doing in terms of practices and relationships with line managers? How can you beat them by doing things better or differently?
- What unique aspects of your firm (e.g. history leadership, culture, and so on) might allow you to develop and/or maintain a more highly skilled and highly committed workforce?
- What HR practices need to be developed or maintained to exploit these unique aspects of your firm?
- Given your firm's history and culture, what unique HR practices might you be able to implement more efficiently and effectively than your competitors?

4. The role of the Human Resources function in building organizational capability. A constant tension exists in the trade-offs between focusing decision-making and resource allocation on the short-term and long-term in most organizations. This conflict also exists within the HR function. Many HR functions are struggling so hard to meet current needs that they have little time to explore long-term organizational plans. This tendency must be broken if HR executives want to play the role of strategic partner.

For example, a high-tech manufacturing firm has seen tremendous growth in both revenues and headcount over a four-year period. This growth resulted in the HR function struggling to keep up with the hiring and training needs of a firm growing by 40 percent per year. Such growth also made it difficult for the HR function to pay attention to developing the organizational infrastructure necessary to maintain the growth. During the last two years, the HR function in this firm began investing in developing organizational capability through the creation of a succession and developmental planning system for the management team and a HR planning system for the rest of the organization. Without such an investment, the firm's growth prospects would have been substantially limited.

In spite of the need to deliver the traditional HR services to meet the organization's current needs, HR executives must consider the future organization's needs by answering the following questions:

- Which of the firm's resources and capabilities provide temporary or sustainable competitive advantage now? Five years from now? Ten years from now?
- What will be the competitive landscape 5–10 years from now in terms of your firm's product markets and labor markets?
- What kind of human resources will your firm need to compete successfully five years from now? Ten years from now?
- What types of HR practices are needed today to build the organization needed in the future?

Conclusion

This resource-based analysis of human resources has shown that HR executives have a key role in nurturing, developing, and managing the set of HR resources (e.g. human capital skills, employee commitment, culture, teamwork, and so on) that are most likely to be sources of sustained competitive advantage for their organizations. The HR function can also adopt a strategic focus, applying the VRIO framework to identify specific HR resources that provide sources of temporary and/or sustainable competitive advantages. Guidance for HR executives on how to create value from the HR function and act as a partner for the company's strategists has been outlined.

The VRIO framework helps the HR executive to evaluate all of the activities of the function against the criteria of value, rareness, imitability, and organizational exploitation. As discussed, HR activities that are valuable but not rare, or valuable and rare but imitable, are not to be ignored. These are the activities that the function must perform to maintain competitive parity, or to provide temporary competitive advantages. For example, competitor firms are likely to be able to imitate a particular HR selection system that identifies cognitive abilities, technical skills, and/or interpersonal skills that provide value; however, to fail to identify these skills in the selection process can result in a severe competitive disadvantage.

The ultimate quest should be for the HR function to provide the firm with resources *that provide value, are rare, and cannot be easily imitated* by other organizations. This quest entails developing employees who are skilled and motivated to deliver high-quality products and services, and managing the culture of the organization to encourage teamwork and trust. It also requires that HR functions focus more attention on developing coherent systems of HR practices that support these aims.

NOTE

1. On going research study conducted by Patrick Wright.

7 Information technology as a source of sustained competitive advantage*

The field of strategic management focuses on understanding sources of sustained competitive advantages for firms (Porter 1980, 1985; Rumelt, Schendel, and Teece 1991). A variety of factors have been shown to have an important impact on the ability of firms to obtain sustained competitive advantage. Some of these have been discussed in previous chapters of this book—including organizational culture, trust, and human resources.

Information technology (IT) has also been mentioned for its possible role in creating sustained competitive advantages for firms (Clemons 1986, 1991; Clemons and Kimbrough 1986; Clemons and Row 1987, 1991*a*; Feeny 1988; Feeny and Ives 1990; Barney 1991*a*; Powell and Dent-Micallef 1997; Bharadwaj 2000; Ray 2000). While the assertion that IT might be able to create sustained competitive advantage for firms is provocative, work in this area is relatively underdeveloped, both empirically and theoretically (Jarvenpaa and Ives 1990; Powell and Dent-Micallef 1997). Research on IT and competitive advantage has predominantly emphasized 'describing how, rather than systematically why' IT can lead to such an advantage (Reich and Benbasat 1990: 326). Accordingly, the IT literature contains case studies of spectacular IT successes, but few conceptual frameworks designed to encourage and assist IT managers with IT implementation (Powell and Dent-Micallef 1997).

* This chapter draws from Mata, Fuerst, and Barney (1995) and Ray, Barney, and Muhanna (2004).

Indeed, some scholars have become quite skeptical about the potential of IT to be a source of competitive advantage. Several empirical studies exploring IT and performance have found that IT adoption and implementation are not necessarily linked to superior performance. For example, ATM adoption in the banking industry was not positively correlated with performance in studies by Banker and Kauffman (1988) and Floyd and Woolridge (1990). Within five years of IT implementation, 70 percent of the firms studied by Kettinger et al. (1994) had experienced competitive declines in either market share, profits or both. The impacts of IT on entry barriers were studied by Mahmood and Soon (1991) who reported no discernable effects in most industries; where IT impacts were found they tended to reduce, rather than increase, entry barriers. A recent *Harvard Business Review* article suggested that IT—because it was so widely available—was no longer strategically relevant (Carr 2003). In this view, IT may create value firm by increasing internal and external coordinating efficiencies. Firms that do not adopt such IT will have higher cost structures and therefore competitive disadvantages. However, firms cannot expect IT to produce sustainable advantages because most IT is readily available to all firms—competitors, buyers, suppliers, and potential new entrants—in competitive factor markets (Clemons and Row 1991*a*; Powell and Dent-Micallef 1997).

This chapter uses resource-based theory to evaluate the potential of IT to be a source of competitive advantage for firms, both temporary and sustained. After discussing how IT can create economic value, the ability of five key attributes of IT—customer switching costs, access to capital, proprietary technology, technical IT skills, and managerial IT skills—to generate sustained competitive advantage is evaluated. The chapter concludes by summarizing some recent empirical results on the relationship between IT and competitive advantage (Ray, Barney, and Muhanna 2004; Ray, Muhanna, and Barney 2005).

The value of IT

Traditionally, most research in strategic IT has focused on the ability of IT to add economic value to a firm by either reducing a firm's costs or differentiating its products or services (see McFarlan 1984; Porter and

Millar 1985; Bakos and Treacy 1986; Wiseman 1988). For example, when Wal-Mart adopted its purchase–inventory–distribution system, it was able to reduce its inventory costs (Ghemawat 1986; Huey 1989; Stalk, Evans, and Shulman 1992). On the other hand, GE was able to differentiate its service support from its competitors by means of its call center technology (Benjamin et al. 1984; Porter and Millar 1985), and Otis Elevator similarly differentiated its service operations thanks to its Otisline system (McFarlan and Stoddard 1986; Balaguer 1990). In all these cases, the judicious use of IT either reduced these firms' costs of operations or increased their revenues by differentiating their products or services, or both, and therefore created value for these firms.

Indeed, there is little doubt that, in a wide variety of circumstances, IT can add value to a firm. However, as suggested earlier, IT adding value to a firm—by reducing costs and/or increasing revenues—is not the same as IT being a source of sustained competitive advantage for a firm. For example, when Wal-Mart adopted its purchase–inventory–distribution system, it gained a competitive advantage over its closest rival, K-Mart. However, K-Mart did not remain idle and developed its own similar system (Steven 1992). With respect to this system, Wal-Mart gained only a temporary, but not sustained, competitive advantage (Barney 1994*a*). Put another way, Wal-Mart's purchase–inventory–distribution system was valuable, but value, per se, is a necessary but not sufficient condition for a sustained competitive advantage.

IT and sustained competitive advantage

Five attributes of IT have been suggested as possible sources of sustained competitive advantage in the literature. These five attributes are evaluated here using resource-based logic.

CUSTOMER SWITCHING COSTS

At one time, it was suggested that customer switching costs could create competitive advantages for some firms. This logic was summarized in the 'create-capture-keep' paradigm (Clemons and Kimbrough 1986; Clemons and Row 1987, 1991*b*; Feeny and Ives 1990). In this paradigm, certain customers are forced to make supplier-specific investments in acquiring IT. Once made, these investments make it possible for IT suppliers to appropriate a disproportionate share of the value created by IT—an example of holdup as described by Williamson (1975). Firms that did not make these specific investments, or firms that buy IT from suppliers that do not engage in holdup, will have competitive advantages over firms that are captured by opportunistic suppliers.

While this argument is consistent with transactions cost theory, changes in the nature of IT over the years have made it less important for firms to make supplier-specific investments to obtain and use IT. Without such investments, holdup cannot occur and the results of holdup cannot benefit some firms more than others. Indeed, even in those areas of IT where specific investments are still required—such as in enterprisewide systems sold by firms like PeopleSoft—increasingly sophisticated contracts seem to have reduced the threat of opportunism in these exchanges. Moreover, these contracting skills are available to most firms (Mayer and Argyres 2004). All of this suggests that supplier-specific investments are unlikely to be a source of competitive advantage for firms in the acquisition and use of IT.

ACCESS TO CAPITAL

The capital needed to develop and apply IT—whether in the form of debt, equity, or from retained earnings—has been suggested as a source of sustainable competitive advantage for at least some firms (McFarlan 1984). The logic underlying this assertion is straightforward. First, IT investments can be very risky, and thus the capital needed to make these investments can be very costly. Second, IT investments can require huge amounts of this risky capital. It may often be the case that only a few firms competing in a particular product market will have the financial capability needed to acquire the necessary capital to make certain IT investments. Thus, the few firms that are able to acquire the needed capital to make these investments can gain a sustained competitive advantage from them.

Two kinds of uncertainty can be considered as the major sources of risk in IT investments, and are, therefore, determinants of the cost of capital required to make those investments: technological uncertainty and market uncertainty. Technological uncertainty reflects the risk that an IT investment may not meet its expected performance targets in a timely way. Specific sources of technological uncertainty in IT investments include (McFarlan 1981): (*a*) failure to obtain the anticipated IT results because of implementation difficulties, (*b*) higher than anticipated implementation costs, (*c*) longer than anticipated implementation time, (*d*) technical performance below what was anticipated at the outset of the investment, and (*e*) incompatibility of the developed IT with selected hardware and software.[1]

When they were first developed, airline reservation systems were characterized by high levels of technological uncertainty. Their development required the solution of a number of unforseen problems, which reflected the technological limitations and scarce experience available at the time. These problems were solved in part by IBM's direct involvement and commitment in the development of these systems (see Copeland and McKenney 1988, for details).

Market uncertainty, on the other hand, reflects risks related to the customer's acceptance of new IT products or services. Market uncertainty was a major cause of failure for the Pronto and ZapMail systems. Even though these systems met their technical objectives, they were not adopted by customers. The Pronto system, an early foray into electronic banking, did not attract enough customers in six years to break even and had to be abandoned (Gunther 1988; Clemons and Weber 1990). Similarly, low-cost substitutes led to the failure of Federal Express's ZapMail, a system designed to transmit facsimile documents through a nationwide network (Keller and Wilson 1986; Wiseman 1988).

Of course, not all IT investments are large, nor are they all risky. If IT investments are not large and risky, then it is likely that many firms will have access to the capital necessary to make them. In this context, access to capital is not likely to be a source of sustained competitive advantage. On the other hand, some IT investments may be both large and very risky. However, even in this context, access to capital for IT investments, per se, is not likely to be a source of sustained competitive advantage for firms. Consider, for example, several firms with identical IT resources and capabilities seeking capital to make particular IT investments. While these investments may be both risky and large, and because these firms are about equally skilled in making IT investments, the risks of these investments are not heterogeneously distributed across these firms. According to resource-based theory, firm attributes that are not heterogeneously distributed across firms will only be a source of competitive parity. While the capital used by these firms to make these IT investments will be risky and large, it will not be any more so to any one of these firms than it is to the others (Barney 1986*a*). Furthermore, technological or market uncertainty is usually resolved once a first mover has been able to successfully implement a system. Therefore, these risks actually affect first movers more than followers (Lieberman and Montgomery 1988), and consequently, in many circumstances, technology followers can have access to lower cost of capital than technology first movers.

Of course, this simple example makes the strong assumption that competing firms have the same resources and capabilities in making IT investments. Obviously, this will often not be the case. Different firms may be differentially skilled in managing the technical and market risks associated with particular kinds of IT investments. Put another way, firms that are more skilled in managing their IT investments face fewer technical and market risks than less skilled firms. These more skilled firms will have access to lower cost of capital than less skilled firms and will be able to pursue IT investments that are not available to less skilled firms. Consequently, some firms may gain competitive advantages over other firms through their IT investments.

However, in this situation it is inappropriate to conclude that access to capital, per se, is a source of competitive advantage. Rather, it is the special resources and capabilities of some firms that enable them to manage the technical and market risks more efficiently, and allows them to gain an advantage. If these resources and capabilities are valuable (which in this case, they are) and heterogeneously distributed across competing firms (again in this case, they are), they can be a source of at least a temporary competitive advantage. Whether the skills needed to manage technical and market risks are imperfectly mobile (i.e. whether they reflect a firm's unique history, are causally ambiguous, or socially complex) and thus sources of sustained competitive advantage, is discussed in later sections of this chapter.

Even small firms, with apparently small debt capacity and few retained earnings, can overcome capital market disadvantages if they have access to the required IT investment resources and capabilities. These small firms can cooperate in their IT investments, gaining access to both the needed skills and the required capital (Cash and Konsynski 1985; Vitale 1986; Clemons and Knez 1988; Clemons and Row 1992). For example, such cooperative efforts were used in the development of the European airline reservation systems, Amadeus and Galileo, to overcome the problems of a single firm acquiring large amounts of capital needed to develop such systems (Etheridge 1988).

PROPRIETARY TECHNOLOGY

Technology that can be kept proprietary has also been suggested as a source of sustained competitive advantage (Bain 1956; Porter 1980). Although proprietary technology can be protected through patents or secrecy (Porter 1980), IT applications are difficult to patent (Jakes and Yoches 1989). Moreover, even if they could be patented, there is evidence that patents provide little protection against imitation (Mansfield, Schwartz, and Wagner 1981; Mansfield 1985). Thus, secrecy is the only alternative for keeping IT proprietary.

Clearly, if a firm possesses valuable proprietary technology that it can keep secret, then that firm will obtain a sustained competitive advantage. The fact that the technology is proprietary suggests that it is heterogeneously distributed across competing firms; the fact that it is secret suggests that it is imperfectly mobile. However, most research indicates that it is relatively difficult to keep a firm's proprietary technology secret, and thus, it is unlikely that proprietary technology will be a source of sustained competitive advantage. This is especially true for IT (Clemons and Row 1987).

A wide variety of factors act to reduce the extent to which proprietary IT can be kept secret. Workforce mobility, reverse engineering, and formal and informal technical communication all act to reduce the secrecy surrounding proprietary technology (Lieberman and Montgomery 1988). Thus, if one firm finds itself at a competitive disadvantage to another because that other firm has some proprietary IT application, the disadvantaged firm can hire away one or more of the individuals who developed the advantaged firm's application; it can purchase that application and discover its character through reverse engineering; it can discover the nature of the application through informal discussions with developers or users; or it can read published reports about the nature of the proprietary application and duplicate it in that way. Put another way, while a particular firm may gain a 'head start' (i.e. a temporary competitive advantage) from its proprietary IT application, competing firms are usually not disadvantaged in imitating that technology by history, causal ambiguity, or social complexity. Thus, that proprietary technology usually is not a source of sustained competitive advantage.[2]

IT has become, to a large extent, generic and available to most firms (Clemons and Row 1987, 1991*b*). Even complex systems that used to be immune from imitation are now broadly available from numerous sources. For example, the software used in airline reservation systems currently can be acquired from the companies that developed them for internal purposes (Etheridge 1988; Hopper 1990). As this diffusion of IT continues, the ability of proprietary technology to be a source of competitive advantage—sustained or temporary—continues to erode.

TECHNICAL IT SKILLS

A third possible source of sustained competitive advantage from IT may be a firm's technical IT skills (Copeland and McKenney 1988). Technical skills refer to the know-how needed to build IT applications using the available technology and to operate them to make products or provide services (Capon and Glazer 1987). Examples of such technical skills might include knowledge of programming languages, experience with operating systems, and understanding of communication protocols and products. These technical skills enable firms to effectively manage the technical risks associated with investing in IT, as discussed previously.

While technical skills are essential in the use and application of IT, they are usually not sources of sustained competitive advantage. Although these skills are valuable, they are usually not heterogeneously distributed across firms. Moreover, even when they are heterogeneously distributed across firms, they are typically highly mobile. For instance, firms without the required analysis, design, and programming skills required to make an IT investment can hire technical consultants and contractors. Specifically, airlines acquired technical expertise for developing their complex airline reservation systems by hiring programmers from other airlines and by making alliances with other carriers and hardware vendors (Copeland and McKenney 1988).

This mobility of technical IT skills shows that such skills are usually explicit and codifiable by means of equations, procedures, blueprints, etc. Since codifiable knowledge 'can be communicated from its possessor to another person in symbolic form, the recipient becomes as much "in the know" as the originator' (Winter 1987: 171). These codifiable skills are easy to transmit and receive (Teece 1988). Thus, technical skills can easily diffuse among a set of competing firms.

If a firm is at a competitive disadvantage because of its inadequate technical IT skills, it has a variety of obvious solutions. For example, this firm could train its own employees in the relevant technical skills, hire new employees that already have the technical skills, ask its employees to take various classes to learn the relevant technical skills, etc. In all these ways, a firm at a competitive disadvantage could solve its technical problems and regain competitive parity in technical IT skills. Consequently, though there's no question that technical IT skills are valuable to the firm, they rarely meet both additional conditions of being heterogeneously distributed across firms and highly immobile. Without meeting these conditions from resource-based theory, it is unlikely that technical IT skills can be used to sustain a competitive advantage.

MANAGERIAL IT SKILLS

Technical skills are not the only skills required to build and use IT applications. A second broad set of skills are managerial skills (Capon and Glazer 1987). In the case of IT, managerial skills include management's ability to conceive of, develop, and exploit IT applications to support and enhance other business functions. Examples of important IT management skills include: (*a*) the ability of IT managers to understand and appreciate the business needs of other functional managers, suppliers, and customers; (*b*) the ability to work with these functional managers, suppliers, and customers to develop appropriate IT applications; (*c*) the ability to coordinate IT activities in ways that support other functional managers, suppliers, and customers; and (*d*) the ability to anticipate the future IT needs of functional managers, suppliers, and customers. Managerial IT skills enable firms to manage the market risks associated with investing in IT. Firms can acquire technical IT skills by hiring programmers and analysts. They then use their managerial IT skills to help programmers and analysts fit into an organization's culture, understand its policies and procedures, and learn to work with other business functional areas on IT-related projects.

That these managerial skills are valuable is almost self-evident. Without them, the full potential of IT for a firm will almost certainly not be realized. How frequently different competing firms will possess similar IT management skills is an empirical question. However, it is reasonable to expect that close working relationships among those in IT and between IT and other business functions are not all that common, and thus, these relationships may be heterogeneously distributed across firms.

Unlike technical IT skills, managerial IT skills are often developed over longer periods through the accumulation of experience by trial-and-error learning (Katz 1974). Skills developed in this way are called 'learning-by-doing' skills (Williamson 1975). For example, friendship, trust, and interpersonal communication can take years to develop to the point where IT managers and managers in other business functions are able to effectively work together to create and exploit novel IT applications. Thus, history is important for developing these skills. Managerial skills in many cases are tacit (Castanias and Helfat 1991) and may involve hundreds to thousands of small decisions that cannot be precisely imitated. As long as these skills are part of the 'taken-for-granted' part of a firm's skill base, they may remain causally ambiguous. Finally, the development and use of many of these managerial skills depend on close interpersonal relationships between IT managers and those working in the IT function, between IT managers and managers in other business functions, and between IT managers and customers. Thus, the development of these skills is often a socially complex process. Therefore, if managerial IT skills are valuable and heterogeneously distributed across firms, then they usually will be a source of sustained competitive advantage, since these relationships are developed over time; and they are socially complex and thus not subject to low-cost imitation.

Of course, while many managerial IT skills are developed over long periods and are causally ambiguous and socially complex, not all such skills have the attributes needed to be sources of sustained competitive advantage. In general, when managerial IT skills can be written down, codified, and transferred at low cost and with little loss in richness or understanding, those skills are not likely to be sources of sustained competitive advantage. On the other hand, when managerial IT skills cannot be written down, codified, or transferred at low cost or without significant loss of richness and understanding, those managerial IT skills may be a source of sustained competitive advantage.

Consider two examples. It has been suggested that management's understanding of the potential for IT to be a source of competitive advantage was important for American Airline's ability to develop the SABRE system (Copeland and McKenney 1988). Moreover, the close relationship between American Airline's IT personnel and personnel in other business functions enabled these groups to work together, to make and learn from mistakes, and to build on successes in a way that led to the SABRE system. If management at American Airline had not been committed to the innovative use of IT, or if relationships between the IT function and other business functions had not been cooperative, the SABRE system may never have been developed or implemented. Imitation of the SABRE system was slowed, while other airlines developed the IT management skills necessary to develop these systems.

Wal-Mart's purchase–inventory–distribution system, which has allowed a reduction in its cost of sales 2–3 percent below the industry average, is another example of the importance of managerial IT skills in creating sustained competitive advantage. A competitively interesting note about this just-in-time system is that it applies very little proprietary technology and uses very few inimitable IT technical skills. Instead, IT is used to support constant and direct communication among Wal-Mart's stores, distribution centers, and suppliers. It is this constant communication and the relationships it builds that has enabled Wal-Mart to retain its competitive advantage despite the successful efforts of many of Wal-Mart's competitors to imitate Wal-Mart's hardware and software (Stalk, Evans, and Shulman 1992). Put differently, while Wal-Mart's technical IT skills have been imitated, its IT management skills have been shown to be a source of sustained competitive advantage.

Part of Wal-Mart's advantage results from its ability to link its IT function with its stores, its distribution centers, and even with its suppliers. This suggests that managerial IT skills are relevant not only in linking different functions within the same firm, but may also be important in linking different firms in ways that generate IT-based competitive advantages through strategic alliances. It may also be the case that managerial IT skills can be used to link a firm with its customers (Jackson 1985). In all these cases, if the linkages are valuable, if they are possessed by relatively few competing firms, and if they are socially complex (and thus imperfectly mobile), they may be sources of sustained competitive advantage.

Empirical examination of resource-based arguments

Recently, some of the empirical implications of these arguments have been examined (Ray, Barney, and Muhanna 2004; Ray, Muhanna, and Barney 2005). This research focused on the role of IT investments in the customer service function in North American insurance companies. These studies examined the impact of the capital required to implement IT, the quality of a firm's current IT, the level of a firm's IT technical skills, and one aspect of a firm's IT managerial skills—the quality of the relationship between IT and customer service managers—on the ability of IT to give a firm a competitive advantage in the customer service function.

Previous research has shown the value of IT in improving customer service in insurance. IT enables customer service workers to gain quick access to a customer's policies, evaluate the nature of a customer's problems, and help address these problems—either directly or by routing a customer to the correct person in the organization. Given these implications of IT for customer service, it is not surprising that insurance companies in North America have spent billions of dollars on IT over the last several years. However, as suggested earlier in this chapter, such investments are not necessarily a source of competitive advantage for a firm in this relatively mature industry.

Surveys were used to collect information about the IT budget, the quality of a firm's current customer service IT, the level of a firm's technical IT skills, and the quality of the relationship between IT and customer service managers within a firm. Several measures of customer service quality were obtained, both from the survey and from a variety of government sources. The study hypothesized that the IT budget, the quality of a firm's current customer service IT, and the level of a firm's technical IT skills would all be unrelated to the relative level of a firm's customer satisfaction. This was because, as suggested in this chapter, all these attributes of IT are tangible and are likely to rapidly diffuse among competitors, especially in mature industries like the North American insurance industry. It was also hypothesized that the quality of the relationship between IT and customer service managers—because it was likely to be socially complex and path-dependent in nature—was likely to be correlated with the relative level of a firm's customer satisfaction. It was also hypothesized that IT budget, current technology, and IT technical skills would be positively correlated with relative customer service when the relationship between IT and customer service managers was positive. These last hypotheses were tested using interaction terms in a simple regression.

Results of this analysis were generally consistent with expectations. Current technology and technical IT skills were unrelated to relative customer satisfaction. IT budget was actually negatively correlated—reflecting, perhaps, the fact that when a firm's customer satisfaction numbers drop, it must spend more on IT than its competitors. While not technically consistent with the hypothesized relationship between IT budget and relative customer satisfaction, this negative relationship is at least consistent with the notion that spending on IT, per se, is only likely to be a source of competitive parity.

The quality of the relationship between IT and customer service managers was positively correlated with relative customer satisfaction, as were the interactions between this variable and current IT and IT technical skills. That is, not only does the relationship between IT and customer service managers have a direct positive impact on customer satisfaction—measured in a variety of ways—but it also makes it possible to leverage a firm's current technology and technical IT skills to improve customer satisfaction. All these results are consistent with the resource-based arguments developed in this chapter.

Conclusions and implications

Of the five attributes of IT studied in this chapter, the resource-based logic suggests that only IT managerial skills are likely to be a source of sustained competitive advantage. IT management skills are often heterogeneously distributed across firms. Moreover, these skills reflect the unique histories of individual firms, are often part of the taken-for-granted routines in an organization, and can be based on socially complex relations within the IT function, between the IT function and other business functions in a firm, and between the IT function and a firm's suppliers or customers.

This analysis—and subsequent empirical research—has important implications for both researchers and managers. For researchers, resource-based theory suggests that the search for IT-based sources of sustained competitive advantage must focus less on IT, per se, and more on the process of organizing and managing IT within a firm. It is the ability of IT managers to work with each other, with managers in other functional areas in a firm, and with managers in other firms that is most likely to separate those firms that are able to gain sustained competitive advantages from their IT and those that are only able to gain competitive parity from their IT. These skills, and the relationships upon which they are built, have been called managerial IT skills in this chapter. Future research will need to explore, in much more detail, the exact nature of these managerial IT skills, how they develop and evolve in a firm, and how they can be used to leverage a firm's technical IT skills to create sustained competitive advantage.

Also, while the ability of five widely cited potential IT-based sources of sustained competitive advantage has been examined in this chapter, there may be other attributes of IT whose competitive implications have not been fully evaluated. Resource-based theory provides a framework that can be used to evaluate these competitive implications. Additional conceptual work will be required to describe these other IT attributes and their relationship to resource-based theory. Moreover, empirical tests of the arguments presented here and other resource-based arguments about IT attributes will also need to be conducted.

This analysis also has important implications for IT managers. First, simply because IT managerial skills are the only likely source of sustained competitive advantage discussed in this chapter, it does not follow that other attributes of IT are competitively unimportant. For example, while technical IT skills are not likely to be a source of sustained competitive advantage, they may be a source of temporary competitive advantage. A firm may be able to get an IT-based head start on its competition based on these technical skills (i.e. they may be heterogeneously distributed among competing firms, but not imperfectly mobile). Moreover, even when such a head start is not possible, it is still essential that a firm be as technically skilled in its IT as its competitors. After all, managerial IT skills can only be used to leverage a firm's technical IT skills if those skills exist in a firm. Responsible IT managers will constantly compare their technical skills with their competitors and seek to meet, or exceed, their competition's level of technical competence.

Second, this analysis suggests that, in addition to developing and maintaining a technically competent IT organization, IT managers also should seek to develop close working relationships with managers in other business functions and even with managers in other firms. Clearly, these relationships are sometimes difficult to build and often difficult to maintain. However, it is these kinds of relationships that will enable the IT function to leverage its technical IT skills to address real business problems. Moreover, to the extent that these kinds of relationships are heterogeneously distributed across a firm's competitors, they are likely to be a source of at least a temporary competitive advantage. Indeed, since these relationships are, by definition, socially complex, they are also likely to be imperfectly mobile and thus a source of sustained competitive advantage.

Finally, this analysis suggests that using IT to gain sustained competitive advantage is not likely to be easy. Indeed, if it was relatively simple for firms to use IT in this way, then IT would not be imperfectly mobile and therefore not a source of sustained competitive advantage. The fact that it is often difficult to develop IT managerial skills, relationships between the IT function and other business functions are often slow to evolve, and the technical orientation of many of those in the IT function can clash with the business orientation of others in a firm is good for those firms who have been able to develop these IT managerial skills. This implies that other firms will have a difficult time imitating these skills, and therefore they can be a source of sustained competitive advantage.

NOTES

1. See Clemons and Weber (1990) for a broader classification of technological risks for IT projects.
2. Indeed, there is even some evidence that suggests that the cost of imitating another firm's proprietary technology is often much less than the cost to the original firm of developing that technology (Lieberman and Montgomery 1988).

Part III

RBT and Organizational Strategies

8 Resource-based theory and vertical integration*

In a world of corporate refocusing, downsizing, and outsourcing, one of the most critical strategic decisions that senior managers must make is determining their firm's boundary. Questions such as, 'Which business activities should be brought within the boundary of the firm?' and, 'Which business activities should be outsourced and managed through some form of strategic alliance?' and, 'Which business activities should be outsourced and managed through some form of "arm's-length" market process?' are all essential in determining a firm's boundary. Firms that bring the wrong business activities within their boundaries risk losing strategic focus and becoming bloated and bureaucratic. Firms that fail to bring the right business activities within their boundaries risk losing their competitive advantages and becoming 'hallow corporations' (Jones 1986; Postin 1988).

Fortunately, there is a well-developed approach for determining a firm's boundary in the field of strategic management and organizational economics. Called *transactions cost economics*, TCE, (Williamson 1975, 1985), this theory specifies, in some detail, the conditions under which firms will want to manage a particular economic exchange within their organizational boundary, the conditions under which firms will want to manage an exchange through some form of strategic alliance, and the conditions under which firms will want to manage an exchange through some form of market contracting.

Moreover, not only is this theory well developed, it is also remarkably simple. Indeed, in its most popular version, this theory requires managers to consider only a single characteristic of an economic exchange—the

* This chapter draws from Barney (1999).

level of transaction-specific investment in an exchange—in order to make decisions about whether to include that exchange within the boundary of a firm. Exchanges characterized by low transaction-specific investments should be managed through arm's-length market relations; those characterized by moderate levels of transaction-specific investment should be managed through intermediate strategic alliances; those characterized by high levels of transaction-specific investment should be brought within the boundaries of a firm and managed through hierarchical means. This last type of governance constitutes vertical integration.

Not only is TCE a highly developed and simple theory for determining a firm's boundary, it has been subjected to numerous empirical tests. Many of the empirical tests of this theory have been consistent with its major predictions (Mahoney 1992; Barney and Hesterly 2006), and thus support the major boundary-defining prescriptions of TCE. Some of the secondary predictions of TCE, especially those that deal with the role of uncertainty in determining a firm's boundaries, do not receive as consistent support as its major predictions. Also, many transactions cost predictions do not seem to hold well in high technology industries (Mahoney 1992). However, despite these qualifications, to date, the simplest conclusion one can make about transactions cost economic analyses of firm boundary decisions is that this form of analysis seems to work.

So, in the face of this well-developed, empirically robust theory, what if anything does resource-based theory have new to say about vertical integration and defining a firm's boundary? The answer is—quite a bit.

As it is currently developed, TCE tends to ignore firm resources and capabilities in making vertical integration decisions. This theory takes the productive capability of firms in an exchange as given and only focuses on how gains from trade in an exchange are to be allocated among those firms. Resource-based theory explicitly focuses on the productive resources and capabilities of firms and explores the possibility that the choice of governance cannot be separated from analyzing how the tangible and intangible resources controlled by firms in an exchange create value in that exchange.

Managers are often mystified by the small role that resources and capabilities play in transactions cost explanations of vertical integration. 'After all', they argue, 'isn't the reason that we make choices about how to govern our various business activities simply an effort to discover the best way to gain access to the resources and capabilities we need to be successful? And aren't some firms simply better at doing some things than other firms? Shouldn't these capability differences have an impact on my decisions about which business activities I want to include within my firm's boundaries and which I want to manage through alliances or market processes? And in making these decisions, wouldn't common sense suggest that the resources and capabilities controlled by my firm, and the resources and capabilities controlled by my potential exchange partners, are important in deciding our firm's boundary?'

The purpose of this chapter is to explain the conditions under which a firm's decisions about how to manage its different business activities should be significantly affected by the resources and capabilities it controls and the resources and capabilities that its potential exchange partners control. When these conditions hold—conditions that are particularly common in newly created, rapidly evolving, high technology industries—firms should make boundary decisions that vary significantly from what would be suggested by traditional transactions cost analyses.

A brief summary of transactions cost economic analyses of firm boundary decisions

In order to set the groundwork for this discussion, it is helpful to begin by briefly summarizing transactions cost logic as applied to vertical integration decisions. Three sets of concepts are important in understanding TCE as applied to firm boundary decisions: governance, opportunism, and transaction-specific investment.

In TCE, governance is simply the mechanism through which a firm manages an economic exchange. While there are a wide range of governance options available to most firms, these different governance mechanisms can generally be grouped into three broad categories: market governance, intermediate governance, and hierarchical governance. Firms use *market governance* to manage an exchange when they interact with other firms across a nameless and faceless market and rely primarily on market-determined prices to manage an exchange. Firms use *intermediate governance* when they use complex contracts and other forms of strategic alliances, including joint ventures, to manage an exchange. Finally, firms use *hierarchical governance* when they bring an exchange within their boundary. In hierarchical governance, parties to an exchange are no longer independent. Rather, some third party ('the boss') has the right to direct the actions taken and decisions made by the parties to an exchange.

Transactions cost economics suggests that two issues are important when deciding which of these governance approaches to use: the cost of a governance mechanism and the threat of opportunism in an exchange. In general, the more elaborate the governance, the more costly the governance (D'Aveni and Ravenscraft 1994). Thus, the cost of using market governance to manage an exchange is less than the cost of using intermediate governance to manage an exchange. In turn, the cost of using intermediate governance to manage an exchange is less than the cost of using hierarchical governance to manage an exchange. If all managers had to worry about was minimizing the cost of governance, they would always choose non-hierarchical forms of governance over hierarchical forms of governance, and they would always draw the boundaries of their firm very narrowly.

However, managers also must consider the threat of opportunism in an exchange. *Opportunism* in an exchange exists when a party to that exchange takes unfair advantage of other parties to that exchange. The threat of opportunism in an exchange is a function of the level of transaction-specific investment in that exchange.[1] A *transaction-specific investment* is any investment that is significantly more valuable in a particular exchange than in any alternative exchange. The threat of opportunism exists when one party to an exchange has made a transaction-specific investment, while others have not made such an investment. The firms that have not made these investments can 'hold up' firms that have.

According to transactions cost logic, firms can use governance to mitigate the threat of opportunism. In general, the more elaborate the governance mechanism, the more effective it will be in reducing the threat of opportunism created by transaction-specific investment. Thus, when exchanges are characterized by very high levels of transaction-specific investment, hierarchical governance can be used to reduce the threat of opportunism. When exchanges are characterized by moderate levels of transaction-specific investment, intermediate governance can be used to reduce the threat of opportunism. And when exchanges are characterized by low levels of transaction-specific investment, opportunism is not really a threat, and firms should opt for the least costly form of governance available—market governance.

Thus, the logic for determining a firm's boundary—at least according to TCE—is: when the level of transaction-specific investment in an exchange is high, the high cost of hierarchical governance is more than offset by the ability of this form of governance to reduce the threat of opportunism, and thus hierarchy is preferred over intermediate or market forms of governance. When the level of transaction-specific investment is moderate, intermediate forms of governance are preferred over hierarchical forms of governance, since the moderate threat of opportunism does not justify the extra cost of hierarchical governance. Intermediate governance is also preferred over market governance, in these conditions, because there is some threat of opportunism that cannot be managed through market governance. Finally, if the level of transaction-specific investment is low, then the threat of opportunism is also low, and the least costly form of governance—market governance—is preferred.

Note that in this entire discussion, never once do questions about the relative resources and capabilities of a firm and its exchange partners arise. Firm resources and capabilities simply do not play a significant role in traditional transactions cost analyses of firm boundaries.

Resource and capability considerations in firm boundary decisions

Only three apparently minor additions to traditional transactions cost logic lead to the conclusion that resources and capabilities can be an important determinant of a firm's boundary; and hence its vertical integration strategy. First, it must sometimes be the case that a firm does not possess all the resources and capabilities it needs to be competitively successful. Second, it must be very difficult (i.e. costly) for a firm without a particular resource or capability that it needs to be successful to create that resource or capability on its own. Third, it must be very difficult (i.e. costly) for a firm without a resource or capability that it needs to be successful to gain access to that resource or capability by acquiring a firm that already has it. When these three conditions hold, the application of traditional transactions cost logic will lead managers to make boundary decisions that put the competitive success of their firm at risk. In these settings, resource-based theory suggests very different governance choices than transactions cost theory. In particular, in these settings, firms may find it necessary to adopt nonhierarchical forms of governance to gain access to resources and capabilities they need to be successful—but resources and capabilities they cannot create on their own and that they cannot gain access to by acquiring another firm—even though such forms of governance might subject a firm to high levels of opportunism.

RESOURCE AND CAPABILITY DIFFERENCES ACROSS FIRMS

It is self-evident that firms can vary in the resources and capabilities they possess. Over time, firms, even if they are operating in the same industry, make different choices in strategy, technology, geographic location, and so forth. These differences in choice can exist for a wide variety of reasons, including the personal preferences of managers in a firm, uncertainty in the competitive environment facing firms, the financial constraints a particular firm faces at a particular time, and so forth. Many of these choices can create important resource and capability differences across firms—the condition of resource heterogeneity first discussed in Chapter 3.

Consider, for example, Toyota and GM. Both these firms operate in the global automobile industry. And yet, even the most casual observer can document important differences in the resources and capabilities of these two firms. Toyota has well-documented resources and capabilities in lean production (Womack, Jones, and Roos 1990). It is, on average, able to manufacture very high-quality cars at very low cost. Despite years of effort, most observers agree that GM—at least that part of GM that is not the Saturn Division or the NUMMI joint venture with Toyota—still has not fully developed this lean production capability.

This is not to suggest that GM does not possess resources and capabilities, resources and capabilities that even Toyota does not possess. For example, GM has developed a very extensive distribution system in North America, a capability that Toyota does not have (but would probably like to have).

Numerous examples could be cited at this point in the discussion. This is because it is so common for firms, even firms in the same industry, to differ significantly in the resources and capabilities they possess. Suffice it to say that, if anything, important capability differences across firms, even firms in the same industry, are the rule, not the exception to the rule. Indeed, in general, the only time that capability differences across firms in an industry are not likely to exist is when the structure of an industry completely determines strategic choices of firms in that industry (Bain 1968). In this setting, surviving firms will all have made the same, or at least strategically equivalent, choices over time—choices that, in the long run, should lead these firms to develop the same sets of resources and capabilities. However, research in industrial economics suggests that industry structure completely determines firm strategy only rarely, and thus firms in an industry should have identical sets of resources and capabilities only occasionally (Scherer 1980).

Implicitly, TCE acknowledges that firms may have significant capability differences. For without significant capability differences, there would be no potential gains from trade. With no potential gains from trade, it would not be necessary for firms to engage in exchanges that, in turn, would have to be governed. Thus, a theory about governance choices made by firms implicitly assumes that firms must differ in the resources and capabilities they possess. Thus, technically speaking, observing that firms can vary significantly in their resources and capabilities does not change the exchange conditions traditionally studied by TCE. However, capability differences are discussed here both as a matter of logical completeness and as a matter of emphasis. While it is true that capability differences are implicitly part of any transactions cost analysis, these differences generally do not receive the attention that they often should.

Moreover, not only can firms differ in their resources and capabilities, but it can sometimes be the case that, in order for a firm to be competitively successful, it must have access to resources and capabilities that it does not currently possess. In this setting, a firm with a capability disadvantage has three basic choices: it can gain access to these resources and capabilities by cooperating with firms that already possess them (either through market or intermediate forms of governance), it can create these resources and capabilities on its own (a form of hierarchical governance), or it can gain access to them by acquiring a firm that already possesses them (another form of hierarchical governance).[2] The difficulties that can sometimes attend the two hierarchical governance solutions to a firm not possessing all the resources and capabilities it needs to be successful are discussed below.

COSTLY TO CREATE RESOURCES AND CAPABILITIES

Not only can there be significant capability differences across firms, even if firms are operating in the same industry, but these capability differences can last for long periods. Capability differences can last for long periods because it can be very costly for firms without a capability to create that capability. Indeed, as long as the cost of creating a capability is greater than any benefit that could be obtained from possessing a capability, a firm will find it in its rational self-interest to not create that capability. This can be true even if possessing a capability would be very beneficial, as long as the cost of creating a capability is very high. This is the assumption of resource immobility first mentioned in Chapter 3.

There are numerous reasons why it might be very costly for a firm to create a particular capability on its own (Dierickx and Cool 1989; Barney 1991*b*). Four of these reasons, originally described in Chapter 3 and particularly important in the case of vertical integration are: (*a*) the ability to create a capability in a cost-effective way may depend on unique historical conditions that no longer exist, (*b*) the creation of a capability may be path-dependent, (*c*) a capability may be socially complex and thus costly to create, and (*d*) the actions a firm would need to take to create a capability may not be fully known.

The role of history

Sometimes, the ability of a firm to create resources and capabilities in a cost-effective way may depend on a firm being in the 'right place at the right time' in history. As history moves on, these opportunities can only be recreated at very high (perhaps infinitely high) cost. A firm that did not happen to be in the right place at the right time may find it to be essentially impossible to create a particular capability in a cost-effective manner. This was the case for Caterpillar, originally described in Chapter 3.

Path dependence

Sometimes, in order to create a particular capability, a firm must go through a long and difficult learning process. When there is no way to 'short circuit' this learning process, it is said to be path dependent. When learning processes are path dependent, decisions made early on in the creation of a capability can have profound impacts on the capability that is actually created in a firm. While other firms may want to create this particular capability for themselves, if they have made decisions that have already put them on another capability creation path, they will need to undo those decisions, and change their trajectory to the path that will ultimately lead to the creation of the capability they wish to possess. However, all these efforts can take time and can be very costly. Thus, in general, when resources and capabilities are path dependent, they are likely to be very costly to create.

Consider, for example, the capability that some Japanese firms have to work cooperatively with their suppliers. Many US manufacturers have coveted these resources and capabilities, in order to gain access to the low-cost, high-quality supplies that seem to be available to at least some Japanese firms (Dyer and Ouchi 1993). However, quick creation of these resources and capabilities among many US manufacturers has been elusive. This difficulty is understandable when it is recognized that many Japanese firms have been working with the same network of suppliers for over 500 years. The experience that develops over 500 years is costly to create in a short period.

Social complexity

In addition to the role of history and path dependence, sometimes it will be very costly for a firm to create a particular capability because that capability is socially complex in nature. Examples of these socially complex firm resources and capabilities might include a firm's culture (see Chapter 4), its reputation among customers and suppliers (Klein, Crawford, and Alchian 1978), its trustworthiness (see Chapter 5), and so forth. These kinds of resources and capabilities can enable a firm to pursue valuable business and corporate strategies. Firms without these resources and capabilities may find it difficult to conceive of, let alone implement, these same strategies.

However, even though the value of these socially complex resources and capabilities in enabling a firm to pursue valuable economic opportunities may be known, it may still be very difficult for a firm without these resources and capabilities to create them. Socially complex resources and capabilities are generally beyond the ability of managers to change in the short term (Porras and Berg 1978*a*, 1978*b*). Rather, these socially complex resources and capabilities evolve and change slowly over time.[3] It is difficult to buy and sell trust, friendship, and teamwork. A firm without these kinds of socially complex resources and capabilities may find it very difficult to create them on their own.

Consider, for example, the economic performance of the set of 'visionary' firms identified by Collins and Porras (1997) in their book, *Built to Last*. These well-known firms—including General Electric, Hewlett-Packard, Johnson & Johnson, Merck, Sony, Wal-Mart, and Disney—are all organized around unique visions of their roles in the economy, their responsibilities to their customers and suppliers, and their commitment to their employees. These socially complex visions have had a profound effect on the decisions these firms have made and the strategies they have pursued. Moreover, over the long run, these firms have provided a much higher return to shareholders than competing firms that are not organized around these socially complex sets of values and commitments.[4] Despite the well-documented success of these visionary firms over many decades, many of their direct competitors have simply been unable to create their own unique visions and thus have been unable to generate the same level of economic performance. When resources and capabilities are socially complex—as the visions of these high performing firms are—it can be very difficult to create them.

Causal ambiguity

Finally, sometimes it is simply not clear what actions a firm should take to create a particular capability. When the relationship between actions a firm takes and the resources and capabilities it creates is causally ambiguous, it can be very difficult to create a particular set of resources and capabilities.

Causal ambiguity about how to create a particular set of resources and capabilities exists whenever multiple competing hypotheses about how to create a particular set of resources and capabilities exist and when these hypotheses cannot be rigorously tested. These conditions are particularly likely when the sources of a firm's resources and capabilities are taken-for-granted, unspoken, and tacit attributes of a firm (Reed and DeFillippi 1990). Such organizational attributes have been described as 'invisible assets' (Itami 1987), and can include an organization's culture (Barney 1986*b*) and its unwritten operational routines (Nelson and Winter 1982).

Clearly, possessing some kinds of invisible assets may enable a firm to create certain kinds of resources and capabilities. However, when the assets needed to create resources and capabilities are invisible, it can be very difficult for firms seeking to create these resources and capabilities to know what they should do to create them. As long as there are multiple competing hypotheses about what a firm needs to do to create a particular set of resources and capabilities, a condition of causal ambiguity obtains, and firms cannot be sure about what they must do to create them. Not knowing what to do to create a set of resources and capabilities clearly increases the difficulty of creating them.

Thus, in some situations, firms without certain resources and capabilities will find it very difficult and costly to create these resources and capabilities on their own. Whenever the creation of a capability depends on history or is path dependent, whenever a capability is socially complex, or whenever its creation is causally ambiguous, it may be very difficult for firms without a capability to create it on their own.

COSTLY TO ACQUIRE RESOURCES AND CAPABILITIES

If firms cannot create resources and capabilities on their own, they can still use hierarchical governance to obtain access to those resources and capabilities by acquiring other firms that already possess them. However, when it is very costly to acquire firms that already possess these resources and capabilities, this approach to gaining access to them can be foreclosed. Stated more precisely, whenever the cost of acquiring another firm in order to gain access to important resources and capabilities it possesses is greater than the benefit that can be gained through this acquisition, acquiring another firm to solve a firm's capability disadvantages will not be chosen.

It is well known that acquiring firms must usually pay a premium in order to acquire a target firm (Barney 1997). However, paying a premium, per se, to acquire a firm does not necessarily mean that a firm has implemented a foolish strategy. This is especially true when the acquired firm possesses resources and capabilities that are essential to an acquiring firm's competitive success and cannot be created by the acquiring firm on its own in a cost-effective way.

However, there may be other liabilities associated with using an acquisition to gain access to another firm's resources and capabilities that may drive the cost of acquisition up to the point that it is greater than any value that could have been created by gaining access to resources and capabilities. These other liabilities raise the effective cost of acquiring a firm, and fall into several categories: (*a*) legal constraints on acquisitions, (*b*) the interests of a target firm's owners, (*c*) the impact of an acquisition on the value of a target firm's resources and capabilities, (*d*) market uncertainty and the lack of strategic flexibility associated with an acquisition, (*e*) how broadly applicable the acquired capability would be in the acquiring firm, (*f*) the acquisition of unwanted 'baggage' in the target firm, and (*g*) the difficulty of leveraging acquired resources and capabilities throughout an acquiring firm.

Legal constraints on acquisitions

Most obviously, sometimes one firm may want to acquire another, in order to gain access to resources and capabilities possessed by this other firm, only to discover that important legal barriers to that acquisition exist. These barriers can be of at least two types: antitrust barriers to acquisition and local ownership barriers to acquisition.

Microsoft, for example, several years ago concluded that it wanted to purchase Intuit, the firm that had developed and marketed the most successful home accounting software on the market—Quicken. There was little doubt that such an acquisition would have benefitted Microsoft—assuming a reasonable price for Intuit could have been negotiated. Not only would Microsoft have gained access to Intuit's programming capability, they would also have gained access to its installed base of users and to its reputation in this home accounting software market. However, this acquisition did not pass antitrust scrutiny, and Microsoft had to find another approach for entering this software application market.[5]

Countries, for their own political reasons, can place ownership restrictions on domestic firms, thereby making it illegal for a nondomestic firm to acquire a domestic firm. Obviously, this represents a significant barrier to completing an acquisition. If a domestic firm possesses resources and capabilities that a nondomestic firm needs, and if a nondomestic firm is unable to develop these resources and capabilities on its own, it will have to find some alternative to acquisition to gain access to those resources and capabilities.

Interests of a target firm's owners

Sometimes, the owners of a firm that possesses valuable resources and capabilities may not want to sell that firm. This is especially common for privately held, or closely held, firms. In this setting, firm owners often perceive important nonpecuniary benefits from ownership, including social status in a geographic region, the maintenance of an important family tradition, personal loyalty to employees, and so forth. In these settings, a reluctance to sell will have the effect of driving the price of an acquisition up, often to the point that it is no longer economically viable. When this occurs, a firm seeking access to resources and capabilities possessed by this other firm will have to find an alternative to acquisition to gain this access.

For example, Publicis SA is one of the largest advertising agencies in Europe. Founded by Marcel Bleustein-Blanchet in 1926 in Paris, Publicis has grown from a small French operation to a large integrated network of agencies providing a broad range of advertising, communications, and public relations services throughout Europe. In the midst of the consolidation of the global advertising market characterized by numerous mergers and acquisitions, Publicis consistently resisted being acquired. Indeed, Bleustein-Blanchet once turned down an acquisition offer from Saatchi & Saatchi by saying, 'Not even for 100 million francs would I sell Publicis.' Still independent, Publicis entered into a strategic alliance with the US advertising firm Foote, Cone & Belding (FCB). However, for FCB to gain access to Publicis' resources and capabilities, it had to find an alternative to acquisition (Kanter 1993). This alternative was a joint venture.

The impact of acquisition on resource value

Sometimes, the acquisition of a firm can reduce the value of the resources and capabilities an acquiring firm is seeking in the acquired firm. Consider, once again, Publicis. One of this firm's greatest assets was its long-term contracts with several large French companies, many of which were at least partially owned by the French government. However, these French clients strongly preferred working with a French advertising agency. If Publicis had been acquired by, say, a US advertising agency, the very thing that the US agency was trying to purchase—Publicis' relationship with large French companies—would have been put in jeopardy. In this context, a firm interested in gaining access to Publicis' resources and capabilities would simply have to find an alternative to acquisition, since the act of acquiring Publicis would have destroyed the resources and capabilities being sought (Kanter 1993).

Strategic flexibility and uncertainty

Under conditions of high market uncertainty, it may not be possible for a firm to know, with certainty, what resources and capabilities it will need to successfully compete in the long run. In this setting, a firm has a strong incentive to retain its flexibility, to move as quickly as possible to create the required resources and capabilities when uncertainty is resolved.

In this highly uncertain environment, acquiring another firm in order to gain access to its resources and capabilities is a less flexible governance choice than, say, using intermediate or market governance to gain access to that capability. If one firm acquires another in order to gain access to a particular capability, only to discover that this capability turns out to not be valuable, this firm will have to sell off the firm it originally acquired, since the capability it purchased when it bought this firm has turned out to not be valuable. On the other hand, if a firm uses intermediate or market governance to gain access to a particular capability, only to find that that capability is not economically valuable, the costs of withdrawing from that form of governance are generally much lower than the costs of selling a previously acquired firm.

Indeed, there is strong empirical support that suggests that, under conditions of high market uncertainty, firms prefer gaining access to the resources and capabilities of other firms through various forms of strategic alliances (as forms of intermediate governance) rather than through acquisitions (Kogut 1991). Only after the market uncertainty facing a firm is resolved do firms use acquisitions to gain access to these resources and capabilities. In the meantime, firms prefer to remain flexible in order to avoid the costs associated with acquiring firms only to discover that the resources and capabilities thus acquired turn out to not be economically valuable.

How broadly applicable a capability is in the acquiring firm

Another reason why acquiring another firm to gain access to its resources and capabilities may be very costly is that the capability that is being acquired, while essential, is only applicable in a narrow range of activities in the acquiring firm or for a very short period in the acquiring firm. This could happen, for example, if the required resources and capabilities are only relevant in a small number of stages of the value chain of the firm contemplating an acquisition. Once this stage of the value chain is completed, the resources and capabilities of the firm it acquired may no longer be needed, and this firm should be sold off—a process we have already seen can be more costly than withdrawing from a market or intermediate forms of governance.

Consider, for example, a firm developing a new product. Suppose that this new product requires the use of some specialized technology resources and capabilities that are not required in any of this firm's other products. A very reasonable way for this firm to gain access to these resources and capabilities would be for it to enter into some form of market or intermediate governance relationship with a firm that already possessed these specific technical resources and capabilities. Then, when the development of this product was complete, the relationship between these two firms could be severed at low cost.

Acquiring the firm with these specialized technical resources and capabilities is a much more costly solution. Certainly, acquiring this firm might facilitate the use of these technical resources and capabilities in the development of the new product, since using a hierarchical form of governance should be able to solve any transaction-specific investment problems that might arise between these two firms if nonhierarchical forms of governance were used to manage this exchange. However, the cost of dismantling this hierarchical form of governance would be much higher than the cost of dismantling nonhierarchical forms of governance. And since the firm needing access to these technical resources and capabilities knows that it only needs them for the development of a particular product for a relatively short period, this firm knows that it will almost certainly want to divest itself of this firm once this specific product is developed. To avoid these almost certain costs, a firm may opt for less hierarchical forms of governance, even if those forms of governance do not fully protect it from potential opportunistic actions of its exchange partner.

The acquisition of unwanted baggage and diffused resources and capabilities

Also, acquiring another firm almost always involves acquiring resources and capabilities that the acquiring firm does not need or want (Hennart 1988; Kogut 1988). Firms are bundles of resources and capabilities that are often difficult to disentangle. A particular capability may not be conveniently located in a single division, or a single group, in another firm. Rather, that capability may be spread across multiple individuals, divisions, and groups around the world in another firm. These kinds of diffused resources and capabilities cannot be easily separated from the firm where they are operating. In this setting, a firm seeking to gain access to the diffused resources and capabilities of another firm may have to acquire the entire firm to do so.

Whenever an entire firm is acquired, both desirable and undesirable resources and capabilities are acquired. Moreover, an acquiring firm must pay for both the resources and capabilities it desires, and the resources and capabilities it does not desire—because some other firm may desire precisely the same resources and capabilities that this firm finds undesirable. If the desirable resources and capabilities can be separated from the undesirable resources and capabilities in the acquired firm, the problem of acquiring unwanted capability baggage in an acquisition can be solved by simply spinning off those parts of the acquired firm that are not important to the acquiring firm. While there may be some costs associated with selling off these unwanted parts of the firm (costs that increase the effective cost of using acquisitions as a way to gain access to another firm's resources and capabilities), at least the firm can gain access to just those parts of another firm that are strategically most relevant.

However, when a firm's resources and capabilities are diffused throughout its organization, it may be impossible to separate the desirable from the undesirable, the core from the baggage. In this setting, acquiring the baggage in order to gain access to some important resources and capabilities significantly increases the cost of acquisition. Indeed, the effective cost of the acquisition can rise to the point that it is greater than whatever benefit would have been created by gaining access to an acquired firm's resources and capabilities.

Leveraging an acquired firm's resources and capabilities

Even if none of the other problems with acquiring another firm to gain access to its resources and capabilities exists, such an acquisition can still be very costly. This is because it is often difficult to leverage the acquired resources and capabilities across the relevant parts of the acquiring firm's operations.

Research indicates that many acquisitions fail (Porter 1987). By far, the most important reason for this failure is the inability of acquiring firms to take full advantage of the resources and capabilities of the firms they have acquired (Haspeslagh and Jemison 1987). These difficulties in integration stem from differences in culture, systems, approach, and so forth. Such differences can significantly raise the effective price of an acquisition designed to provide a firm the resources and capabilities it needs to be competitively successful. Thus, even if a firm knows that another firm has the resources and capabilities needed to be competitively successful, it does not follow that this firm will always be able to acquire this other firm to gain access to its resources and capabilities. Even if an acquisition occurs, difficult leveraging problems can emerge, preventing a firm from gaining the capability access it needs. Of course, these integration difficulties increase dramatically if an acquisition is in any sense unfriendly.

Bringing resources and capabilities back into governance choices

When the three conditions outlined in this chapter exist—when a firm does not possess all the resources and capabilities it needs to be competitively successful, when it is very costly for firms without resources and capabilities to create them on their own, and when acquiring another firm to gain access to its resources and capabilities is very costly—the major predictions and prescriptions of TCE with regard to governance choices can change. It is not that problems of opportunism stemming from transaction-specific investment are unimportant when these three conditions exist. Rather, it is simply that additional considerations come into play—considerations that can lead firms to make very different governance choices than would be expected if transaction-specific investment and opportunism were the only issues that were being considered.

Imagine a situation where one firm requires the resources and capabilities possessed by a second firm, where the threat of opportunism stemming from transaction-specific investment in an exchange between these firms is very high, and the three other conditions mentioned in this chapter exist. The threat of opportunism due to high transaction-specific investment suggests that, all things being equal, a firm would prefer to use hierarchical governance to manage this exchange rather than either intermediate forms of governance or market forms of governance.

As suggested earlier, there are two ways that a firm could use hierarchical governance to gain access to these valuable resources and capabilities. First, it could create these resources and capabilities within its own organizational boundaries. However, if, for any of the reasons described above, the cost of creating these resources and capabilities is high, this governance option may not be available to a firm. Second, it could gain access to these resources and capabilities by acquiring a firm that already possesses them. However, if, for any of the reasons described above, the cost of acquiring this firm is high, this governance option also may not be available to a firm.

In this setting, a firm may find it too costly to choose hierarchical forms of governance to gain access to a capability. If the value of gaining access to this capability is greater than the cost of any opportunism that might occur by using nonhierarchical forms of governance to manage this highly transaction-specific investment, this firm will opt for nonhierarchical forms of governance, and accept any residual opportunism as simply part of the cost of obtaining access to a very valuable capability.

Put differently, rather than simply being driven by the value of gaining access to a capability and the threat of opportunism stemming from transaction-specific investments, governance choices in this setting are driven by: (*a*) the value of gaining access to a capability, (*b*) the cost of opportunism due to transaction-specific investment in an exchange, (*c*) the cost of creating a capability, and (*d*) the cost of acquiring another firm to gain access to a capability. If the cost of creating a capability and the cost of acquiring another firm to gain access to a capability are greater than the cost of opportunism due to transaction-specific investment, but less than the value created by gaining access to a capability, firms will choose nonhierarchical forms of governance to gain access to this capability rather than hierarchical forms of governance. This is an example of a firm engaging in an exchange characterized by high levels of transaction-specific investment rationally choosing to manage this exchange with nonhierarchical forms of governance.

Of course, even when a firm in this situation decides to choose nonhierarchical forms of governance to manage exchanges with high levels of transaction-specific investment, it will not abandon efforts to minimize the threat of opportunism in this exchange. Assuming that both intermediate and market forms of governance are available to this firm, and assuming (as does traditional TCE) that intermediate forms of governance are more effective at controlling the threat of opportunism than market forms of governance, it seems reasonable to expect that a firm in this situation will prefer the use of intermediate forms of governance over market forms of governance.

How common are these exchange conditions?

At this point, a careful reader is probably asking: so what? All this discussion of the value of gaining access to a capability, the cost of creating a capability, and the cost of acquiring a firm to gain access to a capability is only relevant if the conditions described above actually exist in some industries. If these conditions are very rare, then the issues raised here are managerially irrelevant. However, while ultimately the frequency with which these conditions exist in different industries is an empirical question, we believe that these conditions are not uncommon, at least in some types of industries. In fact, there is a class of industries where these three conditions, if anything, are probably quite common. These industries are newly created, rapidly evolving, high technology industries. Examples of these industries include biotechnology, microelectronics, certain sectors of computer software, and so forth. Consider how likely it is for these kinds of industries to have the three conditions described in this chapter.

CAPABILITY DIFFERENCES ACROSS FIRMS

Because these industries are newly created, it is not unusual for different firms in them to have very different sets of resources and capabilities. The homogenizing effects of industry structure, mergers and acquisitions, and consolidation have not yet occurred in these kinds of industries, assuring that important capability differences are likely to exist across firms that operate in them. Firms in these industries often find that they need resources and capabilities that they do not possess if they are to be competitively successful. Thus the first of the three conditions described in this chapter seems likely to exist in these kinds of industries.

COSTLY TO CREATE RESOURCES AND CAPABILITIES

Resources and capabilities in these industries are also often costly to create. History matters in these industries, and technology trajectories of different firms are highly path dependent. For example, firms that desire to create the capability of large scale manufacturing in the biotechnology industry almost certainly must have first created the capability to successfully manufacture in smaller batches (Pisano 1995). Firms that want to create the capability of writing complex software must first create the capability to write software modules within these complex programs, and second, they must create the capability of continuously integrating these modules to create their software products (Blackburn, Hoedemaker, and Van Wassenhove 1996). There is no known way to short circuit these path-dependent processes.

Firms in these industries also vary in the extent to which they use socially complex resources and capabilities pursue strategic objectives. Research in the pharmaceutical industry, for example, suggests that some firms are very skilled at integrating product development efforts across multiple scientific disciplines, while other firms are less skilled in this way (Henderson and Cockburn 1994). These socially complex differences between firms are costly to overcome in the short to medium term.

Finally, given the high level of uncertainty in these industries, there can be a great deal of causal ambiguity about how to develop resources and capabilities that are critical to success in them. Often, this is due to the underdeveloped scientific knowledge that underpins these industries. For example, in biotechnology manufacturing, even the most capable firms are often unable to successfully complete all their manufacturing efforts, let alone able to explain to other firms how to create this capability (Pisano 1995). This lack of scientific knowledge, together with the thousands of small decisions that make up some of the core processes in these industries, makes causal ambiguity in these industries very high, and the cost of creating at least some strategically important resources and capabilities essentially infinite.

Taken together, these attributes of newly created, rapidly evolving, high technology industries suggest that it will often be costly for firms to create at least some competitively important resources and capabilities on their own, and thus that the second condition described in this chapter may frequently exist in these industries.

COSTLY TO ACQUIRE RESOURCES AND CAPABILITIES

The cost of acquiring another firm to gain access to its resources and capabilities can also be very high in these newly created, rapidly evolving, high technology industries. Over and above any legal, ownership, and asset value constraints that might exist, high uncertainty about the future puts a premium on maintaining flexibility in these industries leading firms to avoid using less flexible acquisitions as a way to gain access to a firm's resources and capabilities (Pisano 1995). Given the rapidly changing technical needs of firms in these kinds of industries, it is not unusual for a very specific capability to only be required by a firm for a limited range of activities or for a very short period for highly specialized purposes. Indeed, research in these industries has shown that the entire time scale of competition is much shorter than in other kinds of industries (Eisenhardt and Brown 1998). Temporariness increases the cost of using acquisitions to gain access to resources and capabilities. It is also not uncommon for resources and capabilities in firms operating in these kinds of industries to be highly diffused across the firm—implying that acquiring these firms may often lead to acquiring bundles of unwanted resources and capabilities along with those resources and capabilities that are desired through an acquisition. Finally, differences in culture, differences in procedures, and other differences among firms in these kinds of industries can make it very difficult to integrate new acquisitions to gain full access to the resources and capabilities in these firms.

Taken together, these attributes of newly created, rapidly evolving, high technology industries suggest that it will often be costly to acquire other firms in order to gain access to their resources and capabilities, and thus that the third condition described in this chapter may frequently exist in these industries.

Newly created, rapidly evolving, high technology industries are not the only industries that have the characteristics described in this chapter. Further, all exchanges in this type of industry will not necessarily have all these characteristics. Considerations of transaction-specific investment and opportunism are not suggested as being irrelevant in this type of industry. Clearly, whatever form of governance that firms in this type of industry choose to gain access to a capability, they will attempt to build in safeguards that have the effect of reducing the threat of opportunism as much as possible. What has been proposed here, however, is that gaining access to valuable resources and capabilities in this type of industry may take issues well beyond transaction-specific investment and opportunism into consideration. All things being equal, firms in this type of industry should adopt less hierarchical forms of governance than what would be predicted by traditional TCE. Moreover, in these types of industries, firm resources, and capabilities will play a very significant role in determining a firm's governance choices.

Discussion

Thus, in the end, managerial concerns about not including their own firm's resources and capabilities and the resources and capabilities of potential exchange partners into consideration when making firm boundary decisions are warranted. Sometimes, it makes sense to cooperate with another firm through market or intermediate forms of governance just because that firm possesses certain resources and capabilities that cannot be accessed in any other cost-effective way. That there may be risks of opportunism associated with gaining access to these special resources and capabilities is true. But the costs associated with opportunism may be less than the benefits associated with gaining access to these special resources and capabilities.

Choosing a firm's boundary, thus, is not just about reducing the threat of opportunism; it is also about creating economic value by assembling the right mix of resources and capabilities through a combination of both hierarchical and nonhierarchical forms of governance.

Recent empirical work supports the conclusion that resource considerations are important for making vertical integration decisions, over and above transactions cost considerations. For example, an in-depth case study by Argyres (1996) found that firms will outsource when suppliers possess superior capabilities, except when firms decide to accept the temporary higher costs associated with developing capabilities in-house. Argyres also found that firm capabilities mattered most in vertical integration decisions when there was either very little overlap of the resources controlled by two firms or when there was substantial overlap in these resources.

Leiblein and Miller (2003), in an empirical study of semiconductor firms make or buy decisions, found that firm-level capabilities and strategies independently and significantly influence firms' vertical boundary choices. Firms having greater experience with a particular process technology were more likely to internalize manufacturing activities than firms lacking such production experience. Similarly, firms with high levels of sourcing experience were more likely to outsource their production than firms that did not have such experience. While empirical research on the role of capabilities in vertical integration decisions is still developing rapidly, there is some reason to believe that resource considerations play an important, and sometimes independent role compared to transactions cost considerations.

NOTES

1. At least a moderate level of uncertainty is also required for transaction-specific investment to be a potential source of opportunism in an exchange. Without some uncertainty, it would always be possible for firms in an exchange to write a contract that fully anticipates all possible states of that exchange, and the rights and responsibilities of each exchange partner in those different states. With such a contract, the threat of opportunism could always be completely eliminated. Unfortunately, as suggested earlier, research on the impact of uncertainty on firm governance choices has not received the consistent empirical support that research on the impact of transaction-specific investment on governance choices has received (see Mahoney 1992; Barney and Hesterly 1996, for reviews of this empirical literature). For this

reason, transaction-specific investment as a source of opportunism is highlighted in this review of transactions cost logic.

2. Intermediate governance can be used to resolve a firm's lack of capabilities problem in at least two ways. First, as mentioned in the body of the chapter, intermediate governance can be used to gain access to another firm's capabilities, with little or no effort on the part of a firm without capabilities to create them. Second, a firm can use intermediate governance to learn how to create the capabilities it does not possess. However, in order to simplify the discussion, and with no loss of generality, this second use of intermediate governance will be treated as a special case of using hierarchical governance to create a capability.
3. This, itself, is yet another example of the importance of path dependence in developing some capabilities.
4. Collins and Porras (1997) estimate that $1 invested in their sample of 18 'visionary firms' in 1926 would have been worth $6,536 in 1995, while $1 invested in a matched sample of firms competing over this same time period in the same industries as the 18 visionary firms would have been worth $415 in 1995.
5. See 'Will Regulators Get Tougher on M&A', *Mergers and Acquisitions*, vol. 31, n 1, July–August, 1996, pp. 42–51 for a discussion of the specific antitrust issues in the Intuit Microsoft case.

9 Resource-based theory and corporate diversification*

A firm implements a corporate diversification strategy when it operates multiple businesses within its boundaries. This strategy is one of the most studied phenomena in the field of strategic management (Berg 2001). A wide variety of theoretical tools have been used to understand this phenomenon, everything from agency theory (Jensen and Meckling 1976) to portfolio theory. Depending on these different theoretical perspectives, corporate diversification has been characterized as a systematic waste of shareholder's money (Lang and Stulz 1994; Berger and Ofek 1995, 1999), as having no impact on shareholder wealth (Bradley, Desai, and Kim 1988; Graham, Lemmon, and Walf 2002; Villalonga 2004), and as having a positive impact on shareholder wealth (Elgers and Clark 1980; Jensen and Ruback 1983; Schipper and Thompson 1983; Matsusaka 1993; Hubbard and Palia 1999).

Resource-based theorists, almost from the beginning, have also been interested in the causes and consequences of corporate diversification (Wernerfelt 1989; Chatterjee and Wernerfelt 1991). Indeed, one of the most cited explanations of corporate diversification—that firm's diversify to exploit their core competencies (Prahalad and Bettis 1986; Prahalad and Hamel 1990)—is very consistent with, and an early contributor to, resource-based theory.

This chapter summarizes this traditional resource-based approach to understanding corporate diversification. In addition, this chapter proposes an alternative approach to understanding resource-based theory. Where the traditional theory combines the assumption that firms may have different resources and capabilities that can create value in multiple business

* This chapter draws from Barney (2002) and Wang and Barney (2006).

settings and the assumption that the value of these resources sometimes cannot be realized using market forms of governance to explain the emergence of corporate diversification, the alternative approach focuses on how firms can use corporate diversification to create one type of resource—firm-specific human capital investments—in the first place.

Resources, market failures, and corporate diversification

In their very influential article, Prahalad and Hamel (1990) define a firm's core competence as 'the collective learning in the organization, especially how to coordinate diverse production skills and integrate multiple streams of technologies.' Such core competencies have many of the attributes of resources and capabilities described in Chapter 3 of this book: They are likely to be path dependent, causally ambiguous, and socially complex.

However, the existence of core competencies, per se, is a necessary, but not sufficient explanation of why firms will adopt a corporate diversification strategy. Consider the following. Suppose a firm possesses a core competence, A, that can be applied in its current industry, I, but can also be valuably applied in a second industry, II. Since this single competence is valuable in both these industries, these industries are, by definition, strategically related (Markides and Williamson 1994).

However, what different ways can this firm realize the value of its core competence, A, across these two industries I and II? One option, of course, would be for this firm to simply begin operations in industry II and then make sure that those inside this firm that are in charge of operating the business inside of industry II exploit competence A in doing so. Alternatively, this firm could acquire a firm that is currently operating in industry II, and by integrating this newly acquired business into its boundary, take advantage of competence A. Both these approaches to realizing the potential value of competence A in industry II adopt hierarchical forms of governance (Williamson 1975). And in both these cases, a firm can be said to be implementing a strategy of corporate diversification.

However, hierarchy is not the only way this value can be realized. At least two alternatives present themselves. First, this firm could form an alliance with a firm currently operating in industry II, and realize the potential value of competence A this way. Alternatively, this firm could license its competence A to a firm currently operating in industry II. These intermediate and market forms of governance would enable a firm to realize the value of its core competence, but would not require a firm to actually change the mix of businesses it engages in within its own boundaries. That is, these firms would not necessarily have to implement a corporate diversification strategy to realize the value of the core competence A.

It was Teece's original (1982) insight that in order for it to be economically efficient for a firm to operate multiple businesses within its boundary, not only must there be core competencies that can create value across these multiple businesses (although Teece did not use the term 'core competence'—it had not yet been invented), but that the value of these core competencies could not be realized through intermediate or market forms of governance. Neither valuable core competencies nor market failures, by themselves, were sufficient to explain the existence of diversified firms. However, together, they could explain these types of organizations.

Of course, Teece's original argument (1982) was developed out of TCE, with its emphasis on transaction-specific investment and the threat of opportunism as primary determinants of a firm's governance choices. However, in this case, TCE and resource-based theories are clearly complementary. Transactions cost economics arguments suggest that high levels of transaction-specific investment lead to hierarchical governance. Resource-based theories suggest that exploiting core competencies that are path dependent, causally ambiguous, and socially complex will often require exchange partners to make high levels of transaction-specific investment. Thus, by bringing these two theories together, it follows that in order to exploit their core competencies, firms will often have to bring multiple businesses within their boundaries, that is, firms will need to implement corporate diversification strategies.

A vast amount of empirical research has attempted to assess the validity of these arguments. Currently, there is broad consensus that related diversification (where a firm exploits a core competence in its diversification efforts) creates more economic value than unrelated diversification (where a firm does not exploit a core competence in its diversification efforts) (Palich, Cardinal, and Miller 2000). This result is consistent with the RBT/TCE arguments presented here. After all, if a firm is not exploiting a core competence in its diversification strategy, then it is not likely that transactions to implement its diversification strategy would be subject to market failures, and thus, it is not likely that such transactions will need to be brought within the boundaries of a firm. If such transactions are brought within the boundaries of a firm, then the inefficiencies created will lead to low levels of performance. Thus, related diversifiers—where the exploitation of core competencies is more likely to lead to market failures—are likely to outperform unrelated diversifiers.

While there is broad consensus that related diversification outperforms unrelated diversification, there is less consensus about whether diversification—of any kind—outperforms no diversification, a so-called focused or single business strategy. In their very influential papers, Lang and Stultz (1994) and Comment and Jarrell (1995) showed that diversified firms traded at a significant discount compared to a portfolio of focused firms operating in the same industries as a diversified firm. This result suggested that, on average, diversification—including diversification designed to exploit core competencies—destroyed economic value. One explanation of this result was that the organizational costs of implementing corporate diversification—including the cost of inefficient internal capital markets (Gomes and Livdan 2004)—were simply greater than any value created by exploiting core competencies across multiple businesses.

A second group of scholars, including Campa and Kedia (2002), Villalonga (2004*a*, 2004*b*), and Miller (2004), showed that, controlling for a firm's growth options in its current businesses, that corporate diversification either did not destroy value or might even create value for its shareholders. Suppose, for example, a firm was generating significant free cash flow in a mature or declining business. In such industries, there are limited growth options and it might make sense for a firm to invest some of its free cash into business opportunities that have more significant growth options. This would especially be the case if these growth options exploited one or more core competencies possessed by a firm (Miller 2004). Using a two-stage methodology, many of these authors were able to document either that diversification did not destroy value, or that it, in fact, did create value for a firm's shareholders.

However, even more recently, Mackey and Barney (2006) have shown that this diversification premium literature is incomplete. In particular, when a firm with limited growth options generates free cash flow, it has two broad options: First, it can use this cash to invest in new business activities (i.e. it can engage in related corporate diversification) or, second, it can give this cash back to its shareholders, either in the form of a dividend or a stock buyback program. Employing the same two-stage methodology used by previous scholars, but simultaneously controlling both for the likelihood of a firm to diversify (because of limited growth options) and the likelihood of a firm to give cash back to its shareholders (through dividends or stock buybacks), Mackey and Barney (2006) find that firms that only give cash back to their shareholders create economic value, firms that give cash back and diversify do not create or destroy value, and firms that just diversify destroy value. These results hold even if the level of strategic relatedness in the diversification strategies used by a firm are controlled for. Once again, these results are consistent with the observation that the costs of diversification may be greater than the benefits created by exploiting a firm's core competencies.

Diversification and the creation of core competencies

Much of this corporate diversification literature takes the existence of core competencies as given and asks, 'What is the most efficient way to exploit the value of these core competencies?' Diversification is one of the answers that is provided to this question.

However, a logically prior question is also possible. That question is: 'Where do core competencies that might be exploited across multiple businesses come from in the first place?' In answering this question, it is possible to show that over and above any effect that core competencies might have on diversification, diversification might have an impact on the development of core competencies.

Indeed, there is a paradox at the heart of current resource-based theories of superior firm performance. On the one hand, these theories recognize that employee firm-specific investments are among the most important sources of economic rents for firms (Barney 1991*a*). Employee firm-specific investments—including employee knowledge of how a firm operates, knowledge about a firm's key suppliers and customers, and knowledge about how to work effectively with other employees—often meet the criteria established in resource-based logic for generating sustained competitive advantages (Dierickx and Cool 1989; Barney 1991*a*).

The rents generated by these firm-specific investments are often shared between a firm's employees and its owners (Becker 1964; Hashimoto 1981; Rumelt 1987) and thus can be a source of wealth for both the employees and the owners.[1]

On the other hand, a great deal of research in organizational economics suggests that employees who make firm-specific investments risk opportunistic actions by the firms in which they invest (Williamson 1985). Once employees make firm-specific investments, firms can systematically extract wealth from these employees and employees have few ways they can protect themselves. Indeed, the hazards associated with making firm-specific investments are so significant that, absent some protection, current theories suggest that employees will avoid making firm-specific investments altogether (Alchian and Demsetz 1972).

A great deal of research has documented ways that employees can protect themselves against the threat of opportunistic behaviors if they make firm-specific investments (Williamson 1975, 1985). Additional work has identified ways that firms can credibly reassure employees that they will not behave opportunistically in such settings (Jensen and Meckling 1976; Grossman and Hart 1986; Castanias and Helfat 1991; Rajan and Zingales 1998). With these protections and reassurances in place, current theory seems to suggest that employees will be willing to make firm-specific investments.

However, beyond the threat of opportunism that plagues specific investments made by employees, there is another risk accepted by employees making these investments that has received less attention in the literature.[2] This is the risk that the value of the underlying assets controlled by a firm—the assets that an employee makes investments specific to—will fall. If these assets drop in value, then the value of the investments made by employees that are specific to these assets will also fall. This will be the case even if none of the parties in this exchange engage in opportunistic behaviors. Employees may be very reluctant to make firm-specific investments when the future value of a firm's underlying assets is very risky, even if protections and reassurances are in place that effectively eliminate any threat of opportunism in this exchange.

Here, the implications for both employees and firms of these risky assets are examined. For employees, it is shown that risky core firm assets can reduce employee incentives to make firm-specific investments, even when there is no threat of opportunism in these exchanges. Some actions firms can take to address concerns employees might have about making specific investments in risky firm assets are discussed. These actions include directly compensating employees for risk bearing and engaging in a particular type of corporate diversification—resource-based product market diversification. This latter mechanism is then explored in detail, and the implications of this analysis for the theory of diversification are then discussed. We begin by developing a simple model of employee decisions about whether to invest in firm-specific human capital that depends both on the threat of opportunism in this exchange and the riskiness of the value of a firm's underlying assets.

A MODEL OF EMPLOYEE DECISIONS TO MAKE FIRM-SPECIFIC INVESTMENTS

Two kinds of resources are important in a model of the employee decision to make firm-specific investments: (*a*) the rare and costly to imitate resources controlled by a firm that an employee is contemplating making specific investments in, and (*b*) the resources controlled by an employee that will be modified if specific investments are made. Here, the first kind of resource is called a 'core firm resource' and the second kind is called a 'human capital resource'.

Of course, not all the resources controlled by a firm are rare and costly to imitate—that is, not all the resources controlled by a firm are core firm resources as defined here. Indeed, many noncore firm resources, that is, many firm resources that are not rare or costly to imitate, may be necessary if a firm is to gain competitive advantages and earn economic rents. However, these common and imitable resources do not separate firms that have the potential to gain competitive advantages from those that do not have this potential. These firms are separated by the rare and costly to imitate resources they do and do not control.

It is also the case that just possessing rare and costly to imitate resources, by itself, is usually insufficient for a firm to generate economic rents. In addition, employees need to know how to exploit these resources through the strategies a firm pursues. As Porter (1991: 108) argued, 'resources are not valuable in and of themselves, but they are valuable because they allow firms to perform activities.'

Noncore firm resources are neither rare nor costly to imitate, and thus can be exploited by nonspecific human capital investments made by a firm's employees. However, core firm resources will generally require highly firm-specific investments in human capital if they are to be exploited in a firm's strategies. That is, employees must understand the nature of these core resources, develop a working knowledge of how they can be used in conceiving of and implementing strategies, and how they can be protected and nurtured over time if they are to be fully exploited in creating competitive advantages and economic rents. These human capital investments have little value in alternative settings, but can create a great deal of value in a particular firm.

Now, consider an employee, i, of a firm choosing an optimal level of human capital investment specific to a firm's core resource. The amount (units) of specific investments made by this employee is denoted as x_i. It is further assumed that the payoff that the employee is expected to appropriate from the total rent generated *per unit* of his/her specific investment (in combination of the core resource of the firm) is a fraction, $a(0 < a < 1)$, of the total expected amount of rent generated per unit of his/her specific human capital investment, r_i. r_i is in turn an increasing function of the value of the firm's core resource, V. The more valuable the core resource, the more potential rents can be generated from this core resource $(\partial r_i/\partial V > 0)$. Thus, the amount of rents appropriated by the employee is ar_i.

Also, assume that the employee incurs an opportunity cost while making specific human capital investments. The opportunity cost comes from the fact that instead of making specific human capital investments, the employee can alternatively make general human capital investments, for example, developing skills that improve his/her marketability. Since general human capital does not suffer the problem of value loss in case of transferring across business settings, the payoff from the employee's per unit general human capital investment is denoted as $\bar{w}_i$, which is assumed to be a constant.[3]

The total units of human capital investments, including both specific and general, is denoted as n (n can also be thought of as the total hours the employee devotes to making these investments). Since x_i is the total amount of specific investments, the amount of general investments is then $(n - x_i)$. Thus, the employee's total payoff, denoted as w_i, includes the payoffs from both his/her specific human capital investments $(x_i a r_i)$ and his/her general human capital investments $[(n - x_i)\bar{w}_i]$:

$$w_i = a x_i r_i + (n - x_i)\bar{w}_i. \tag{9.1}$$

The employee then chooses the optimal amount of firm-specific investments, x_i, that maximizes his/her utility. The employee's concern over the risk associated with the payoff from his/her investments can be captured using a risk-averse utility function. The particular form of standard mean variance utility function is thus chosen to capture the idea that employee utilities increase with the expected amount of payoff from his/her investments, $E(w_i)$, but decrease with the risk associated with this payoff, $\text{var}(w_i)$ (Sargent 1987). It follows that the employee solves the following utility function, subject to his/her payoff constraint[4]:

$$\begin{aligned} \max_{x_i} U &= E(w_i) - \frac{A}{2}\text{var}(w_i) \\ \text{where } w_i &= a x_i r_i + (n - x_i)\bar{w}_i. \end{aligned} \tag{9.2}$$

A is the absolute risk-averse parameter that captures the employee's degree of risk aversion. Without loss of generality, the parameter, A, is normalized to 1 $(A \equiv 1)$. The wealth constraint shows that when the employee increases his/her level of specific human capital investment (higher x_i), his/her total wealth will covary more with the expected rents generated per unit of specific human capital investment.

From the first-order condition with the normalized risk-aversion parameter $(A \equiv 1)$, the optimal amount of specific human capital investment chosen by the employee can be obtained as follows (please see appendix of this chapter for a more detailed derivation):

$$x_i^* = \frac{aE(r_i) - \bar{w}_i}{\text{var}(a r_i)}. \tag{9.3}$$

This equation has several important implications. First, the numerator of this equation suggests that the optimal amount of specific human capital investments an employee chooses to make (or, an employee's incentive to specialize), x_i^*, depends on the amount of rents the employee is expected to appropriate, $aE(r_i)$, relative to the rents from risk-free general human capital investments. This is perfectly consistent with previous research in organizational economics which suggests that employee investments in firm-specific human capital can generate economic rents, but the willingness of employees to make these investments depends on how much of the rent they expect to be able to appropriate (Grossman and Hart 1986; Hart and Moore 1990; Castanias and Helfat 1991, 2001; Rajan and Zingales 1998, 2001). Moreover, a small amount of rent appropriation suggests that an employee expects significant opportunistic actions on the part of a firm, while a large amount suggests that an employee does not expect such actions. Efforts by employees to contractually protect themselves from opportunism, and efforts by firms to reassure employees that they will not behave opportunistically, can both be interpreted as efforts to guarantee that the employees will realize their expected amount of rent appropriation and thereby increase the likelihood that these employees will make specific human capital investments that generate economic rents.

Second, x_i^* is inversely related to $\text{var}(ar_i)$, the risk associated with the amount of rent that the employee expects to appropriate per unit of his/her specific human capital investment. This establishes a basis for the analysis in this chapter: the incentives for an employee to make specific human capital investment are negatively affected by the *risk* to the per unit payoff from his/her specific human capital investment. As r_i, the rents generated from an employee's specific human capital investment, increases with V, the value of the core resource owned by the firm, so does the payoff to the employee from his/her per unit specific investment, ar_i. It then follows that the riskiness of this payoff, $\text{var}(ar_i)$, should also increase with the riskiness of the value of a firm's core resources. That is, when the value of a firm's core resource falls, so does the value of employee firm-specific investments and the potential payoff the employee obtains from these investments. Therefore, the riskier is the value of a firm's core resources, the lower the employee's incentives to make specific human capital investments.

A lower level of firm-specific human capital investments, in turn, reduces the total amount of rents that can be generated from the underlying core resources and the amount of rents that is eventually appropriated by the firm. In this setting, the firm has a motive to adopt mechanisms to mitigate employee concerns over the risk to the value of the core resource to induce employees to make these rent generating investments.

MANAGING THE RISK OF FIRM CORE RESOURCES AND EMPLOYEE INCENTIVES TO MAKE FIRM-SPECIFIC INVESTMENTS

Thus, in order for a firm to induce its employees to make firm-specific investments, not only must potential opportunism problems in this exchange be managed, but firms must also discover ways of managing the risks associated with making human capital investments that are specific to a firm's risky core resources. Two possible solutions to this problem are considered here: (*a*) compensating employees directly for accepting these risks, and (*b*) using resource-based related diversification to mitigate these risks.

Compensating employees for risk bearing

The most straightforward solution to the employee incentive problem stemming from the riskiness of a firm's core resources seems to be for the firm to directly compensate employees it needs to make firm-specific investments for bearing this risk. That is, to get these 'key employees' to make firm-specific investments, pay them to do so. Theories and empirical findings in the strategic management literature indeed suggest that diverse stakeholders, including a firm's employees, suppliers, and customers, often demand compensation for risk bearing (Aaker and Jacobson 1990; Amit and Wernerfelt 1990; Miller 1998; Deephouse and Wiseman 2000; Miller and Chen 2003). The expected amount of payment to the employees should be based on an estimation of the risk to the value of firm core resources to which these employees are making specific human capital investments.

These observations lead to the following proposition:

> Proposition 1: The higher is the risk associated with a firm's core resources, the more likely that the firm's key employees will have a larger amount of total expected compensation.

On the other hand, compensating employees for risk bearing has some limitations in functioning as an effective employee incentive mechanism.

First, it can be very difficult to write and enforce a compensation contract described above (Titman 1984; Hart 1995). Bounded rationality linked with environmental uncertainty make it difficult, if not impossible, to identify all the future states of nature that would affect the value of a firm's core resources. Even if these states could be anticipated, their specific effects on the value of core resources and employee specific investments remain challenging to quantify. Because firm core resources are rare, nontradable and employee specific human capital investments are nontangible, both are difficult to value.

Moreover, the firm may default on the terms of compensation contract in the case of severe negative economic outcome. For example, a firm may approach bankruptcy when it no longer has valuable assets that allow it to continue to operate. In such case, terms of contract cannot be effectively enforced.

Second, although compensating employees for risk bearing can to some extent create incentives for them to make firm-specific human capital investments, it directly increases firm expenditures and thus imposes costs on the firm (Miller and Chen 2003). When the risk associated with firm core resources is very high, it becomes increasingly expensive for the firm to compensate employees for risk bearing despite the motivational benefits of such compensation. As the risk associated with a firm's core resource increases, for a given amount effort to make firm-specific investments, the employee will demand higher compensation resulting in higher marginal cost per unit effort and no corresponding increase in the expected revenue for the firm. Therefore, it may not pay for the firm to motivate the employees beyond a certain point through compensation, because the utility of an additional unit of effort to make firm-specific investment is worth less to the firm than the cost of motivating the employees for an incremental unit of effort. Thus, the optimal compensation schedule often does not fully compensate the employees for risk bearing (Shavell 1979). This of course will leave the employees to reduce efforts and underinvest in firm-specific human capital.

Due to the limitations associated with compensating employees for risk bearing and the costs of such compensation imposed on the firm, sometimes the firm may be better off finding additional ways to reduce the risk associated with core resources. Resource-based product market diversification is one such alternative.[5]

Resource-based corporate diversification

Generally, the value of a firm's core resource is determined in the product markets where that resource is deployed (Barney 1991*a*; Peteraf 1993; Bowman and Amrosini 2000). This implies that if the firm's core resources can be deployed in multiple product markets, the value of the resource in one product market is likely to be different from that in the other product markets. Moreover, a change in the value of a core resource in one product market may not necessarily affect its value in a different product market. This suggests that the risk associated with core resources can be reduced by exploring the applicability of these core resources in other product markets and to diversify accordingly.

Note that diversifying into multiple product markets through deploying a firm's core resource does not directly reduce the risk to the resource value in each *individual* product market. However, as long as the factors that lead to changes in one product market are not perfectly correlated with those in another product market, uncertainty in one product market that has a significant effect on the value of the core resource in that particular market is not likely to have a similar effect on that in another market. Therefore, through diversifying into product markets with less than perfectly correlated environmental factors, the overall risk associated with the value of the core resource can be reduced. This risk reduction, in turn, can potentially increase the employees' incentives to make human capital investments that are specific to a firm's core resources.[6] Generally speaking, the positive effect of resource-based product market diversification on employee incentives is expected to increase with the level of the risk associated with the firm's core resources in the firm's original market(s).

These observations lead to:

> Proposition 2: The higher is the risk associated with a firm's core resources, the more likely that the firm will diversify into other product markets based on these core resources.

To the extent that resource-based product market diversification can substitute for compensating employees for risk bearing as the means of facilitating employee to make firm-specific human capital investments, the ability for a firm to engage in resource-based diversification can reduce the need for the firm to pay employees for risk bearing. Therefore,

Proposition 3: Ceteris paribus, firms that have diversified based on their core resources will subsequently compensate their key employees at a lower level than if they have not diversified in this way.

Note that the arguments above are built on the implicit assumption that management is able to implement a resource-based diversification strategy in such a way that the risks of existing businesses of the firm are not altered. However, to the extent that the existing businesses are disturbed, the effect of resource-based diversification on risk reduction and therefore on employee incentives should be discounted accordingly.

IMPLICATIONS FOR THEORIES OF DIVERSIFICATION

Note that the pattern of diversification and the definition of resource relatedness discussed above are in spirit very close to those based on the concept of the 'strategic asset' in the resource-based theory of diversification (e.g. Teece 1982; Markides and Williamson 1994, 1996). To the extent that a *core firm resource* is rare and costly to trade, the diversification pattern predicted here, that is, diversification by deploying core firm resources, resembles the resource-based theory of corporate diversification, which argues that multibusiness organizations exist to exploit core competencies (Teece 1982; Mahoney and Pandian 1992; Peteraf 1993).[7] However, there are some important differences in the pattern of corporate diversification derived from this theory of diversification and traditional resource-based theories of diversification. These differences are manifest in the path and the scope of diversification.

Diversification path

Traditional resource-based logic suggests that diversification is appropriate when a firm's resources are applicable across the multiple businesses a firm engages in (Montgomery and Wernerfelt 1988; Markides and Williamson 1994; Silverman 1999). The logic developed here suggests that risk reduction, in addition to the ability to apply firm resources across multiple businesses, may motivate diversification. This suggests that a diversifying firm will look to exploit its current resources and capabilities in its diversification moves, but that it will also look for businesses where it can apply those resources that have cash flows that are uncorrelated with its current business activities. This suggests the following:

> Proposition 4: Firms that diversify into businesses that exploit their current core resources and that have a pattern of cash flow that is not highly correlated with their current businesses will generate higher levels of employee firm-specific investment than firms that diversify into businesses that only exploit their current core resources but have a pattern of cash flow that is highly correlated with their current businesses.

Diversification scope

Traditional resource-based logic suggests that there are often decreasing returns associated with diversification. This is because, generally, firms will diversify into the highest return related business first, the second highest return related business second, and so forth. Barring an exogenous shock that changes the value of a firm's core assets, the last diversification moves made by a firm that exploit a particular core resource are likely to be less valuable than the first few diversification moves made by a firm that exploited the resource.

The theory of diversification developed here also suggests that returns from risk reduction (i.e. the willingness of employees to make firm-specific investments that have rent-generating potential) will also have decreasing returns. This is because portfolio risk is generally a concave function of the number of assets in the portfolio (Elton and Gruber 1995), which implies that with the increase in the number of businesses a firm diversifies into, the overall risk to the value of the core resources falls but at a decreasing rate. A decreasing incremental amount of risk reduction is then likely to lead to decreasing returns for the firm.

However, while both core competence-exploitation and risk reduction may be characterized by decreasing returns, these two benefits of diversification may not move together over time. Figure 9.1 shows that as a firm diversifies further away from its original businesses, both the marginal advantage obtained from exploiting core competencies and that obtained from providing incentives for employees to specialize are expected to decrease; and the marginal cost of diversification is expected to increase. When considering each effect separately, the optimal scope of the firm is determined by the point where the marginal revenue of diversification

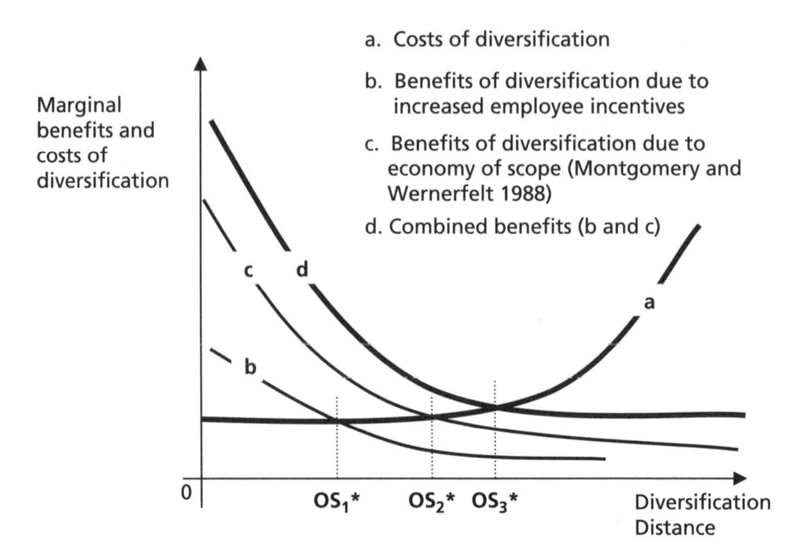

Figure 9.1. The determinants of the optimal scope of a firm

Notes: OS_1* is the optimal scope when only the benefit from employees' increased investment incentives is considered; OS_2* is the optimal scope when only the benefit from economies of scope is considered; OS_3* is the optimal scope when both the benefits of economies of scope and employee incentives are considered

equals marginal cost (OS_1* and OS_2* in Figure 9.1). However, when both effects are considered, the optimal diversification distance is at OS_3*, where the marginal revenue of diversification from the combined effects equals to the marginal cost of diversification.

Of course, the analysis in Figure 9.1 assumes that the benefit from exploiting core competencies, which is determined by the applicability of core firm resource (or strategic asset) in other product markets, and that from providing employee investment incentives, which is determined by the degree of reduction in risk to the core resource value, are not correlated. To the extent these benefits are correlated, the optimal diversification scope would be less than OS_3^* (Figure 9.1). Some strategy scholars have suggested that businesses that exploit the same underlying core resources can nevertheless have very different patterns of cash flow over time (e.g. Prahalad and Hamel 1990; Markides and Williamson 1994, 1996), implying a low correlation between these two benefits from diversification. However, the extent to which these benefits are correlated is ultimately an empirical question. All this suggests the following:

> Proposition 5: When the benefits of realizing economies of scope and increased employee incentives to specialize are not perfectly correlated, a firm will diversify more widely than when only one of the benefits is considered. And the optimal diversification scope increases with a decrease in the correlation between the two benefits.

Finally, it is worth noting that this emphasis on risk reduction from diversification is also related to the argument of agency theory, in which diversification is used to reduce overall firm risk exposure. The agency argument, however, considers diversification as an outcome of conflicts between shareholder and managers since it reduces managers' employment risk, but at the expense of the shareholders of the firm (Amihud and Lev 1981). In contrast, this part of this chapter argues that shareholders as well as employees (including managers) potentially gain from the firm's diversification, because diversification encourages employees to join the firm and to invest in firm-specific knowledge and skills. Another notable difference between these two perspectives is that central to our argument is 'resource-based' diversification (related), which reduces risks associated with the core resources. In contrast, agency theory emphasizes conglomerate diversification (unrelated), which leads to financial risk reduction, that is, it smoothes cash flow at the corporate level, but does not effectively reduce the risk of the underlying core resources.

Conclusion

This chapter shows that resource-based logic can be used to explain how firms leverage core competencies to operate in multiple businesses simultaneously, and to explain how corporate diversification can be used to help develop one very important type of core competency—firm-specific human capital investments. In this sense, corporate diversification is both the effect of core competencies and the cause of core competencies.

Obviously, of these two arguments, the former has received much more attention than the latter. However, the second argument has some potentially interesting implications for the study of diversification, generally, and for resource-based theory, in particular.

With regard to the study of diversification, the model developed here uses a simple linear rent sharing scheme between the employee and firm.

Since firm rents are assumed to be normally distributed, so is the amount of payoff to the employee's specific investments, suggesting a symmetric upside and downside risk associated with the employee's payoff. However, sometimes a nonlinear payoff function, such as an option-like function with a component of payment that is fixed, seems to be a more plausible assumption. These issues concerning the interaction between the payment and rent sharing function and the shape of the distribution of uncertain outcomes may be an interesting research direction to be explored in the future.

Second, we have focused attention on the discussion of the role of core resources and resource-based diversification as an important mechanism for reducing the risks associated with these core resources. Nevertheless, it omits some other relevant strategic questions that deserve future research attention. For example, when implementing a resource-based diversification strategy, what noncore resources should be internalized with the core resources? How should firm strategies be different in utilizing these different types of resources? How do complementary noncore resources affect the risk associated with core resources? While it is beyond the scope of this chapter to include the discussion of these issues, future research along this path will help complete a theory of core resources and employee incentives.

A third area that requires further research efforts is related to the limitation of the applicability of the current framework. The ideas here are most applicable to firms that face moderate levels of uncertainty, but not to those that operate in either very stable or extremely volatile environments. In a stable environment, the value of a firm's core resource is also likely to be stable and rents generated from the resource and employee specific human capital can be sustained over a long period. In this setting, employees have stronger incentives to specialize and appropriate their share of the rents. On the other hand, in an extremely volatile environment, rents may become so short-lived that inducing employees to make specific investments can be too costly. Furthermore, when changes in environmental factors render the core firm resource itself obsolete, diversification by deploying the core resource would no longer be effective in preserving the value of the resource. In this case, a better strategy for the firm is to develop capabilities that enable the firm to efficiently adapt to constantly changing and fast-evolving environments. Although the recent dynamic capabilities literature (Teece, Pisano, and Shuen 1997) helps address this issue, it is clearly an area that deserves further research attention.

More broadly, this second line of inquiry raises a fundamental question that is largely unanswered in resource-based theory: Where do valuable, rare, and costly to imitate resources come from? This analysis suggests that a firm's equityholders have an interest in a firm pursuing a diversification strategy in order to induce employees to make firm-specific investments, thus suggesting that valuable, rare, and costly to imitate resources may reflect strategic choices made by firms. However, this is only one way these kinds of resources might emerge for a firm and additional work is required to understand the exact processes by which these resources are created.

NOTES

1. How much of the rents will be appropriated by the employees, and how much will be appropriated by the firm's owners depends on the relative bargaining power of each party (Coff 1999).
2. Agency theory (e.g. Jensen and Meckling 1976; Shavell 1979; Holmstrom and Milgrom 1987; Eisenhardt 1989*a*) also stresses the existence of a trade-off between risk and incentives, but with a specific interest in optimal contract design and appropriate corporate governance mechanisms under varying levels of outcome uncertainty, risk aversion, and information. This argument differs in at least two aspects. First, although the agency literature also concerns itself to the effect of risk considerations on agent incentives, it does not directly address the specific incentive problems associated with employees making specific human capital investments. Second, due to contract incompleteness, the optimal contract design emphasized in the agency literature is rarely the first-best solution (e.g. Shavell 1979). Thus, it almost always leaves room for firms to adopt strategic risk management mechanisms such as resource-based diversification strategies.
3. In order to focus our attention on the pure effect of resource risk on employee incentives to make *specific* human capital investments, we implicitly assume that *general* human capital investments are risk free. But in reality general human capital investments may not be completely riskless. Incorporating the riskiness of general human capital would make investment in firm-specific human capital even more attractive relative to general human capital.
4. The mean variance risk-averse utility function is originally derived from exponential utility function, which has the form $U(C) = -e^{-AC}$, where A is called the Arrow-Pratt index of absolute risk aversion, given by $A = -U''(C)/U'(C)$. C is the income (payoff) distributed normally with mean, μ, and standard deviation, σ^2. It can then be derived that the agent's expected utility is $EU(C) = -e^{-A(\mu-(A/2)\sigma^2)}$. Hence, the objective of the employee is to maximize $U = \mu - (A/2)\sigma^2$, which is the same utility function used in the article.

5. A strategy of resource-based related diversification directly deals with the risk to core resource value. This makes such a risk reduction mechanism more appealing in the context of this argument than some other potential firm-level risk management mechanisms such as financial hedging and unrelated diversification. However, these alternative mechanisms may be effective in reducing overall firm-level risk exposure, but the risk to the value of the fundamental core resources is not likely to be significantly affected. See Miller (1992, 1998) for a detailed discussion of these alternative firm-level risk management tools.
6. Note that in addition to the need for employees to make human capital investments that are specific to a firm's core resource, a diversified firm may also need to induce its employees to make investments that are specific to a specific product market that the firm operates in. This usually requires different firm policies such as appropriate compensation mechanisms not specifically addressed here. However, this consideration should not directly affect the arguments made here as long as the firm requires employees to make substantial specific investments at the core resource level.
7. Note that a 'core resource' as defined here is not exactly the same as a 'strategic asset'. While a strategic asset can be a source of firm rents, a core resource itself does not generate rents. It can only be source of rents when it is combined with specific human capital investments by employees. Moreover, Markides and Williamson (1994, 1996) argue that in addition to realizing economies of scope, diversification may help improve a firm's current strategic assets and build new ones.

Appendix: Derivation of Equation (9.3)

Plugging the employee payoff constraint $w_i = ax_i r_i(V) + (n - x_i)\bar{w}_i$ into the utility function, $U = E(w_i) - \frac{A}{2}\text{var}(w_i)$, we then have

$$U = E(w_i) - \frac{A}{2}\text{var}(w_i) = ax_i E(r_i) + (n - x_i)\bar{w}_i - \frac{A}{2}[x_i^2 \text{var}(ar_i)],$$

which is to be maximized with respect to x_i. With normalized risk-aversion parameter ($A \equiv 1$), the first-order condition (with normalized A) for x_i is:

$$U'_{x_i} = aE(r_i) - \bar{w}_i - x_i \text{var}(ar_i) = 0$$

The x_i^*, the amount of specific human capital investments that maximize the employee's utility, can be obtained by solving the above equation for x_i.

$$x_i{}^* = \frac{aE(r_i) - \bar{w}_i}{\text{var}(ar_i)}.$$

10 Resource-based theory and mergers and acquisitions*

A senior manager at a major US corporation was recently overheard describing how her firm had successfully 'snatched' a strategically important acquisition from a bevy of competing firms. Her enthusiasm for this acquisition was contagious. Not only did this acquisition add economic value to her firm in the short term, she argued, it also created important long-term strategic advantages.

This manager's enthusiasm reflects the widespread belief, among managers and academics alike, that merging with or acquiring strategically related firms can increase the economic value of successful bidding firms (Salter and Weinhold 1979). A great deal of effort has gone into describing the sources of strategic relatedness that exist between a bidding and target firm (Lubatkin 1987; Singh and Montgomery 1987), and how this relatedness is translated into economic profits for the shareholders of bidding firms once an acquisition is completed (Haspeslagh and Jemison 1987).

This 'relatedness hypothesis' in mergers and acquisitions has not gone untested. Unfortunately, results are not consistent with these managerial or academic expectations. Lubatkin (1987), for example, found no significant difference in returns to bidding firm shareholders for strategically related and unrelated acquisitions. Also, Singh and Montgomery (1987), despite controlling for the type and degree of strategic relatedness between bidding and target firms, found that these acquisitions did not generate superior returns for shareholders of bidding firms. Singh and Montgomery (1987) did find that the shareholders of related target firms obtain higher profits than the shareholders of unrelated target firms. Indeed, the results of numerous studies, reviewed in Porter (1987) and Jensen and Ruback

* This chapter draws from Barney (1988).

(1983) support this same conclusion: In mergers and acquisitions, the shareholders of target firms benefit, and the shareholders of bidding firms do not lose.

These results may at least partially reflect difficult sampling, measurement, and other methodological problems associated with the event study methods used in this research (Lubatkin 1987; Singh and Montgomery 1987). However, the view developed in this chapter is that the theory of mergers and acquisitions that underlies this empirical work is also incomplete. While acquiring a strategically related firm may create economic value, in many circumstances this increased value is distributed in the form of high returns to the shareholders of acquired *target firms* rather than to the shareholders of successful bidding firms. Thus, strategic relatedness is not a sufficient condition for the shareholders of bidding firms to earn superior returns: in order for relatedness to generate such returns, a variety of specific conditions must be met.

The purpose of this chapter is to specify the conditions under which relatedness in mergers and acquisitions can be a source of superior returns for shareholders of bidding firms. Not surprisingly, these conditions turn on the attributes of the resources and capabilities that bidding firms are attempting to leverage through their acquisition strategies. The chapter begins by providing a financial definition of relatedness, and then describing the conditions under which acquiring a strategically related target will *not* generate superior returns for the shareholders of bidding firms. Next, conditions where relatedness will generate superior returns for shareholders of bidding firms, including the existence of private and unique synergistic cash flows, inimitable and unique synergistic cash flows, and unexpected synergistic cash flows, are discussed. The chapter concludes by discussing the implications of these arguments for research and practice.

A financial definition of relatedness

From a financial point of view, two firms are related when the net present value (NPV) of the cash flow of the combination of these firms is greater than the sum of the NPVs of the cash flows of these firms acting independently (Copeland and Weston 1983):

$$\text{NPV}(A + B) > \text{NPV}(A) + \text{NPV}(B) \tag{10.1}$$

where NPV (X) is the discounted NPV of the cash flows generated by firm X (Copeland and Weston 1983). When the inequality in equation (10.1) holds, a synergistic cash flow is created if firm A acquires firm B.

A variety of possible sources of relatedness and synergy in mergers and acquisitions have been cited in the literature (Williamson 1975; Benston 1980; Eckbo 1983; Jensen and Ruback 1983; Stillman 1983; Harrison et al. 1991; Goold and Campbell 1998; Hitt, Harrison, and Ireland 2001) Salter and Weinhold (1979), for example, argued that key business skills and product market positions are two potentially important sources of relatedness. From a broader perspective, Lubatkin (1983) classified nine types of relatedness between bidding and target firms into three categories: technical economies (e.g. marketing and production economies), pecuniary economies (e.g. market power), and portfolio economies (e.g. risk reduction). Jensen and Ruback (1983) identified eleven potential sources of strategic relatedness between bidding and target firms. In this chapter, relatedness between two firms can reflect any one, or any combination, of these sources, as long as equation (10.1) is satisfied.

Mergers or acquisitions between related firms will have no impact on the wealth of shareholders of bidding firms when the price paid for a target firm is exactly equal to the difference between the NPV of the cash flow of the target and bidder firms combined, and the NPV of the cash flow of the bidding firms alone. This price, P, is simply the value added to the bidding firm by acquiring a target:[1]

$$P = \text{NPV (A + B)} - \text{NPV (A)} \qquad (10.2)$$

Note that P does not depend on the value of the target firm acting as an independent business, but rather on the value that the target firm creates when it is combined with the bidding firm. If a bidding firm pays $P + k$ for a target, then that firm has acquired a firm that adds P dollars in additional value (i.e. NPV (A + B) − PV (A)) for the price $P + k$. If $k = 0$, then a bidding firm has paid the price P for an addition to its cash flow worth exactly P, and thus the wealth of bidding firm's shareholders is unaffected. If $k > 0$, then this acquisition represents a real economic loss to the shareholders of the bidding firm. If $k < 0$, then the shareholders of the bidding firm will obtain a positive economic return. Thus, specifying the conditions under which a bidding firm's shareholders will obtain superior returns from mergers and acquisitions reduces to specifying the conditions under which the price of an acquisition or merger will be less than P, that is, specifying the conditions under which $k < 0$.

Competitive parity for bidding firms from acquiring related targets

Strategic relatedness between bidding and target firms, as defined in equation (10.1), is not a sufficient condition for the shareholders of bidding firms to earn competitive advantages from mergers or acquisitions (Jensen and Ruback 1983; Lubatkin 1983). If the value of the combined cash flow of target and bidding firms is publicly known, if several potential bidding firms can all obtain this cash flow, and if semi-strong capital market efficiency holds (Fama 1970), then shareholders of bidding firms will, at best, gain only competitive parity from acquisitions. In this setting a 'strategically related' merger or acquisition may create economic value, but this value will be distributed in the form of superior returns to the shareholders of target firms. This conclusion follows directly from the equilibrium expected in perfectly competitive markets (Hirshleifer 1980), in this case the market for corporate control (Jensen and Ruback 1983).

The price of a target firm in such markets will rapidly rise to its NPV *in creating synergies with bidding firms*, that is, k will tend to 0. The price of a target will not be less than this level, for if it were, another bidder, seeing an opportunity for superior returns, would drive the price up (Barney 1986*a*).[2] Bidding firms that complete a merger or acquisition in this setting will not obtain superior returns, even if they are completely successful in exploiting anticipated relatedness with a target, for the value of that relatedness will be reflected in the price of a target (Barney 1986*a*), and thus distributed as superior returns to the shareholders of acquired target firms.[3]

Different bidding firms may have different types of relatedness with target firms, and these competitive dynamics still unfold. All that is required is that these different bidding firms value targets at the same level. However, in real markets for corporate control, it seems likely that when different bidding firms value the acquisition of targets at the same level, the type of relatedness that exists between one bidder and targets is likely to be quite similar to the type of relatedness that exists between other bidders and targets.[4] This homogeneity in relatedness leads to a homogeneity in the valuation of targets, which in turn leads to zero economic profits for bidders on acquisition.

The frequency with which markets for corporate control are perfectly competitive in this manner is ultimately an empirical question. However, in general these conditions seem at least plausible. It is not difficult to imagine a set of similar firms pursuing the same strategy in an industry all becoming interested in a particular type of acquisition to implement that strategy. In this setting, perfect competition dynamics are likely to unfold, and firms that successfully acquire a target are likely to earn zero economic profits for their shareholders. In all likelihood the manager who successfully 'snatches' a target from several competing firms will have paid a price for that target that fully anticipates any competitive advantages associated with that acquisition. Such acquisitions cannot be expected to generate superior returns for the shareholders of this successful bidding firm.

Empirically, Ruback's analysis (1982) of DuPont's takeover of Conoco suggests that this acquisition probably occurred in a perfectly competitive market. Also, Singh and Montgomery's research (1987), which showed that strategically related acquisitions created more economic value than unrelated acquisitions, but that this value was captured by the shareholders of acquired firms, suggests that these acquisitions occurred in perfectly competitive markets.

Superior returns to bidding firms from acquiring related targets

Thus the existence of bidder and target relatedness, per se, is not a source of superior returns to the shareholders of bidding firms. However, if a market for corporate control is imperfectly competitive, then bidding firms may be able to obtain a superior return for shareholders from implementing merger and acquisition strategies. Three ways that these markets can be imperfectly competitive—including (*a*) when private and uniquely valuable cash flows exist between a bidder and target, (*b*) when inimitable and uniquely valuable cash flows exist between a bidder and target, and (*c*) when unexpected synergistic cash flows exist between a bidder and target—are examined below. The first two of these cash flows reflect valuable, rare and private and valuable, rare, and costly to imitate resources controlled by bidding firms.

PRIVATE AND UNIQUELY VALUABLE SYNERGISTIC CASH FLOWS

One way such an imperfectly competitive market could exist is when a target is worth more to one bidder than it is to any other bidders—and when no other firms, including bidders and targets, are aware of this additional value. The price of a target will rise to reflect public expectations about the value of a target. Once acquired, however, the performance of this special bidder will be greater than expected, and this will generate superior returns for its shareholders.

Consider, for example, the simplest case where the combined cash flow between bidder A and target firms has an NPV of $12,000, whereas the combined cash flows of all other bidders and targets have an NPV of $10,000. Suppose also that, while no other firms are aware of A's unique status, they are aware of the value of the cash flow of all other bidders combined with targets (i.e. $10,000). If the current cash flow of all bidders has an NPV of $5,000, then firm A will obtain a superior return from acquiring a target if it pays less than $7,000 ($P = \$12{,}000 - \$5{,}000$), while all other bidders will obtain a superior return from acquiring a target if they pay less than $5,000 ($P = \$10{,}000 - \$5{,}000$). All publicly available information in this market suggests that a target is worth $5,000. Thus, the price of targets will rise to this level, ensuring that if bidding firms, besides firm A, acquire a target, they will not obtain superior returns.

If there is only one target in this market for corporate control, then firm A will be able to bid $\$5{,}000 + \varepsilon$, that is, just slightly more than any other bidder, to obtain the target. At this level, firm A obtains a superior return of ($\$7{,}000 - (\$5{,}000 + \varepsilon)$), that is, the added value of the combined cash flow minus the price of obtaining that additional cash flow. No other firm will bid higher than firm A because, from these firms' point of view, the acquisition is simply not worth more than $5,000. If there are several targets in this market for corporate control, then firm A, along with several other bidding firms, will all pay $5,000 for a target. While all other successful bidding firms will not obtain superior returns from their bidding activities, firm A will obtain a $2,000 economic profit.

For firm A to obtain this return, the existence of its uniquely valuable synergistic cash flows with targets cannot be known by other firms, both bidders and targets. If other bidding firms know about this additional value associated with acquiring a target, they are likely to try to duplicate this value for themselves. Typically, this would be accomplished by other firms duplicating the type of relatedness that exists between A and targets by acquiring the resources and capabilities that create technical economies, pecuniary economies, diversification economies, or some combination of these types of relatedness between A and targets. Once other bidders acquired the resources and capabilities necessary to obtain this more valuable combined cash flow with targets, they would be able to enter into bidding, thereby increasing the likelihood that the shareholders of successful bidding firms would earn zero economic profits.

The acquisition of these resources and capabilities would not even have to be completed before bidding began, because bidding firms can anticipate that they will be able to acquire them at some point in the future, and thus the NPV of the expected combined cash flow with a target for these bidders is the same as for A (Barney 1986*a*). In this setting the price of an acquisition will rise to the point where $k = 0$. Firm A is shielded from this perfect competition if other bidding firms are unaware of the higher synergistic cash flow available to A and the sources of this higher synergistic cash flow (Lippman and Rumelt 1982).

Target firms must also be unaware of A's uniquely valuable synergistic cash flow for A to obtain superior returns from a merger or acquisition. If target firms are aware of this cash flow and its sources, they can inform other bidding firms. These bidding firms could then adjust their bids to reflect this higher value, and the competitive dynamics discussed previously would reduce superior returns obtained by bidders to a fully competitive level. Target firms are likely to inform bidding firms in this way because increasing the number of bidders with a more valuable combined cash flow increases the likelihood that target firms will extract all the economic value created in a merger or acquisition (Jensen and Ruback 1983; Turk 1987). Although there may be many different managerial motives behind target firms seeking out 'white knights' as alternative merger partners after an acquisition attempt has been made, the effect of such actions

Table 10.1. NPV of synergistic cash flows and NPV of four idiosyncratic bidding firms ($)

	Firm A	Firm B	Firm C	Firm D
NPV of synergistic cash flows with targets	12,000	11,000	10,000	9,000
NPV of independent cash flows	3,000	5,000	3,000	2,000

is to increase the number of fully informed bidders for a target. This, in turn, reduces the superior returns that successful bidding firms obtain.

Thus far, it has been assumed that only one firm had a more valuable combined cash flow with targets (in the example, worth $12,000). However, the argument also applies to the more complex case when several firms have combined cash flows with targets greater than what is publicly known. As long as the number of targets is greater than or equal to the number of firms with these more valuable combined cash flows, each of these bidding firms can complete an acquisition, and each can earn varying amounts of superior returns (depending on the value of each of these bidding firm's combined cash flows) for their shareholders.

The impact of private and uniquely valuable synergistic cash flows on superior returns for shareholders of bidding firms even holds when different bidding firms all have different independent cash flows, and when they all have different combined cash flows with targets, that is, where each firm acting in a market for corporate control is unique. Consider the example outlined in Table 10.1. The NPV of the cash flows of firms A, B, C, and D in this table vary from $5,000 to $2,000, and the NPV of the combined cash flows with targets range from $12,000 to $9,000. From equation (10.2) it is clear that firm A must pay less than $9,000 for a target to obtain superior returns, firm B less than $6,000, firm C less than $7,000, and firm D less than $7,000.

If information is publicly available suggesting that firms with the right resources and capabilities can obtain an incremental growth in cash flow worth $7,000 from acquiring a target, then several things are likely to occur. First, firm B is likely to add to its resources and capabilities those attributes that allow firms C and D to obtain a $7,000 NPV increase from acquiring a target. Next, the price of a target is likely to rise to $7,000. If there are several target firms available, all the firms in Table 10.1 will be able to acquire a target, but only firm A will make a superior return (equal to $2,000). If only one target is available, only firm A will complete the acquisition or merger, and its abnormal return, though still positive, will be slightly smaller (\$2,000 – ε). If there are not enough targets for all bidding firms, then which firms (B, C, or D) will complete an acquisition is indeterminate, although whichever of these firms does will not obtain a superior return. In this case, as well, firm A will complete an acquisition and still earn a superior return for its shareholders equal, in total, to \$2,000 – ε.

Adding a fifth firm (firm E) that is identical to firm A in Table 10.1 highlights the requirement that the number of firms with a more valuable synergy with targets must be less than or equal to the number of targets in order for these bidding firms to obtain superior returns. If there are two or more targets, then both firms A and E can execute an acquisition for such returns. However, if there is only one target, then firms A and E are likely to engage in competitive bidding, perhaps driving the price of this target up to the point where $k = 0$ (i.e. to \$9,000) and in this process shifting superior returns from their shareholders to the shareholders of acquired firms.

INIMITABLE AND UNIQUELY VALUABLE SYNERGISTIC CASH FLOWS

The existence of a firm with private and uniquely valuable synergistic cash flows with targets is not the only way that a market for corporate control can be imperfectly competitive. If other bidders cannot duplicate the uniquely valuable combined cash flow of one bidder and targets, then competition in this market for corporate control will be imperfect, and the shareholders of this unique bidding firm will earn superior returns. In this case the existence of uniquely valuable combined cash flows does not need to be private, for other bidding firms cannot duplicate these cash flows, and thus bids that substantially reduce returns to the shareholders of this special bidding firm are not forthcoming.

Typically, other bidding firms will be unable to duplicate the uniquely valuable combined cash flow of one bidder and targets when the relatedness between this bidder and targets stems from some nonimitable resources or capabilities controlled by this bidding firm. Such resources and capabilities tend to be path dependent, causally ambiguous, socially complex, or have other attributes that increase the cost of their imitation identified in the resource-based literature (Dierickx and Cool 1989; Barney 1991*a*). Barney (1986*b*) has given several examples of inimitable resources and capabilities, including a firm's culture, its unique history, its product reputation, etc. If any of these resources and capabilities are rare and, when combined with a target, generate a more valuable cash flow than any other bidders can obtain when combined with a target, then the shareholders of these firms will obtain superior returns from acquisitions. This would occur even if all firms in this market for corporate control were aware of this more valuable synergistic cash flow and its sources. This superior return will not be obtained by the shareholders of target firms because competitive bidding dynamics cannot unfold when the sources of a more valuable synergistic cash flow are inimitable.

As before, the number of firms with this special synergistic cash flow with targets must be less than the number of targets for the shareholders of these firms to obtain superior returns. If there are more of these special bidders than there are targets, then these firms are likely to engage in competitive bidding for targets, once again shifting superior returns from bidding to target firm shareholders.

If the number of bidding firms with these special attributes is less than the number of target firms, then these bidding firms enjoy some of the advantages of a monopolist, and the level of superior return they obtain will be approximately the same as for bidding firms with private and uniquely valuable synergies. However, if the number of special bidders and number of targets are the same, the market for corporate control takes on many of the attributes of a bilateral monopoly. In this setting, the level of return obtained by shareholders of bidding firms depends on their negotiating skill (Hirshleifer 1980), and is thus indeterminant. When all bidders and targets know the value of a target for a particular bidder, this negotiated price is likely to fall somewhere between the value of targets for firms with the highest value combined cash flows and the value of targets for other bidding firms.

Of course, it may be possible for a unique and inimitable synergistic cash flow to also be private. Indeed, it is often the case that those attributes of a firm that are inimitable are also difficult to describe (Barney 1991*b*), and thus can be held as proprietary information. In this case the analysis of superior returns associated with unique and valuable synergistic cash flows presented earlier applies.

UNEXPECTED SYNERGISTIC CASH FLOWS

The analysis thus far has adopted, for convenience, the strong assumption that the NPV of synergistic cash flows between bidders and targets are known with certainty by individual bidders. This is, in principle, possible, but certainly not likely. Most acquisitions and mergers are massively complex (Jensen and Ruback 1983), involving numerous unknown and complicated relationships between firms (Ruback 1982). In these settings, unexpected events may occur after an acquisition has been completed, making the synergistic cash flow from an acquisition or merger more valuable than what was anticipated by bidders and targets. The price that bidding firms will pay to acquire a target will only equal the expected value of that target when it is combined with the bidder. The difference between the unexpected synergistic cash flow actually obtained by a bidder and the price the bidder paid for the acquisition is a superior return for the shareholders of this bidding firm.

Of course, by definition, bidding firms cannot expect to obtain unexpected synergistic cash flows. Unexpected synergistic cash flows, in this sense, are surprises, a manifestation of a firm's good luck, not its skill in acquiring targets (Barney 1986*a*).

Implications for research on mergers and acquisitions

This discussion has several important implications for research on mergers and acquisitions. First, the analysis suggests that much of the work on mergers and acquisitions has been conducted at too aggregate a level to inform managers of bidding firms when these strategies will generate superior returns for their shareholders (Halpern 1983). This is true even for research that has investigated the link between strategic relatedness in a merger or acquisition and returns to shareholders of bidding firms. Relatedness, per se, does not generate superior returns for bidding firms. Rather, synergistic cash flows stemming from relatedness will lead to superior returns for shareholders of bidding firms when those cash flows are private and unique, inimitable and unique, or unexpected. These cash flows, in turn, will be generated by rare and private resources, or rare and costly to imitate resources and capabilities controlled by bidding firms that create economic value when combined with the resources and capabilities of target firms. Future research will need to partition related mergers and acquisitions into these much finer categories in order to study how strategic relatedness is translated into superior returns for the shareholders of bidding firms.

Second, the role of unexpected synergistic cash flows in generating superior returns for bidding firm shareholders from mergers and acquisitions reemphasizes the role of luck in studying returns to the strategic actions of firms (Lippman and Rumelt 1982; Barney 1986*a*). While luck is a difficult variable to work with, especially in prescriptive models of competitive strategy, its continued emergence in analytical work suggests its importance. Simply observing that an acquisition generated superior returns for the shareholders of a bidding firm does not imply that a uniquely valuable synergistic cash flow existed between this bidder and the acquired target. Nor do such returns necessarily imply that managers in this firm are skilled in discovering or exploiting relatedness between themselves and targets. Bidding firms can simply be lucky.

Finally, the impact that managerial actions in bidding and target firms can have on the distribution of the value created in a related acquisition deserves further attention. It has already been shown in the literature that target firms can obtain superior returns for their shareholders by increasing the number of well-informed bidders (Jensen and Ruback 1983; Turk 1987). This process can be short-circuited if managers in bidding firms are able to keep the existence of a uniquely valuable synergistic cash flow with targets private. How managers in bidding firms might be able to keep this information private (McKelvey 1982), and the implications of this private information for the regulation of securities markets (Bettis 1983), deserve ongoing attention.

Implications for practice

The arguments presented here also have important implications for managers seeking to implement merger and acquisition strategies. First, while the conditions under which these strategies will generate average and superior returns have been emphasized, this analysis also suggests that mergers and acquisitions can lead to below average returns for the shareholders of successful bidding firms. This will occur when bidding firms overestimate the value of targets, and thus the price paid for a target will be greater than the economic value that a target brings to the bidding firm. Research by Salter and Weinhold (1979), and others, suggests that bidding firms typically overestimate the value of targets by *underestimating* the costs of exploiting synergies with targets. Even when markets for corporate control are imperfectly competitive, such miscalculations can generate economic losses for successful bidding firms. To avoid these miscalculations, bidding firms must become very skilled at understanding the nature of the strategic relatedness between themselves and target firms. With this understanding, bidding firms reduce the likelihood of overestimating the value of targets, and increase the likelihood of gaining at least competitive parity from mergers or acquisitions.

To move beyond competitive parity, the arguments presented here suggest that bidding firms must develop a second skill, over and above the ability to evaluate relatedness between themselves and targets. This second skill is the ability of a bidding firm to understand and value strategic relatedness between *other* bidding firms and targets. Firms cannot expect to obtain superior returns from acquiring targets when several other bidding firms all value these targets in the same way. In these kinds of markets for corporate control, perfect competition dynamics are likely to unfold, and the economic value of a target in creating competitive advantages for a bidding firm is likely to be reflected in the price that a bidding firm must pay for a target. Thus, in order to obtain expected superior returns from acquisitions, firms must complete acquisitions only in imperfectly competitive markets for corporate control.

Distinguishing between perfectly competitive and imperfectly competitive markets depends on the ability of a firm to value the relatedness of other bidders with targets, and compare that value with their own relatedness with a target. If other bidders value the target in the same way as a particular firm does, perfect competition dynamics are likely to unfold, and successful bidding firms can only expect zero economic profits. If other bidders value the target at a lower level than a particular bidder, then this peculiar bidding firm may earn superior returns from acquiring the target. To earn expected superior returns from acquisitions, it is not enough for managers to be good at spotting and valuing relatedness between their own firm and targets; they must also be good at spotting and valuing relatedness between other firms and targets.

NOTES

1. To simplify the discussion, it is assumed throughout the chapter that cash flows are net of any transactions costs. Equation (10.2) also generalizes to the case where bidder and target firms are not related. In this case, P is simply the NPV of the target, a conclusion consistent with theory in finance (Copeland and Weston 1983).
2. Semistrong capital market efficiency implies that potential bidding firms will have sufficient capital to engage in bidding, for as long as $k < 0$, an acquisition investment will have a positive net present value (Fama 1970).
3. The lack of actual multiple bids for a target does not imply that perfect competition does not exist. A bidding firm, in anticipation of other potential bidders, may make an initial bid where k is equal to 0, or even larger than 0. In this case the threat of anticipated competition for a target leads to zero economic profits for the shareholders of bidding firms completing an acquisition (Barney 1986*a*).
4. This assumption has recently been relaxed in a working paper being developed by Rich Makadok and Russ Coff at Emory University. The results are generally consistent with the arguments developed here.

Part IV

RBT: The Research Frontier

11 Resource-based theory: empirical research*

In 1916, Albert Einstein predicted the existence of gravity waves. Given how small these waves were supposed to be—10^{-18} of a millimeter—Einstein was convinced that this implication of his general theory of relativity would never be examined directly. Initially, the existence of these waves was only examined indirectly, by observing that pulsars were losing mass at a rate consistent with the existence of gravity waves. However, more recently, a new generation of wave detection technology has been introduced. Drawing on the computing power of thousands of personal computers linked in a voluntary network, physicists now believe that it may be possible to directly observe gravity waves, though it may take many years to refine the technology and complete the data analysis (Lafferty 2005).

Godfrey and Hill (1995) observed that resource-based theory—along with TCE and agency theory—incorporated difficult to observe concepts as independent variables. These authors wondered if it would ever be possible to directly test resource-based theory. Initially, they reasoned, resource-based empirical work would have to focus on examining the observable implications of a firm's resources and capabilities, rather than examining those resources directly. However, more recently, several scholars have begun to develop techniques for measuring at least some aspects of these previously difficult to observe concepts. Although it may take many years to refine this measurement technology and complete the data analysis, there is now a growing belief that it may be possible to measure resources and capabilities and therefore to directly test the implications of resource-based theory (Dutta, Narasimhan, and Rajiv 2005).

* This chapter draws from Barney and Arikan (2001) and Barney and Mackey (2005).

In reviewing these stories, in no way is it being suggested that resource-based theory has the same theoretical status as Einstein's theory of general relativity. Rather, these stories are reviewed only to point out that the evolution of science—whether it is experimental physics or empirical social science—often involves the development of new approaches to measurement and testing that make what were once impossible to test theories testable. Indeed, in the ever-growing literature that now constitutes the 'resource-based view', a great deal has been learned over the last several years about how to test this theory (Barney and Arikan 2001). The purpose of this chapter is to highlight some of these lessons.

Testing resource-based theory

Resource-based theory makes a few central assumptions about the nature of resources and capabilities, their impact on a firm's performance, and the sustainability of these performance differences. These assumptions help define the kinds of empirical work that is required to test resource-based theory.

THE QUESTION OF VALUE

It is now widely understood that resources—the tangible and intangible assets controlled by a firm that enable it to create and implement strategies (Barney 2002)—only have the potential to generate economic value if they are used to do something (Porter 1991). Of course, the thing that resources—and their close conceptual cousin, capabilities (Amit and Schoemaker 1993)—are supposed to do is to enable firms to create and implement strategies.

This simple insight actually suggests a way that researchers can measure the potential of a firm's resources to create value: To measure this potential, measure the value created by the strategies a firm creates and implements using its resources. Put differently, since resources have no value in and of themselves and only create value when they are used to implement strategies, researchers should examine the value these strategies create to infer the potential value of a firm's resources.

Of course, there is substantial literature that describes the ability of different strategies to create economic value. A wide variety of such strategies have been described, including cost leadership, product differentiation, vertical integration, flexibility, tacit collusion, strategic alliances, corporate diversification, mergers and acquisitions, and international strategies, to name just a few (Barney 2002). Much of this work identifies the conditions under which these strategies will and will not create economic value.

For example, a cost leadership strategy creates value if and only if it enables a firm to reduce its costs below those of competing firms (Porter 1980). A product differentiation strategy creates value if and only if it enables a firm to charge higher prices for its products than a firm that is not differentiating its products (Porter 1980). A corporate diversification strategy creates value if and only if it exploits an economy of scope that cannot be realized through market contracting (Teece 1980).

There has been less work that links specific firm resources and capabilities with the ability to create and implement these kinds of firm strategies. This is largely because currently available typologies of firm resources are very broad in scope, for example, Barney's distinction (2002) between financial, physical, human, and organizational resources. Further work developing this type of typology is likely to facilitate the examination of the link between resources, in general, and the ability to conceive of and implement specific strategies.

However, that there has been limited work that links specific resources to particular strategies does not mean that there has been no work in this area. Indeed, several papers have examined the linkages between particular resources and capabilities and specific strategies. Most of this work is carried out on a limited sample of firms within a single industry. This helps establish the link between the resources and strategies in question. But, taken as a whole, this work suggests an approach to linking resources to strategy and thereby examining the potential of resources to create economic value by enabling firms to create and implement strategies. Consider a couple of examples of this research.

In 1994, Henderson and Cockburn were interested in understanding why some pharmaceutical firms were more effective in developing new patentable drugs than other pharmaceutical firms. It is well known that patents are a source of economic value in the pharmaceutical industry

(Mansfield, Schwartz, and Wagner 1981)—contingent on the demand for particular drugs, firms with large numbers of patented drugs will usually have higher revenues than firms with smaller numbers of patented drugs. The specific resource that Henderson and Cockburn were able to identify that enabled some firms to have more patents than other firms was something they called 'architectural competence'—the ability to facilitate cooperation among the different scientific disciplines required to develop and test a new pharmaceutical drug. Firms with high levels of this competence were able to patent more drugs than firms with low levels of this competence. Henderson and Cockburn's research showed that architectural competence had the potential to generate economic value when it was used to develop new patentable drugs.

More recently, Ray, Barney, and Muhanna (2004) examined the relationship between the ability of two functional areas—the IT function and the customer service function—and the level of customer service in a sample of North American insurance companies. Again, it is widely recognized that customer service is an information intensive function in most modern insurance companies, and that the careful use of IT can enhance the ability of customer service professionals to meet their customers' needs. Customer satisfaction, in turn, is related to a variety of economically important variables, including customer retention. What Ray, Barney, and Muhanna (2004) were able to do is to develop a measure of the level of cooperation between the IT and customer service functions in a sample of insurance firms and demonstrate that this relationship—a socially complex resource—has the potential to create economic value when it is used to develop customer service-specific IT applications.

Besides demonstrating that it is possible to examine the potential of a resource to create economic value by examining the value consequences of the strategies a firm creates and implements by using these resources, these—and related—papers have several other things in common. First, they are examples of what might be called 'quantitative case studies'. That is, they examined the relationship between a firm's resources and the value of its strategies in a narrow sample of firms, typically a sample of firms drawn from a single industry. This enabled these authors to clearly identify industry-specific resources and capabilities and to build industry-specific measures of these resources. Then, using traditional quantitative techniques, they examined the relationship between these measures of firm resources and attributes of a firm correlated with a firm's economic performance.

Of course, it is difficult to generalize this research beyond the specific industry contexts within which it is done. That architectural competence is related to the number of patents in pharmaceutical firms may or may not say anything about the relationship between architectural competence and innovation in other firms in other industries. That the level of cooperation between IT and customer service has an impact on the level of customer service in North American insurance companies may or may not say anything about the relationship between this type of cooperation and customer service in other firms in other industries.

Although these papers have limited generality at the level of the specific resources and strategies studied, their results are quite general from a broader perspective. Each of these papers—and the several others that apply a similar empirical logic (e.g. Combs and Ketchen 1999)—show that at least some firm resources have the potential to generate economic value if they are used to create and implement certain strategies. Over time, as more of these quantitative case studies are done, our ability to specify the conditions under which resources can be used to create and implement strategies that create economic value will be enhanced.

Second, many of these studies examine the value potential of a firm's resources at a level of analysis below that of the firm. Not surprisingly, the most correct level of analysis at which to examine the relationship between a firm's resources and its strategies is at the level of the resource, not the level of the firm. However, the firm is usually the unit of accrual. We are likely to learn a great deal more about the relationship between resources and strategies if scholars are able to 'get inside' the firm, where resources reside, rather than simply correlate aggregate measures of resources with aggregate measures of the value of a firm's strategies.

Finally, the central independent variables in both of these papers—architectural competence in Henderson and Cockburn (1994) and IT–customer service cooperation in Ray, Barney, and Muhanna (2004)—focus on a particular type of organizational resource. This type of resource has been described as socially complex (Barney 1991*b*), and it has been linked to the sustainability of a firm's competitive advantage. Empirically examining these sustainability issues is examined in the next section of this chapter.

SUSTAINING COMPETITIVE ADVANTAGES

It is now widely understood that resources only have the potential to create economic value, and that that potential is only realized when a firm uses its resources to create and implement strategies. It is perhaps not as widely recognized that the ability of other firms to imitate a particular firm's strategies does not depend on the attributes of those strategies, per se, but rather on the attributes of the resources and capabilities that enabled that firm to create and implement its strategies in the first place. Put differently, just as resources only have the potential to create value through their impact on a firm's strategies, so too strategies only have the potential to be costly to imitate because of the nature of the resources that enabled a firm to choose and implement its strategies.

By their nature, strategies are relatively public. That is, when a firm implements its strategies, it is usually not very long before other firms are able to articulate what those strategies are. This is especially the case when a firm's strategies are logical and coherent.[1] What are not always so public are the resources and capabilities that enable a firm to create and implement its strategies.

Resource-based theory suggests that valuable strategies that are created and implemented using resources that are widely held or easy to imitate cannot be a source of sustained competitive advantage (Barney 1991*b*). In this context, a firm has a sustained competitive advantage when it is one of only a few competing firms that is implementing a particular value-creating strategy and when this competitive situation lasts over extended periods.

Resource-based theory also makes specific predictions about the characteristics of resources and capabilities that make some more difficult to imitate than others.[2] For example, Lippman and Rumelt (1982) suggest that causally ambiguous resources are more likely to be costly to imitate than resources that are not causally ambiguous. Barney (1986*b*) suggests that resources and capabilities a firm already controls are more likely to be costly to imitate than resources it acquires from competitive factor markets. Barney (1986*b*) suggests that socially complex resources and capabilities—the particular resource he examined in this paper was a firm's culture—are more likely to be costly to imitate than resources that are not socially complex. Dierickx and Cool (1989) suggest that resources characterized by time compression diseconomies, asset stock interconnectedness, and asset mass efficiencies are more likely to be costly to imitate than resources without these attributes. Finally, in a summary, Barney (1991*a*) suggests that path dependent, causally ambiguous, and socially complex resources are more likely to be costly to imitate than resources without these attributes.

Of course, each of these assertions implies testable hypotheses about the imitability of different types of resources. A study that examined, say, path dependent resources that enabled a few competing firms to create and implement value-creating strategies, but where numerous firms were able to imitate these strategies once they were initially implemented would be very inconsistent with resource-based theory. So too would a study that examined resources that did not possess any of these special attributes but nevertheless enabled a few competing firms to create and implement value-creating strategies, but where numerous firms were unable to imitate these strategies once they were initially implemented. In the first study, path dependence would not be a source of sustained competitive advantage; in the latter case, the lack of path dependence (or social complexity, or causal ambiguity, or some other attribute of resources supposed to prevent their easy imitation) would be a source of sustained competitive advantage. Both results contradict resource-based theory.

Of course, the empirical requirements to test these hypotheses are nontrivial, but several studies have come close to approximating these requirements. For example, by studying the resource-based determinants of patents, Henderson and Cockburn (1994) come close to examining the sustainability of any competitive advantages that architectural competence might create because patents, as a function of patent law, last a defined and relatively long period—twenty years.[3]

One particularly elegant study that examined the imitability of path-dependent firm resources was published by Barnett, Greve, and Park (1994). In this paper, Barnett, Greve, and Park examined why some commercial banks competing in the state of Illinois during a recession were able to outcompete other banks competing in the same market at the same time. Clearly, banks that were not performing well in this setting had a very strong incentive to imitate the strategies of banks that were performing well. However, Barnett, Greve, and Park hypothesized that one reason the strategies of the banks that were doing well were not subject to quick imitation was that these banks possessed resources and capabilities that enabled them to choose these valuable strategies, and that these underlying resources and capabilities were costly to imitate due to their path dependent nature.

This study did not directly measure the resources that enabled some banks to outperform other banks. However, it did demonstrate that banks that had survived a financial recession previously, systematically outperformed banks that had not survived a financial recession previously. Barnett, Greve, and Park interpreted this finding to suggest that there was something about the historical experience of banks that had survived a previous recession that equipped them with the resources and capabilities—they use the largely interchangeable term 'routines' (Nelson and Winter 1982)—necessary to survive, and even prosper, in a later recession. Of course, this paper would have been even stronger if it could have directly measured these resources and the extent to which they were path dependent in nature. Nevertheless, it is consistent with the general hypothesis that path-dependent resources and capabilities are costly to imitate and thus a source of sustained competitive advantage.

Makadok's study (1999) of economies of scale in the money-market mutual fund industry also supports resource-based assertions. In this case, however, resource-based theory would suggest that since the realization of these economies of scale did not depend on resources or capabilities that are costly to imitate, that strategies that exploit these economies of scale would not be a source of sustained competitive advantage for these firms. If Makadok (1999) had found that economies of scale in this industry had been a source of sustained competitive advantage, this would have been inconsistent with resource-based theory.

Interestingly, these two studies, like the first two studies reviewed in this chapter, are quantitative case studies. That is, they studied a sample of firms drawn from a particular industry, and in the case of Barnett, Greve, and Park (1994), from a particular geographic market. This enabled these scholars to examine the link between specific resources, strategies, and competitive advantage over time.

Unfortunately, neither of these studies measured the attributes of a firm's resources and capabilities directly. This is, perhaps, due to the difficulty of gaining access to this intraorganizational resource-level information over an extended period. Obviously, duplicating Ray, Barney, and

Muhanna's survey methodology (2004) over several years would be very challenging and would delay the publication of any subsequent paper until after all the data had been collected. A recent paper by Leiblein and Miller (2003) on transactions cost and resource-based implications for vertical integration decisions comes closer to meeting this ideal standard than much of the previous work on sustainability of competitive advantages.

Another attribute shared by these two studies is that they were conducted on data over time. Although it is possible to define sustained competitive advantage with respect to the observed inability of firms to imitate a particular firm's resources (Barney 1991*a*), this equilibrium definition of sustained competitive advantage will often be highly correlated with competitive advantages that last a long time. This suggests that time series analyses of various kinds will generally be required to investigate the imitability of different types of firm resources, and thus the sustainability of a firm's competitive advantage. The challenges associated with collecting resource-level information within a firm over time have already been discussed.

THE QUESTION OF ORGANIZATION

Thus, while much work is left to be done, some research has examined what most consider to be the two central assertions of resource-based theory: (*a*) that some resources have the potential to enable firms to create and implement valuable strategies, and (*b*) that such resources can be a source of sustained competitive advantage when they possess attributes that make their imitation costly. However, some versions of resource-based theory also suggest that firms must be organized to take advantage of their resources and strategies if their full economic potential is to be realized (Barney 2002). This emphasis on strategy implementation has received less attention in the resource-based empirical literature.

There are several possible reasons for this relative inattention. First, most strategy scholars are interested in understanding sources of sustained competitive advantage. If a firm's ability to implement strategies is valuable (in the sense described earlier), rare, and costly to imitate, then a firm's strategy implementation capability is a potential source of sustained competitive advantage. In this case, the study of strategy implementation—as a source of sustained competitive advantage—is indistinguishable from other studies of the sources of sustained competitive advantage.

Indeed, some of the studies reviewed thus far could easily be reinterpreted as if they were examining the competitive consequences of a firm's ability to implement its strategies. Thus, Henderson and Cockburn's study (1994) could be reinterpreted as a strategy implementation study by suggesting that architectural competence is the ability that some firms have to implement their patenting strategies more effectively than other firms. In this sense, because the ability to implement a strategy can be thought of simply as another type of resource or capability, strategy implementation can be thought of as just another possible source of sustained competitive advantage.

This is one reason why research on the ability of firms to develop new capabilities—so-called 'dynamic capabilities' (Teece, Pisano, and Shuen 1997)—has captured the interest of so many strategy scholars. Such dynamic capabilities can also be reinterpreted in strategy implementation terms: A dynamic capability is the ability that some firms have to create new capabilities, capabilities whose potential value can only be realized when a firm implements new strategies that build on these new capabilities.

However, another perspective on the question of organization is that organization includes all those dimensions of implementing a firm's strategies that are, in principle, imitable, but are nevertheless important if a firm is to gain competitive advantages. Barney (2002) calls these dimensions of strategy implementation 'complementary resources', because these implementation skills—things like an organization's structure, its management controls, and its compensation policies—are not sources of competitive advantage by themselves, but are nevertheless important if a firm realizes the full competitive potential of its resources and strategies.

Examples of resource-based empirical research

These principles about testing resource-based research have been applied in a wide variety of disciplines, not just strategic management. The remainder of this chapter describes some of these tests.

RESOURCE-BASED RESEARCH IN STRATEGIC MANAGEMENT

Not surprisingly, to date, strategic management scholars have conducted the most empirical tests of resource-based logic. These tests examine several important assertions derived from the theory, including: (*a*) that firm effects should be more important than industry effects in determining firm performance, (*b*) that valuable, rare, and costly to imitate resources should have a more positive impact on firm performance than other kinds of resources, (*c*) that corporate strategies (including mergers, acquisitions, and diversification) that exploit valuable, rare, and costly to imitate resources should generate greater returns than corporate strategies that exploit other kinds of resources, (*d*) that international strategies that exploit valuable, rare, and costly to imitate resources will outperform international strategies that exploit other kinds of resources, (*e*) that strategic alliances that exploit valuable, rare, and costly to imitate resources will outperform other kinds of alliances, and (*f*) that there cannot be a 'rule for riches' derived from strategic management theory.

Industry versus firm effects on firm performance

Resource-based theory suggests that firm effects should have a larger impact on firm performance than industry effects. The following research examines the relative impact of industry attributes and firm attributes on performance.

Initial work done by Schmalensee (1985) and Wernerfelt and Montgomery (1988) on industry versus firm effects in explaining variance in firm performance was inconsistent with resource-based expectations. In particular, this work suggested that industry effects were more important than firm effects. However, in 1991, Rumelt published an article that contradicted these earlier findings. Rumelt (1991) argued that previous work had applied the wrong methods or had used inadequate data to evaluate the relative impact of industry and firm effects on firm performance. After solving these problems, Rumelt's results were consistent with resource-based expectations. Several authors have replicated Rumelt's results (e.g. Brush and Bromiley 1997; McGahan and Porter 1997; Mauri and Michaels 1998). Some of these are critical of Rumelt's findings, but primarily in terms of the small corporate effect that Rumelt (1991) identified (Brush and Bromiley 1997). However, all these replications continue to document that firm effects are a more important determinant of firm performance than industry effects, although the relative size of these effects can vary by industry.

Hansen and Wernerfelt (1989) found that firm factors explained about twice as much variance in profit rates as economic factors. While Collis and Montgomery (1995) reported that where a company chooses to play will determine its profitability as much as its resources. According to Karagozoglu and Lindell (1998), motives behind internationalization of small and medium-sized technology based firms can be explained more with firm-specific characteristics rather than uniform patterns.

Other specific research on firm versus industry effects includes the influence of environmental conditions at founding on mortality rates (Swaminathan 1996), the impact of operating and competitive industry experience (Ingram and Baum 1997), and societal impacts on the acquisition and creation of competencies (Marcus and Geffen 1998). Nickerson and Silverman (1998) studied the buffering effect of high profitability in the for hire trucking industry. Makadok (1998) examined sustainability of first-mover and early-mover advantages in an industry with low barriers to entry and imitation. In addition, proactive environmental strategy and the development of competitively valuable organizational capabilities were considered by Sharma and Vredenburg (1998), and the strategic importance of focusing on being different was studied by Deephouse (1999).

Resources and firm performance

Resource-based theory suggests that valuable, rare, and costly to imitate resources can be sources of competitive advantage. This research examines a variety of different resources that have these attributes to varying degrees and examines their impact on performance.

The bulk of empirical resource-based work in the field of strategic management has focused on identifying resources that have the attributes that resource-based theory predicts will be important for firm performance and then examining whether the predicted performance effects exist. The performance effects of a wide variety of different types of firm resources have been examined, including a firm's history (e.g. Collis 1991; Barnett, Greve, and Park 1994; Rao 1994), employee know-how (e.g. Hall 1992, 1993; Glunk and Wilderom 1998), its integrative capability (e.g. Henderson and

Cockburn 1994), its innovativeness (e.g. Bates and Flynn 1995; McGrath et al. 1996), its culture (e.g. Moingeon et al. 1998), and its network position (e.g. Baum and Berta 1999; McEvily and Zaheer 1999), to name just a few. A wide variety of different methods have been used to examine the performance effects of firm resources including large sample surveys, small sample surveys, case studies, and simulations. Overall, results are consistent with resource-based expectations.

There are, however, a few studies that generate results that are inconsistent with resource-based expectations. For example, Poppo and Zenger's analysis (1995) of vertical integration is more consistent with TCE than resource-based theory. Also, Sherer, Rogovsky, and Wright (1998) do suggest that compensation policy can have an effect on cooperation among a firm's employees, but that environmental conditions are a more important determinant of this cooperation. These and similar results suggest that the conditions under which different resources are and are not valuable requires further development in resource-based theory (Priem and Butler 2001).

Further specific research on the impact of resources and capabilities on firm performance includes the importance of the firm-specific knowledge environment on process development (Pisano 1994), comprehension and deftness within competence developing processes (McGrath, MacMillan, and Venkataraman 1995), codifying and communicating manufacturing capabilities (Zander and Kogut 1995), and contingent combinations of firm-specific resources (Brush and Artz 1999). Miller and Shamsie (1996), in their award-winning *Strategic Management Journal* paper, examined the impacts of property-based and knowledge-based resources on performance in the US film industry. Other knowledge-based research includes studies of stocks and flows of organizational knowledge (De Carolis and Deeds 1999), the negative impacts of nonlocal learning (Greve 1999), integration of knowledge in product development (Hoopes and Postrel 1999), the transfer of intellectual property from universities to business (Stevens and Bagby 1999), and team-based tacit knowledge in the National Basketball Association (Berman, Down, and Hill 2002).

The role of firm resources and organizational attributes in determining entry timing was examined by Schoenecker and Cooper (1998). Ruiz-Navarro (1998) focused on identification and acquisition of complementary capabilities for a turnaround, and Maskell (1998) considered agglomeration of resources in low-tech manufacturing firms. Other researchers evaluated the performance impacts of TQM programs (Reed, Lemark, and Montgomery 1996), appropriating and sustaining rents from human capital (Maijoor and Wittrloostuijin 1996), top management and organizational capital (Glunk and Wilderom 1998), organizational impediments to innovation (Dougherty and Hardy 1996), and modes of interorganizational imitation (Haunschild and Miner 1997). The integration of environmental management concerns in strategic planning processes was studied by Judge and Douglas (1998). Further resources and capabilities that have been investigated include relational capabilities (Lorenzoni and Lipparini 1999), corporate governance (McGuire 2000), localized learning (Maskell and Malmberg 1999), age dependence (Henderson 1999), isolating mechanisms (Oktemgil, Greenley, and Broderick 2000), location of airlines in their rival's hub markets (Gimeno 1999), technological competence and imitability (De Carolis 2003), and managerial foresight associated with patenting breakthrough innovations (Ahuja, Coff, and Lee 2005). While Yeoh and Roth (1999) investigated potential sources of sustained competitive advantage in the pharmaceutical industry, Pettus (2001) identified resource development paths in the deregulated trucking industry. Douglas and Ryman (2003) found that service-related strategic competencies were positively related to financial performance in the hospital industry. Hansen, Perry, and Reese (2004) used a Bayesian hierarchical methodology to examine the relationship between administrative decisions and economic performance over time.

Resources and corporate strategies

Resource-based logic suggests that both tangible and intangible resources can be important in corporate strategies, but only valuable, rare, costly to imitate, and nonsubstitutable resources can be a source of sustained competitive advantage for firms implementing merger, acquisition, and diversification corporate strategies (as discussed in Chapters 9 and 10).

The impact of resources on corporate strategies and competitive advantage has also been examined empirically. One of the most important findings in this area is that SIC-code based measures of strategic relatedness must be augmented by resource-based measures to capture the full performance effects of diversification strategies (e.g. Robins and Wiersema 1995; Farjoun 1998). Moreover, only when the basis of a diversification strategy is valuable, rare, and costly to imitate can firms expect such a strategy to generate superior firm performance (Markides and Williamson 1996). Moreover, while finance scholars have identified an important discount in the value of firms when they begin to diversify (Lang and Stulz 1994), resource-based theorists have shown that this discount either does not exist or is consistent with shareholder's interests when the characteristics of the resources on which a firm's diversification strategies are based are accounted for (Miller 2000, 2004). Similar results have been found in studies on the return to mergers and acquisitions (e.g. Coff 1999).

Further specific research on the impact of resources on corporate diversification strategies includes differences in resource allocations between target and acquiring firms (Harrison et al. 1991), consistency in resource allocations (Harrison, Hall, and Nargundkar 1993), firm-specific factors in multinational performance (Tallman 1991), firm-specific and product-specific characteristics of service firms (Ingham and Thompson 1995), and creating firm-specific advantage in a multinational subsidiary (Birkinshaw, Hood, and Jonsson 1998). Resource deployment was examined in acquisitions in declining industries (Anand and Singh 1997), following horizontal acquisitions (Capron, Dussauge, and Mitchell 1998), in relation to asset divestiture (Capron 1999), and market entry mode (Chatterjee and Singh 1999). In addition, Silverman studied technological resources and diversification decisions (Silverman 1999), and Gupta and Govindarajan (2000) examined subsidiary knowledge stocks and transmission channels. Miller (2004) found that the diversification discount observed *ex post* can be explained in part by firms having lower levels of technological resources *ex ante*. Carow, Heron, and Saxton (2004) examined early-mover advantages in acquisitions and found that strategic pioneers experience positive acquisition announcement returns and outperform other acquirers in acquisition waves in terms of long-term stock price as well. Shamsie, Phelps, and Kuperman (2004) looked at performance differences among late entrants in fifteen different new product categories of household electrical equipment. They found that the ability of a late mover to penetrate the market is strongly linked to its own resources (size and relevance) and its own strategy.

International strategies

Resource-based work on international strategies is a logical extension of the work on diversification strategies cited earlier. However, some attributes of resource-based arguments are highlighted in an international context. For example, this work shows that a firm's resources reflect its country of origin and that these country differences are long lasting (e.g. Karnoe 1995; Jarvenpaa and Leidner 1999). This work also examines the role of different forms of governance in realizing cross-border economies of scope and suggests that the tacitness of the resources used to realize these economies is an important determinant of governance choices (e.g. Zou and Ozsomer 1999).

Further specific research on the role of resources in an international context includes transferring idiosyncratic technologies (Kogut and Zander 1992), international diversification (Hitt, Hoskisson, and Kim 1997; Geringer, Tallman, and Olsen 2000), top management team international business advice network density (Athanassiou and Nigh 1999), the intensity and diversity of host country experience (Luo and Peng 1999), and expatriate staffing of subsidiaries (Gong 2003). Research on Japanese firms examined product-specific competencies and market size (Arora and Gambardella 1997), knowledge diffusion (Appleyard 1996), proprietary assets (Delios and Beamish 1999), and firm strategies and the environment (Kotha and Nair 1995). In addition, Mutinelli and Piscitello (1998) studied skills and entry mode of Italian multinationals, Baldauf, Cravens, and Wagner (2000) examined export performance in Austria, and Nachum and Rolle (1999) considered firm-specific characteristics of advertising agencies in the UK, France, and the United States. The impact of the international experience of CEOs on the degree of internationalization and on financial performance was also investigated by Daily, Certo, and Dalton (2000). Financial implications of specificity and opacity of strategic resources were studied using Spanish manufacturing firms (Vicente-Lorente 2001), and RBV-driven variables were found to explain share values for Czech firms in the privatization period when the capitalistic economy was emerging (Makhija 2003).

Resources and strategic alliances

Closely related to resource-based international research is work that focuses on the impact of resources of strategic alliances. In particular, this work focuses on how firms can use alliances to either exploit their preexisting resources or develop new resources. This latter work integrates insights from research on learning and absorptive capacity with resource-based logic (e.g. Lane and Lubatkin 1998; Shenkar and Li 1999; Dussauge, Garrette, and Mitchell 2000).

Further specific research on the role of resources in determining the performance of strategic alliances includes functional expertise of management teams in high-tech ventures (McGee, Dowling, and Megginson 1995), R&D skill sharing (Sakakibara 1997), firm-specific technological capabilities (Mowery, Oxley, and Silverman 1998), technical education and experience of executives (Tyler and Steensma 1998), and intellectual property rights (McGaughey, Liesch, and Poulson 2000). Combs and Ketchen (1999) contrasted resource-based and organizational economics factors on interfirm cooperation, while Gulati (1999) examined the impact of prior alliances on decisions to enter new alliances. In addition, research on international strategic alliances focused on multinational alliances in China (Luo 1999), and international strategic partner selection (Hitt et al. 2000). Park, Mezias, and Song (2004) found that alliances of e-commerce firms have a positive effect on firm value in an emerging business sector.

Rules for riches

Finally, resource-based logic suggests that it is not possible to deduce rules for riches from strategic management theories, as persistent superior performance depends on valuable, rare, and costly to imitate resources. Rules for riches are rules that any firm can apply to gain sustained competitive advantages and economic rents. In this empirical work, the impossibility of deriving rules from riches from strategic management theory is examined in the context of the difficulty of sustaining competitive advantages through the application of well-known, widely understood, managerial practices. These include the use of reengineering (Walston, Burns, and Kimberly 2000), learning curve logic (Lieberman 1982, 1987), the structure of training programs (Segev, Raveh, and Farjoun 1999), formal long-range planning (Brews and Hunt 1999), and patenting procedures (Mansfield, Schwartz, and Wagner 1981; Mansfield 1985; Schankerman 1998). Difficulties of focusing on a few competencies were investigated by Tripsas (1997) and Miller and Toulouse (1998). In addition, Makadok (1999) found that money-market mutual fund families with larger marginal returns to increasing their scale subsequently do gain market share at the expense of their competitors, but this effect diminishes over time, possibly due to imitation.

RESOURCE-BASED RESEARCH IN OTHER MANAGEMENT DISCIPLINES

While the bulk of empirical research on resource-based theory focuses on strategic management implications of the theory, this theory has had implications in related fields as well. Among the most important of these is HRM (as discussed in Chapter 6). Several other disciplines have begun to explore the empirical implications of resource-based logic. These include marketing, entrepreneurship, management information systems (MIS), operations management, and technology and innovation management. While research approaches vary by discipline, in all these different settings, research examines how various kinds of functional resources affect firm performance in ways that are consistent with resource-based logic.

Human resource management

Resource-based logic suggests that socially complex resources and capabilities should be among the most important sources of sustained competitive advantages for firms. Human resources are examples of socially complex resources and thus it is not surprising that HR theorists have drawn heavily on resource-based logic to examine the impact of human resources and HR policies on firm performance (Wright and MacMahan 1992; Wright, MacMahan, and McWilliams 1994; Barney and Wright 1998).

Some of the earliest work in this area focused on the impact of human resources on cost and quality in manufacturing (Womack, Jones, and Roos 1990; MacDuffie 1995). More recently, this work has focused on various bundles of HR practices that can have the effect of creating significant firm-specific human capital investments (e.g. Huselid and Becker 1997; Harel and Tzafrir 1999) and improving firm performance (Delaney and Huselid 1996). While some of this work has been criticized (Becker and Gerhart 1996), there is little doubt that resource-based logic has had an important impact on human resources research.

Further specific research on human resources includes aligning HRM practices to formulated strategy (Schuler and MacMillan 1984), aligning human capital enhancing HR systems and manufacturing strategies (Youndt et al. 1996), and integrating the HR function with strategic decision-making (Bennet, Ketchen, and Schultz 1998). Interestingly, Gupta and Govindarajan (1984) found no consistent managerial characteristics that would guarantee effective strategy implementation in multinationals. Yet Richard (2000) found that cultural diversity adds value and contributes to competitive advantage in the right context.

Huselid (1995) observed that investment in high performance work practices reflected in lower employee turnover and greater productivity and financial performance. Other studies examined HR management effectiveness (Huselid, Jackson, and Schuler 1997), HR involvement in strategy and perception of HR effectiveness (Wright et al. 1998), and the links between strong employee commitment and generic strategies (Lee and Miller 1999). Koch and McGrath (1996) examined labor productivity in capital intensive firms, while Delery and Doty (1996) considered universal, contingency, and configurational HR performance expectations. Both hard and soft versions of HRM based on theories X and Y were investigated by Truss et al. (1997).

Welbourne and Andrews (1996) examined the impact of HR value and organization-based rewards on IPO performance; Klaas, McClendon, and Gainey (1999) considered idiosyncratic HR practices moderating the degree of outsourcing and perceived benefits; and Gainey and Klaas (2003) looked at the impact of outsourcing of training and development on client satisfaction. In addition, the effects of human capital and social capital on firm dissolution were studied by Pennings, Lee, and van Witteloostuijn (1998). The effects of human capital on the performance of large US law firms were demonstrated by Hitt et al. (2001). Hatch and Dyer (2004) examined human capital as a source of sustainable competitive advantage in semiconductor manufacturing firms. Kor and Leblebici (2005) tested the impacts of interdependencies between human capital deployment, development, and diversification strategies on performance in professional service firms. Employers' participation in school-to-work programs was shown to enable the development of firm-specific human capital capabilities by Linnehan and De Carolis (2005).

Internationally focused research includes HR practices, HR outcomes, and firm performance in Russia (Fey, Bjorkman, and Pavlovskaya 2000), HR practices influencing high mobility of managers in Hong Kong (Field,

Chan, and Akhtar 2000), and strategy–HRM interaction impacts on performance in Singapore firms (Khatri 2000).

Marketing

The role of marketing resources as sources of competitive advantage and their impacts on firm performance has been investigated by many researchers. Specific marketing resources studied include marketing resources and capabilities from foreign direct investments (Hooley et al. 1996), market based and marketing support resources (Hooley et al. 2003), technical knowledge assets enabling bundled products (Ghingold and Johnson 1997), marketing mix reactions to a new entrant (Gatignon, Robertson, and Fein 1997), market knowledge competence (Li and Calantone 1998), industrial distribution channels (Johnson 1999), marketing strategy-making process (Menon et al. 1999), corporate citizenship in internal and external marketing (Maignan, Ferrell, and Hult 1999), redeployment of marketing assets after acquisitions (Capron and Hulland 1999), media reputation (Deephouse 2000), and market orientation (Hult and Ketchen 2001). In addition, Hult, Ketchen, and Slater (2004) examined market orientation using both cultural and information processing elements and found that both approaches contribute to explaining performance, but their effects are mediated by organizational responsiveness. In a study of market dominance, Shamsie (2003) found that advantages from reputation are tied to specific industry characteristics, for example industries with consumer products that are purchased frequently and have lower prices.

Entrepreneurship

Resource-based logic has also been applied empirically in the field of entrepreneurship. Chrisman (1999) examined the resources and capabilities influencing start-ups and regional differences in start-up propensities, while Dean, Turner, and Bamford (1997) considered the factors assisting the postentry phase for new firms. Other studies of small and entrepreneurial firms have focused on basic capabilities (Rangone 1999), as well as firm-specific resources (Borch, Huse, and Senneseth 1999). The impact of resources on performance of small service and retail firms was examined by Brush and Chaganti (1999), and Michael and Robbins (1998) focused on retrenchment among small manufacturing firms during recession. In addition, dynamic capabilities and new product development in high technology ventures were studied by Deeds, De Carolis, and Coombs (2000) in their empirical analysis of biotechnology firms. Consistent with resource-based theory, Choi and Shepherd (2004) found that entrepreneurs were more likely to exploit opportunities when they perceived more knowledge of customer demand for the product, more fully developed enabling technologies, greater managerial capability, and greater stakeholder support.

Management information systems

Strategic roles for resource and capabilities that are based on IT and MIS have been considered by many IT–MIS scholars (as discussed in Chapter 7). Among this research, there have been some empirical studies which have applied resource-based logic. Dent-Micallef and Powell (1998) found that IT investment per se had no effect on performance in the retail service industry. However, when combined with intangible, difficult-to-imitate complementary resources, such as a flexible culture, strategic planning, IT-integration, and supplier relationships, retail firms gained a competitive advantage. Similarly, Ray (2000), in his study of customer service processes in North American insurance firms, found that firm-specific managerial IT knowledge can be a source of sustainable competitive advantage (further explained in Ray, Barney, and Muhanna 2004; Ray, Muhanna, and Barney 2005). Bharadwaj (2000) found that firms with high IT capability outperformed others in a matched sample group in his project that focused on firm-specific IT resources including IT infrastructure, human IT resources, and IT-enabled intangibles (such as customer orientation, knowledge assets, and synergy). Li and Ye (1999) found that IT investments linked to managerial, strategic, and environmental factors had a stronger positive effect on financial performance. In addition, Broadbent, Weill, and Neo (1999) examined IT infrastructure capabilities of firms linked to their strategic context. Tippens and Sohi (2003) found that organizational learning plays a significant role in mediating the effects of IT competency (comprising IT knowledge, IT operations, and IT objects) on firm performance.

Operations management

Resource-based logic has also been applied empirically within the field of operations management, with the same pattern of results as discussed above with IT/MIS research. Powell (1995) found that TQM tools and techniques do not generally produce competitive advantage, but certain tacit, behavioral, imperfectly imitable features such as an open culture, employee empowerment, and executive commitment can be a source of competitive advantage. Knights and McNabe (1997) also examined quality focusing on measurement issues. The alignment between best practices, processes, and manufacturing strategy was investigated by Morita and Flynn (1997). In addition, Klassen and Whybark (1999) studied the pattern of investments in environmental technologies, manufacturing strategy, and performance in the furniture industry. They found that significantly better performance was achieved where management invested in the environmental technology portfolio and allocated resources toward pollution prevention technologies. Hult, Ketchen, and Nichols (2002) examined the effects of supply chain cultural competitiveness as a strategic resource which can improve supply chain outcomes such as on order fulfillment cycle time. Finally, in their study of manufacturing performance, Schroeder, Bates, and Junttila (2002) focused on three manufacturing capabilities (internal learning, external learning, and proprietary processes and equipment) and their findings were consistent with resource-based theory.

Technology and innovation management

Resource-based logic has also been applied empirically within technology and innovation management. Key findings here are consistent with resource-based theory and research. In their study of the acquisition of medical technological innovation and hospital performance, Irwin, Hoffman, and Lamont (1998) found that the relationship is strongest when these technological innovations are valuable, rare, and imperfectly imitable. Similarly, Stuart and Podolny (1996) found that the evolution of technological positions is derived from firm-specific ability to innovate in particular technological subfields that partly shapes their competitive success. Intangible resources and capabilities were the main determinants of profitability for Spanish firms engaged in internal R&D (Del Canto and Gonzales, 1999). Further, Helfat (1997) found that dynamic capabilities enabled firms to stay competitive through changing market conditions in her study of knowledge and asset complementarity in R&D processes.

Other specific research within technology and innovation management included projects on optimal patent policy and innovation (Chang 1995), environmental pollution and competitive advantage in industrial goods manufacturing firms (Morris 1997), and knowledge transfer between customers and suppliers in industrial districts (Albino, Garavelli, and Schiuma 1999). Dutta, Narasimhan, and Rajiv (2005) used stochastic frontier estimation to demonstrate heterogeneity in R&D capabilities in the semiconductor industry.

Exemplars of resource-based research

Three of the articles cited above can be seen as exemplars of how resource-based research can be done. Consider, for example, Henderson and Cockburn's examination (1994) of the impact of 'component competence' and architectural competence on the research productivity of pharmaceutical firms. Henderson and Cockburn measure the value of these competencies by estimating their impact on the research productivity of pharmaceutical firms, under the assumption that pharmaceutical firms with more productive research efforts will outperform pharmaceutical firms with less productive research efforts. They measure the rarity of these competencies by showing that their level varies across competing pharmaceutical firms. And they measure the imitability of these competencies by showing that firm differences in the level of these competencies remain very stable over time. To the extent that high levels of research productivity are valuable in the pharmaceutical industry, Henderson and Cockburn's results are consistent with resource-based theory.

Makadok (1999) provides another paper that rigorously tests resource-based theory. Makadok examines the impact of differential levels of economies of scale on the ability of money-market mutual funds to increase their market share. Makadok measures the value of these economies of scale by first estimating the impact of the size of a family of funds on both its weighted-average risk-adjusted gross yield and its weighted-average expense ratio and then shows that these yields and expenses affect the market share of a family of funds. He measures the rarity of economies of scale by showing that they vary across families of funds. And he examines the imitability of these scale differences by examining their impact on the market shares of families of funds over time. Consistent with resource-based theories, because economies of scale are not path dependent, causally ambiguous, or socially complex, Makadok does not expect these capability differences to be a source of sustained competitive advantage. And, in fact, the impact of scale differences on market share becomes smaller over time—results that are again consistent with resource-based theory.

Hatch and Dyer (2004) provide a third exemplar of resource-based empirical research in their study of the impact of firm-specific investments in human capital on learning-by-doing performance in the semiconductor manufacturing industry. They measured the effects of preemployment screening tests, HR training, deployment of human capital, and inimitability of human capital on learning-by-doing performance. Hatch and Dyer found that firms using screening tests in their selection process were able to more effectively identify employees with the ability to learn and adapt to the new environment. Effective screening enabled firms to move more quickly down the learning curve. Depth of human capital skills was more valuable than breadth of capital skills (training on multiple machines) in influencing learning performance. Firms with greater deployment of human capital to learning activities were able to realize learning advantages. In addition, the importance of firm-specific human capital on learning was demonstrated by showing that defects increased with newly hired employees and as turnover increases. Consistent with resource-based theory, Hatch and Dyer show that managing the selection, development, and deployment of human capital can significantly improve learning-by-doing and firm performance. Further, they provide empirical evidence that rivals cannot quickly or costlessly imitate or substitute for the value of firm-specific human capital.

Conclusion

An overview of key empirical tests of resource-based theory conducted by scholars within strategic management and other management disciplines has been presented in this chapter. Collectively, these studies provide an impressive and comprehensive body of empirical evidence of resource-based theory. Further, the results demonstrate highly consistent findings across the domain of strategy and all of these other management disciplines.

While the ability to operationalize and test resource-based theory has been questioned (Priem and Butler 2001), there is now a significant body of empirical work (as outlined in this chapter) which demonstrates conclusively that resource-based theory can be tested. As resource-based theory has become more widely accepted as a key perspective for research on firm performance, the number of studies has grown markedly and resource-based theory publications have steadily increased.

However, scholars continue to ask, 'How does one measure resources?' Usually, the question they are really asking is 'How does one measure resources easily?' The answer is, of course, that you do not measure resources easily. But as the empirical tests of resource-based theory continue to evolve, what becomes clear is that it is possible to derive testable assertions from this theory and then to collect the data needed to test these assertions.

In 1916, Einstein believed his theory of gravity waves could never be tested. In 1995, Godfrey and Hill were also not optimistic about the testability of many of the central assertions of resource-based theory. It may well be that both these predictions may turn out to be overly pessimistic.

NOTES

1. When firms implement a set of incoherent, self-contradictory strategies, it is often difficult for competitors to know what exactly a firm intends to do. Of course, this is often because this firm, itself, does not know exactly what it intends to do.
2. Recall that imitation can take two forms: direct duplication or substitution (Barney 2002). The arguments developed in this section apply most directly to direct duplication. Further work is required to see if these same arguments apply to resource substitution.

3. Ray, Barney, and Muhanna (2004) try to finesse the sustainability question by arguing that the North American insurance industry is a very mature industry and that the relationship between IT and customer service is well known in the industry. In such a setting, any remaining heterogeneity in the application of IT to the customer service function must be the result of costly to imitate resources and capabilities possessed by some firms but not others. However, because they have only cross-sectional data, they obviously are unable to test this hypothesis directly.

12 The future of resource-based theory

This thing called resource-based theory has come a long way since the mid-1980s, when it was first being formulated by Rumelt (1984), Wernerfelt (1984), and Barney (1986*a*). Beginning with a small group of scholars, resource-based theory grew rapidly until it arguably became the dominant theory in the field of strategic management by the late 1990s. This roughly fifteen-year period saw numerous refinements of the theory, many empirical tests, and several pointed criticisms (e.g. Porter 1991; Priem and Butler 2001; Bromiley 2005). But the central assertions of the theory—that firms often possess different resources and capabilities, that these different resources and capabilities enable some firms to implement valuable strategies that other firms will find too costly to implement, and that these differences among firms can be long lasting—remain pretty much unchanged since its earliest development.

Given this history, a reasonable question becomes: What is next for resource-based theory? Is it possible that this theory will continue to yield new theoretical or empirical insights? If so, in what areas are these insights likely to exist? Or, has this theory run its course, destined to being part of the established base of theory in the field of strategic management, but no longer inspiring new and creative theoretical and empirical work?

Of course, our belief is that resource-based theory has the potential to continue to generate new theoretical and empirical insights. The primary purpose of this chapter is to describe some areas where this potential might be realized. However, before describing where these insights are likely to come from, it might make sense to cite a few areas where we think additional discussion and debate is *not* likely to generate new insights.

Issues that are no longer important

In the development of resource-based theory, a variety of issues have been raised and addressed. While many of these questions have been important in the refinement of this theory, and, in fact, are reflected in the summary of resource-based theory presented in this book, in our view, some of these questions are very unlikely to generate additional insights. Four of these questions are discussed here.

ARE RESOURCES, CAPABILITIES, DYNAMIC CAPABILITIES, AND SO FORTH DIFFERENT, AND DOES IT MATTER?

The definitions of resources provided in Wernerfelt (1984) and Barney (1991*a*) are very broad—Wernerfelt talks of anything in a firm that could be thought of as a strength, Barney includes anything controlled by a firm that can enable it to implement strategies. These definitions were broad for several reasons. First, these broad definitions made it clear that resource-based theory was a broadly applicable theory, not just a 'theory of the middle range' (Merton 1957). In this sense, both Wernerfelt and Barney were trying to show that resource-based theory was at the same level of generality as Porter's positioning theory.

Second, a short list of 'essential resources and capabilities that all firms must possess to gain competitive advantages' could easily have been misinterpreted as suggesting a 'rules for riches'. Rather than focusing on the ability of specific resources to generate competitive advantages, Barney (1991*a*), Dierickx and Cool (1989), and Peteraf (1993) focused on the attributes that a firm's resources and capabilities must have to be a source of sustained competitive advantage.

Finally, since at the time, very little empirical work on the relationship between firm resources and performance had been conducted, it was difficult to know which among all of the resources and capabilities controlled by a firm might ultimately turn out to generate sustained competitive advantages. Again, the theory described the kinds of attributes these resources and capabilities would have—they would be, for example, path dependent, causally ambiguous, and/or socially complex—but it did not specify which specific resources a firm might control would be sources of sustained competitive advantage.

While these broad definitions had their purpose, they were limited in their ability to provide guidance for empirical research. They also made it difficult to teach resource-based theory. In response, a variety of resource typologies were introduced into the literature. Barney (1991*a*), for example, suggested that firm resources might be physical capital, human capital, or organization capital. Stalk, Evans, and Shulman (1992) distinguished between resources and capabilities.

Note that the essential predictions of resource-based theory did not change with the introduction of these typologies. That is, whether the resources in question are labeled 'resources', 'capabilities', 'organizational capital', and so on, the theory predicted that these firm assets were only likely to be a source of sustained competitive advantage when they enabled a firm to implement a strategy that increased the willingness of its customers to pay and/or reduced its costs while simultaneously being path-dependent, causally ambiguous, or socially complex in nature. All these different labels did was parse the very large and unorganized space created by the term 'resources' into a more organized space that could facilitate empirical work and teaching. These labels, by themselves, did not change the central propositions of resource-based theory.

Since these early efforts, there has been a proliferation of labels for the resources controlled by a firm. Some of this proliferation has been helpful. For example, Teece, Pisano, and Shuen (1997) labeled one kind of firm resource 'dynamic capabilities' to focus attention on the ability of firms to develop new capabilities as a source of sustained competitive advantage. Several other authors have used the term 'routine' to refer to resources. This helped draw an important connection between resource-based theory and the evolutionary theory of the firm (Nelson and Winter 1982).

However, changing the label of the independent variable of a theory does not change the central assumptions and assertions of that theory. Thus, what makes resources a potential source of sustained competitive advantage are the same as what make capabilities, dynamic capabilities, routines, and so forth potential sources of sustained competitive advantage. In this sense, resource-based theory is not really about resources, per se, but about the attributes that resources must possess if they are to be a source of sustained competitive advantage. That this theory is called 'Resource-based' is something of an historical accident.[1] It could just as easily have been called 'capability-based' or 'competence-based'—the underlying theory would have remained the same.

One of the unfortunate consequences of this proliferation of labels of the independent variables of this theory is that some have concluded that changing the label means that the theory, itself, is changed, and thus requires a new name. Thus, when knowledge is the independent variable in the theory, the theory is called the 'knowledge-based view', when dynamic capabilities is the independent variable in the theory, the theory is called the 'dynamic capabilities view', and so forth.

Renaming the theory this way, even though the underlying causal linkages between the independent variable in question and sustained competitive advantage remains the same, is roughly equivalent to labeling transactions cost research that examines the relationship between transaction-specific investment and governance as the 'specific investments view' and transactions cost research that examines the relationship between behavioral uncertainty and governance as the 'uncertainty view'. These new names fail to recognize that both of these 'views' apply the same underlying logic about the relationship between opportunism and governance developed by Williamson (1975, 1985) and others. If the causal mechanisms remain unchanged, the theory remains unchanged, even if the specific independent variables change labels.

So, in our view, there likely are differences between resources, capabilities, dynamic capabilities, routines, knowledge assets, and other labels that have been used to describe the independent variables in this class of theories. These fine distinctions may help in empirical tests of the theory. They also can help in teaching. However, unless these different independent variables change the nature of the logic that links a firm's assets with sustained competitive advantage, they are not actually new theories, but rather, a manifestation of a more general theory. In this book, we have called this theory 'resource-based theory'—not because this is somehow the 'best' label that could have been chosen, but because it was the first. Additional names for this theory—including the knowledge-based view or dynamic capabilities view—are only appropriate if these perspectives develop and apply an alternative logic that links a firm's assets and its sustained competitive advantage.

CAN RESOURCES REALLY BE MEASURED?

Over the years, many students and faculty alike have asked the question: How do I measure firm resources? Of course, what they are really asking is: How do I measure firm resources easily? The answer to this second question is: You don't.

With regard to measurement, we have much better theories about how *not* to measure resources than we do about how to measure resources. As suggested by Godfrey and Hill (1995), the essential measurement task is to insure that the independent variables in this theory are not measured by the dependent variable, that is, that the value, rarity, and imitability of a firm's resource is not measured by a firm's high level of performance.

Several critics of resource-based theory have suggested that this is a common way this theory has been tested (e.g. Porter 1991; Priem and Butler 2001). While examples of this tautological form of measurement can be found, mostly in the popular business literature (e.g. Peters and Waterman 1982), no high-quality research journal would publish this kind of work. Even if there are some examples of this approach in the scholarly literature—and we have not found them yet—it is clearly the case that the vast majority (indeed, all) of the research reviewed in Chapter 11 has not applied this tautological approach. Instead, it has developed independent measures of resources and their capabilities and correlated them with independent measures of performance.

This experience in testing resource-based theory suggests some lessons about how to measure resources and their attributes. Many of these were highlighted in Chapter 11. Despite the difficulties in measuring resources and their attributes, the efforts of hundreds of scholars, summarized in Chapter 11, suggest both that resources can be measured, and can be done while avoiding tautological problems.

HOW IS SUSTAINED COMPETITIVE ADVANTAGE DEFINED?

Over the years, several different definitions of competitive advantage and sustained competitive advantage have been published. However, after fifteen years, a single set of definitions seems to be emerging. These definitions were presented in Chapter 1 of this book. The consensus now seems to be that competitive advantage is said to exist when the economic value created by a firm in an industry is greater than the economic value created by the marginal firm in that industry (Peteraf and Barney 2003). Economic value is defined by the difference between the willingness of a firm's customer to pay and that firm's costs. Sustained competitive advantage is simply a competitive advantage that lasts a long period.

There is little doubt that these general definitions will have to be modified to be applied in particular empirical settings. Specific theoretical developments in resource-based theory, for example, game theoretic extensions, may also require some modifications to these definitions. It may even be the case that additional modifications of these general definitions may be forthcoming (Postrel 2004; Lippman and Rumelt 2005*a*, 2005*b*). However, to date, this approach to defining competitive advantage and sustained competitive advantage seems to address many of the theoretical limitations of prior definitions, and does so in a way that is amenable to empirical test.

Interestingly, debates about how these two concepts should be defined has not only led to clearer distinctions in resource-based theory, but has also had an impact on the entire field of strategic management. In this sense, not only are these two definitions applicable in resource-based theory, they seem to be equally applicable to other strategic management theories trying to understand why some firms are outperforming others.

IS RESOURCE-BASED THEORY TAUTOLOGICAL?

As Barney (2001) argued, it is always possible to restate any theory as if it is tautological by failing to incorporate the parameterizations of the independent and dependent variables of that theory in its restatement. Thus, restatements of resource-based theory that fail to incorporate the essential parameterization of this theory say nothing about whether the theory is, at its heart, tautological (Priem and Butler 2001). Indeed, a full statement of resource-based theory makes it clear that the theory is not tautological—an assertion that seems to be supported by the numerous empirical tests of implications of the theory summarized in Chapter 11. This is especially the case since some of these tests generate results that are inconsistent with some of the implications of the theory.

In its most general form, resource-based theory suggests that firms with certain kinds of assets with identifiable attributes can generate sustained competitive advantages. To give these assertions empirical content, resource-based theory asserts that the kinds of assets in question are assets that enable a firm to increase the willingness of its customers to pay for its products and/or reduce its costs to a greater extent than at least some other firms in this firm's industry; that the attributes of these assets include their path dependent, causally ambiguous, and/or socially complex nature; and that a firm has a sustained competitive advantage when it is able to increase the willingness of its customers to pay and/or reduce its costs to a greater extent than at least some other firms in this firm's industry and for a relatively long period.

Note that the definition of competitive advantage (to increase the willingness of its customers to pay and/or reduce its costs to a greater extent than at least some other firms in this firm's industry) is both in the independent and dependent variables of resource-based theory. This leads some to suggest that the theory is tautological. However, since competitive advantage is on both sides of this theoretical equation, the only non-tautological empirical assertions that are part of resource-based theory focus on the attributes of resources (path dependent, causally ambiguous, and/or socially complex) and the length of time a firm is able to sustain a competitive advantage. This is why Barney (2001*b*) asserted that the question of value is exogenous to resource-based theory, and that the theory's predictions focus on the relationship between certain attributes of resources and how long a firm is able to maintain its competitive advantages.

Can resource-based theory be stated as if it was tautological? Yes. Is resource-based theory tautological? No.

Extending resource-based theory

While resource-based theory has been developed and extended broadly, there may still be further opportunities to extend the theory in some meaningful and important ways. Several of these possible extensions are noted here. However, how resource-based theory can be extended ultimately depends on scholarly creativity and innovativeness. What turns out to be the most important extensions of the theory may not even be mentioned here.

ADDITIONAL EMPIRICAL TESTS

The most obvious extensions of resource-based theory will take place through additional empirical tests of the theory. Particularly fruitful tests are likely to have one or more of the following characteristics.[2]

First, future tests of this theory are likely to apply the quantitative case study approach. Since the value of a firm's resources depends so much on the specific industry context within which a firm is operating, studies of samples of firms in a single industry, perhaps over time, are most likely to generate insights about how particular sets of resources generate sustained competitive advantages or not. There is already an emerging tradition of this kind of scholarship in strategic management. This trend seems likely to continue into the future.

This does not mean that large cross-sectional research will have no future impact on resource-based theory. For example, the variance decomposition research summarized in Chapter 11 uses such data. However, on balance, it seems more likely that quantitative case studies of firms in a single industry over time have more potential to generate insights about resource-based theory than large sample, cross-sectional work.

Second, future tests of the theory area are likely to involve comparing the predictions of resource-based theory and other theories in strategic management. Indeed, this kind of comparative work has already been done. While the variance decomposition stream of work did not generate explicit hypotheses to be tested, it nevertheless did pit the explanatory power of resource-based theory against the explanatory power of positioning theory. Overall, firm effects seem to explain more of the variance in firm performance than industry effects, although industry effects continue to exist.

A similar approach has been adopted in research on the theory of the firm. Poppo and Zenger (1998), Leiblein and Miller (2003), Leiblein (2003), and Folta (1998) each derive some theory of the firm hypotheses from several different theories, including resource-based theory and transactions cost economics. Sometimes these theories are rivals, sometimes they are complements. There is little doubt that this kind of research model is likely to generate important insights, both for resource-based theory and for other theories in strategic management.

Finally, there are some early indications that Bayesian methods may be particularly useful in testing resource-based theory (Hansen, Perry, and Reese 2004). Traditional statistical methods focus on estimating mean effects—the average relationship between variables A and B. Resource-based theory is not about the mean, it is about the unusual, the outlier. Indeed, standard statistical practice suggests throwing outliers out of a sample to generate more efficient mean-based statistics. Resource-based theory suggests that, rather than throwing outliers out of a sample, we should study them!

Properly applied, Bayesian statistics enable a researcher to not only estimate mean effects, but also to estimate firm-specific coefficients that describe how two variables are related for a particular firm (Hansen, Perry, and Reese 2004; Mackey 2006). One study of the relationship between diversification strategy and firm performance using Bayesian statistics was able to show that sometimes related diversification adds value to a firm, sometimes it destroys value; that unrelated diversification adds value to a firm, sometimes it destroys value (Mackey 2006). This study was also able to show why the coefficient that linked diversification strategy with firm performance varied by firm. The results are consistent with resource-based theory.

Currently, the number of strategy scholars who understand and can apply Bayesian methods is quite limited. However, this may be one area where there are significant opportunities to extend empirical tests of resource-based theory.

MATHEMATICAL RESOURCE-BASED MODELS

Virtually all social science theory is originally explicated using words and language. This language-based approach can last for some time and generate a significant amount of empirical research. However, despite the many advantages of this type of theory—not the least of which is that it is accessible to anyone who can read—language-based social science theories have one enormous limitation: They are insufficiently precise.

Language is a rich and textured medium. In skilled hands, its subtly and nuance can be used to communicate rich meaning, sometimes communicating many more than a single meaning all at once. When Julius Caesar, in Shakespeare's play of the same name, says, 'Yond Cassius has a lean and hungry look,' he is not actually commenting on Cassius' physical appearance—though Cassius may, in fact, be lean and hungry. He is saying much more about Cassius' ambitions and how those ambitions can manifest themselves in a person's appearance. He is also talking about himself, for he too is 'lean and hungry', even if in fact he is neither lean nor hungry, and maybe a bit afraid—of Cassius, surely, but of himself as well, and what he is becoming. He also is commenting on the state of ancient Rome, where political civility has almost been replaced by the politics of violence, where the traditional contest of wills has almost been superseded by the contest of brute strength—thus the emphasis on Cassius' physical state and its looming presence. All this meaning, and more, in eight simple words.

But this subtly and nuance is a problem for science. Science requires precision, not subtly and interpretation and nuance. Many of the controversies surrounding social science theories, including resource-based theory, are due to the imprecision and multiple interpretations of language. As the limits of our language are reached, it becomes important to restate our theories, including resource-based theory, in rigorous mathematical terms.

Of course, this is already beginning to occur. Important parts of resource-based theory have already been translated into mathematical models (e.g. Adner and Levinthal 2001; Makadok 2001; Makadok and Barney 2001; Adner 2002; Adner and Levinthan 2002; Adner and Helfat 2003; Adner and Zemsky 2005, 2006). This trend is likely to accelerate.

However, this mathematical exposition of the theory is not a simple restatement. The increased precision with which the theory can be stated has several effects, one of which is to generate insights that could not be generated with the verbal theory alone. These insights suggest empirical implications of the theory worthy of further detailed analysis.

The great risk in trading verbal theory for mathematical theory is that developing elegant models becomes a means unto itself. This is a widespread problem in economics, a problem that even many economists agree has adversely affected the field (Debreu 1991). However, with respect to resource-based theory, we are a long way away from this concern. A great deal of progress can still be made in the theory by a greater reliance on mathematical formulations.

Expanding resource-based theory

Additional empirical work and reformulating resource-based theory in mathematical terms are almost inevitable extensions of resource-based theory over the next several years. Possible expansions of resource-based theory, that is, efforts to take the theory where it has yet to go, are more speculative in nature. However, in this speculative vein, several possible expansions of the theory are possible. Some of these are discussed here.

WHERE DO RESOURCES COME FROM?

Resource-based theory takes the existence of heterogeneous firm resources and capabilities as given and examines the impact of these resources for the ability of firms to gain and sustain competitive advantages. The question about where resources come from is only addressed in resource-based theory to the extent that this process may have an impact on the ability of other firms to imitate a particular firm's resources and capabilities. Thus, history, in general, and path dependence, in particular, are important attributes of resources that can have an impact on how costly they are to imitate.

But in another sense, observing that a particular resource was developed in a path dependent way is really just a label for our ignorance about the micro-dynamics of resource development. Why a particular path in a path dependent process was taken; why (or why not) this path is irreversible and inimitable; the impact of paths not taken; and how the decisions made by boundedly rational managers, leaders, and consumers affect the evolution of a path dependent process are all issues we know relatively little about. And what we know often takes the form of interesting stories—organizational autobiographies—that are difficult, at best, to generalize, if only because we can only tell such stories about the paths taken, and not about the paths not taken.

Ultimately, a complete resource-based theory of firm performance would have to include a more general theory of this resource-development process. Such a general theory would acknowledge the role of luck in the development of resources (Barney 1986*a*), but would also recognize the important role of managers taking advantage of their good luck to extend their resource-based advantages.

One area of research that confronts a similar class of problems is entrepreneurship (Barney 2001*b*). Entrepreneurship scholars are beginning to confront the question of how do entrepreneurs assemble a set of resources to exploit market opportunities when the nature of those opportunities, and thus which resources are required to exploit them, may not be known (Alvarez and Barney 2005). How firms are organized in this setting, how property and decision rights are all assigned, and economic profits—if they exist at all—are allocated, are all important questions in this context (Alvarez and Barney 2004, 2005).

Some of these scholars suggest that there may be two fundamentally different ways of solving this central entrepreneurial problem. Some entrepreneurship scholars adopt the assumption that opportunities for competitive advantage exist as objective phenomena, just waiting to be discovered by unusually insightful individuals (Shane and Venkataraman 2000; Shane 2004). Other scholars suggest that opportunities do not exist as objective phenomena, just waiting to be discovered, but instead are created by the actions of boundedly rational individuals just trying to improve their current situation as much as possible (Baker and Nelson 2005).

Of these two theories, the latter—creation theory—seems to be more amenable to helping explain where resources come from, if only because the former—discovery theory—adopts assumptions and an approach that are closely aligned with traditional economic theory. Traditional economic logic, of which resource-based theory is clearly a part, is good at examining what should be done to exploit opportunities that are reasonably well understood. It is less good at examining what should be done to exploit opportunities that do not yet exist. In such settings theories of muddling through (Lindbolm 1959), effectuation (Sarasvathy 2001*a*), and bricolage (Baker and Nelson 2005) provide an alternative to economic logic that resource-based theorists might be able to borrow in developing a theory of where resources come from.

DYNAMIC RESOURCE-BASED THEORIES

A second possible expansion of resource-based theories might be to develop truly dynamic resource-based models. Currently, the core theoretical assertions of resource-based theory are not dynamic: Firms with certain kinds of resources will be able to gain sustained competitive advantages. While the theory focuses on a variety of dynamic processes that are created by these resources and the advantages they create, for example, the dynamics of imitation, the assumption of much of the current theory is that the resources and capabilities that give a firm a competitive advantage are relatively fixed in nature.

Ironically, even dynamic capabilities versions of resource-based theory are static in this sense. That is, the ability of dynamic capabilities to enable firms to develop new capabilities is also assumed to be fixed. While the capabilities a firm develops with its dynamic capabilities may be new, the ability to create new capabilities is assumed to remain constant, and thus dynamic capabilities resource-based models are actually no more dynamic than other versions of this theory.

That resource-based theory is not terribly dynamic in its construction should not be too large a surprise. After all, resource-based theory was originally developed as an alternative (or complement, depending on your point of view) to Porter's positioning theory, and positioning theory is also not very dynamic in its characterization of the competitive process. Yes, the threat of entry is central to positioning theory, just as the threat of imitation is central to resource-based theory. But barriers to entry—because they are attributes of industry—are not assumed to vary much over time. This stability makes the model tractable, both to guide research and teaching. But it is obviously the case that just because rivalry, substitutes, new entry, and so forth generate an attractive industry now does not mean that these are fixed attributes of an industry, that attractiveness is an unchanging attribute of an industry. And so it is with resource-based logic: That a resource is currently valuable, rare, and costly to imitate does not mean that it will always be valuable or rare or costly to imitate.

Resource-based theory does acknowledge this limitation. Barney (1991*a*) for example argued that resource-based propositions hold only as long as there are no Schumpeterian shocks in an industry (Schumpeter 1934). Such shocks can take what had been valuable, rare, and costly to imitate resources and make them either not valuable, or not rare, or not costly to imitate. However, identifying such Schumpeterian shocks as a boundary condition in resource-based theory hardly qualifies as a dynamic expansion of the theory. Again, it is more a label for our ignorance about these dynamics than an analysis of them.

In this sense, the dynamics of competition among resources is a temporal extension of the first expansion of resource-based theory discussed here: Where do resources come from? However, instead asking about the source of resources, dynamic resource-based models will ask: Where are a firm's resources going next? In this sense, current resource-based theory answers only the middle of the three existential questions asked in moral philosophy: Where do we come from, why are we here, and where are we going? Given resource heterogeneity, resource-based theory can explain why some firms are currently able to outperform others. As to the genesis or ultimate fate of these resources, resource-based theory has little to say.

However, it may well be the case that the theories that use entrepreneurial actions to explain where resources come from may also help explain how resources evolve in the future. This is a highly speculative suggestion. However, since at one point the present was yesterday's future, it might be possible to take insights about how the past became the present to understand how the present could become the future. Of course, the business of predicting the next Schumpeterian shock is really the business of fortune-tellers and futurists—and sometimes it is hard to tell the difference. But, it may be possible to predict who is most likely to generate this shock, how incumbent firms with incumbent resources are likely to respond, and when new entrants will overtake incumbents. In this sense, Christensen's work (Christensen 1997; Christensen, Anthony, and Roth 2004) on the innovator's dilemma and using theoretical models to anticipate the evolution of industries—and the value, rarity, and imitability of resources in those industries—are early exemplars.

RESOURCE-BASED THEORY AND THE FIELD OF ECONOMICS

In the mid-1960s, it seemed inconceivable that finance scholars would one day make contributions sufficiently important to the field of economics so that they would be awarded the Nobel Prize in economics.

This happened the first time in 1985, when Modigliani won the prize. It happened again in 1990 when Markowitz, Miller, and Sharpe shared the prize, and in 1997 when Merton and Scholes shared the prize. In this sense, finance is an example of a field, originally dominated by practitioners and largely atheoretical in nature, that matured to the point that it began to make fundamental contributions to its discipline of origin, namely economics.

It may seem inconceivable now that strategic management scholars would ever be taken seriously enough by the field of economics that they would be considered for the Nobel Prize in economics. However, this was just as inconceivable for finance in the mid-1960s as it is for strategic management in 2006. Of course, it is not being suggested that strategic management, in general, and resource-based theorists, in particular, should adopt 'winning a Nobel Prize in economics' as a realistic or worthy goal. However, efforts to have strategic management research, generally, and resource-based theories, in particular, taken more seriously by economics would almost certainly have a positive impact on the expansion of both the field and of this theory.

To facilitate this link between resource-based theory and economics, several things must occur. Some of these are already occurring. For example, mathematical exposition of the theory is likely to make it more attractive to mainstream economists. Publishing theoretical (e.g. Adner and Zemsky 2005) and empirical (e.g. Henderson and Cockburn 1994, 1996) resource-based articles in mainstream economics journals will also facilitate this interaction.

One way that resource-based theory will probably need to expand if it is to begin to have implications for broader discussions in economics concerns the role of social welfare. Historically, strategy scholars have not discussed social welfare at all (Barney and Hesterly 2005). This may have been a matter of personal taste—after all, our major applied audience was firms, not society at large. However, more fundamentally, the once dominant paradigm in the field of strategic management—the positioning perspective—was derived from economic theory in such a way that engaging in strategies to generate competitive advantages could generally be expected to reduce social welfare. When client firms are taking actions to reduce rivalry, tacitly collude, and to erect artificial barriers to entry to retain their high profits, it is difficult for strategy scholars to contribute much to broader conversations about how to maximize social welfare. Indeed, in this context, a good way to maximize social welfare may have been to do away with the field of strategic management!

However, building on Demsetz's observations (1973) about efficiency explanations of heterogeneous firm performance, resource-based theories have always held the potential for developing a theory of heterogeneous firm performance that was also consistent with maximizing social welfare. Such a theory could have a variety of important policy implications, including implications for antitrust policy, patent protection policy, and employment policy—to name just a few. Only a couple of efforts have been published in these areas, and these efforts are tentative at best (Barney 2001; Ellig 2001).

However, it does not seem unreasonable to suggest that this is a potential stream in resource-based theory that could be developed to a significant degree. To the extent that proposed resource-based social policies differed significantly from policies derived from current economic theory, these efforts might actually highlight the link between resource-based theory to the broader economic and social policy issues of the day. Such a linkage might benefit both the fields of strategic management and economics.

Conclusion

Resource-based theory, like the resources it describes in firms, is a path dependent phenomenon. Its evolution from earlier ideas and original articulation in the mid-1980s depended on specific individuals at particular points in time making idiosyncratic decisions that, over time, came to be known as resource-based theory. As with all path dependent processes, luck and chance played a role. Alternative paths—perhaps even more fruitful alternative paths—were rejected in favor of the path taken, although at the time these decisions were made, the future of this theory—and of the field of strategic management—could only be seen imperfectly, through a glass, darkly.

Today, the theory stands poised to extend itself, both empirically and theoretically, and to expand on itself, by asking and answering questions that are beyond its current borders. This too will be a path dependent process, full of uncertainty—the fits and starts of science—whose ultimate destination cannot be known.

But however this theory develops, who will develop it can be known with certainty—it will be the same eclectic group of scholars, curmudgeons to the last, who will not take the status as quo. And in asking new questions and challenging old ideas, we all benefit.

NOTES

1. Birger Wernerfelt first developed this name for the theory. It has always been a source of some confusion since it is so close to resource-dependence theory in organization theory, a theory with which it has nothing in common except the word resource.
2. These issues are discussed in more detail in Chapter 11 and are included in an abbreviated form here just for logical completeness.

BIBLIOGRAPHY

Aaker, D. A. and Jacobson, R. (1990). 'The Risk of Marketing: The Roles of Systematic, Uncontrollable, and Controllable Unsystematic, and Downside Risk', in R. A. Bettis and H. Thomas (eds.), *Risk, Strategy and Management*, vol. 5. Greenwich, CT: JAI Press, pp. 137–60.

Adelman, M. A. (1955). 'Concept and Statistical Measurement of Vertical Integration', in National Bureau for Economic Research (eds.), *Business Concentration and Price Policy*. Princeton, NJ: University Press, pp. 281–322.

Adner, R. (2002). 'When are Technologies Disruptive: A Demand-Based View of the Emergence of Competition', *Strategic Management Journal*, 23(8): 667–89.

—— and Helfat, C. E. (2003). 'Corporate Effects and Dynamic Managerial Capabilities', *Strategic Management Journal*, 24(10): 1011–25.

—— and Levinthal, D. (2001). 'Demand Heterogeneity and Technology Evolution: Implications for Product and Process Innovation', *Management Science*, 47(5): 611–29.

—— —— (2002). 'The Emergence of Emerging Technologies', *California Management Review*, 45(1): 50–66.

—— and Zemsky, P. (2005). 'Disruptive Technologies and the Emergence of Competition', *RAND Journal of Economics*, 36(2): 229–54.

—— —— (2006). 'A Demand-based Perspective on Sustainable Competitive Advantage', *Strategic Management Journal*, 27(3): 215–39.

Ahuja, G., Coff, R. W., and Lee, P. M. (2005). 'Managerial Foresight and Attempted Rent Appropriation: Insider Trading on Knowledge of Imminent Breakthroughs', *Strategic Management Journal*, 26: 91–908.

Akerlof, G. A. (1970). 'The Market for "Lemons": Quality Uncertainty and the Market Mechanism', *Quarterly Journal of Economics*, 84: 488–500.

Albino, V., Garavelli, A. C., and Schiuma, G. (1999). 'Knowledge Transfer and Inter-firm Relationships in Industrial Districts: The Role of the Leader Firm', *Technovation*, 19(1): 53–63.

Alchian, A. (1950). 'Uncertainty, Evolution, and Economic Theory', *Journal of Political Economy*, 58: 211–21.

—— and Demsetz, H. (1972). 'Production, Information Costs, and Economic Organization', *American Economic Review*, 62: 777–95.

Altman, E. I. (1968). 'Financial Ratios, Discriminant Analysis, and the Prediction of Corporate Bankruptcy', *Journal of Finance*, 23: 589–609.

Altman, E. I. (1984). 'A Further Investigation of the Bankruptcy Cost Question', *Journal of Finance*, 39: 1067–89.

Alvarez, S. A. and Barney, J. B. (2004). 'Organizing Rent Generation and Appropriation: Toward a Theory of the Entrepreneurial Firm', *Journal of Business Venturing*, 19(5): 621–35.

——— (2005). 'How Do Entrepreneurs Organize Firms under Conditions of Uncertainty?', *Journal of Management*, 31(5): 776–93.

——— (2006). Toward a Creation Theory of Entrepreneurial Opportunity Formation. Working Paper, Fishers College of Business, The Ohio State University.

Amihud, Y. and Lev, B. (1981). 'Risk Reduction as Managerial Motive for Conglomerate Mergers', *Bell Journal of Economics*, 12: 605–17.

Amit, R. and Livnat, J. (1988). 'Diversification Strategies, Business Cycles, and Economic Performance', *Strategic Management Journal*, 9: 99–110.

—— and Schoemaker, P. J. H. (1993). 'Strategic Assets and Organizational Rent', *Strategic Management Journal*, 14: 33–46.

—— and Wernerfelt, B. (1990). 'Why do Firms Reduce Business Risk?', *Academy of Management Journal*, 33: 520–33.

Anand, J. and Singh, H. (1997). 'Asset Redeployment, Acquisitions and Corporate Strategy in Declining Industries', *Strategic Management Journal*, 18(Summer Special Issue): 99–118.

Andrews, K. R. (1971). *The Concept of Corporate Strategy*. Homewood, IL: Dow Jones Irwin.

Ansoff, H. I. (1965). *Corporate Strategy.* New York: McGraw-Hill.

Appleyard, M. M. (1996). 'How Does Knowledge Flow? Interfirm Patterns in the Semiconductor Industry', *Strategic Management Journal*, 17(Special Issue): 137–54.

Argyres, N. (1996). 'Evidence on the Role of Firm Capabilities in Vertical Integration Decision', *Strategic Management Journal*, 17: 129–50.

Armstrong, I. S. (1982). 'The Value of Formal Planning for Strategic Decisions: Review of Empirical Research', *Strategic Management Journal*, 3: 197–211.

Arora, A. and Gambardella, A. (1997). 'Domestic Markets and International Competitiveness: Generic and Product-Specific Competencies in the Engineering Sector', *Strategic Management Journal*, 18(Summer Special Issue): 53–74.

Arrow, K. J. (1974). *The Limits of Organization*. New York: W.W. Norton.

—— (1985). 'The Economics of Agency', in J. W. Pratt and R. J. Zeckhauser (eds.), *Principals and Agents: The Structure of Business.* Boston, MA: Harvard University Press.

Arthur, W. B. (1983). 'Competing Technologies and Lock-in by Historical Small Events: The Dynamics of Allocation under Increasing Return', Unpublished manuscript, Center for Economic Policy Research, Stanford University.

—— (1984*a*). 'Industry Location Patterns and the Importance of History: Why a Silicon Valley?' Unpublished manuscript, Center for Economic Policy Research, Stanford University.

—— (1984*b*). 'Competing Technologies and Economic Prediction', *Options*, IIASA, Laxenburg, Austria.

—— (1989). 'Competing Technologies, Increasing Returns, and Lock-in by Historical Events', *Economic Journal*, 99: 116–31.

—— Ermoliev, Y. M., and Kaniovski, Y. M. (1987). 'Path Dependent Processes and the Emergence of Macro Structure', *European Journal of Operations Research*, 30: 294–303.

—— —— —— (1994). 'Strong Laws for a Class of Path Dependent Stochastic Processes with Applications', in V. I. Arkin, A. Shiryayev, and R. Wets (eds.), *Proceedings of a Conference on Stochastic Optimization*, Kiev 1984, pp. 87–93.

Athanassiou, N. and Nigh, D. (1999). 'The Impact of U.S. Company Internationalization on Top Management Team Advice Networks: A Tacit Knowledge Perspective', *Strategic Management Journal*, 20(1): 83–92.

Bacharach, S. B. (1989). 'Organizational Theories: Some Criteria for Evaluation', *Academy of Management Review*, 14: 496–515.

Bain, J. S. (1941). 'The Profit Rate as a Measure of Monopoly Power', *The Quarterly Journal of Economics*, 55(2): 271–93.

—— (1956). *Barriers to New Competition.* Cambridge: Harvard University Press.

—— (1968). *Industrial Organization.* New York: John Wiley & Sons.

Baker, T. and Nelson, R. E. (2005). 'Creating Something from Nothing: Resource Construction through Entrepreneurial Bricolage', *Administrative Science Quarterly*, 50(3): 329–66.

Bakos, J. Y. and Treacy, M. E. (1986). 'Information Technology and Corporate Strategy: A Research Perspective', *MIS Quarterly*, 10(2): 107–19.

Balaguer, N. S. (1990). 'OTISLINE (B)', Harvard Business School Case 9-190-149, Harvard Business School Publishing Division, Boston, MA.

Baldauf, A., Cravens, D. W., and Wagner, U. (2000). 'Examining Determinants of Export Performance in Small Open Economies', *Journal of World Business*, 35(1): 61–79.

Banker, R. and Kauffman, R. (1988). 'Strategic Contributions of Information Technology: An Empirical Study of ATM Networks', *Proceedings of the Ninth International Conference on Information Systems*, 141–50.

Barfield, R. (1998). 'Creating Value Through Mergers', *The Banker*, 148(869): 24–5.

Barley, S. P. (1983). 'Semiotics and the Study of Occupational and Organizational Cultures', *Administrative Science Quarterly*, 28: 393–413.

Barlow, J. (1996). 'Clearing the Air at Continental', *Houston Chronicle*, April 7: 1 D.

Barnett, W. P., Greve, H. R., and Park, D. Y. (1994). 'An Evolutionary Model of Organizational Performance', *Strategic Management Journal*, 15(Winter Special Issue): 1–28.

Barney, J. B. (1985*a*). 'Rational Expectations Markets for Strategy Implementation: Asymmetric Expectations, Luck, and the Theory of Strategy', Unpublished, Graduate School of Management, UCLA.

—— (1985*b*). 'Strategizing Processes and Returns to Strategizing', Unpublished, Graduate School of Management, UCLA.

Barney, J. B. (1985*c*). 'Types of Competition and the Theory of Strategy', Unpublished manuscript, University of California, Graduate School of Management, Los Angeles.

—— (1986*a*). 'Strategic Factor Markets: Expectations, Luck and Business Strategy', *Management Science*, 32: 1512–14.

—— (1986*b*). 'Organizational Culture: Can It Be a Source of Sustained Competitive Advantage?', *Academy of Management Review*, 11: 656–65.

—— (1986*c*). 'Types of Competition and the Theory of Strategy: Toward an Integrative Framework', *Academy of Management Review*, 11: 791–800.

—— (1988). 'Returns to Bidding Firms in Mergers and Acquisitions: Reconsidering the Relatedness Hypothesis', *Strategic Management Journal*, 9: 71–8.

—— (1989). 'Asset Stock Accumulation and Sustained Competitive Advantage: A Comment', *Management Science*, 35: 1511–13.

—— (1990). 'The Debate between Traditional Management Theory and Organizational Economics: Substantive Differences or Intergroup Conflict?', *Academy of Management Review*, 15: 382–93.

—— (1991*a*). 'Firm Resources and Sustained Competitive Advantage', *Journal of Management*, 17(1): 99–121.

—— (1991*b*). 'The Resource Based View of Strategy: Origins, Implications, and Prospects', Editor of Special Theory Forum in *Journal of Management*, 17: 97–211.

—— (1994*a*). 'Competitive Advantage from Organizational Analysis', Working paper, Texas A&M University, College Station, TX, 1994.

—— (1994*b*). 'Bringing Managers Back in: A Resource-Based Analysis of Managers in Creating and Sustaining Competitive Advantages for Firms', in *Does Management Matter?* Sweden: Institute of Economic Research, Lund University.

—— (1995). 'Looking Inside for Competitive Advantage', *Academy of Management Executive*, 9(4): 49–61.

—— (1997). *Gaining and Sustaining Competitive Advantage.* Reading, MA: Addison-Wesley.

—— (1999). 'How a Firm's Capabilities Affect Boundary Decisions', *Sloan Management Review*, 40(3): 137–45.

—— (2001*a*). Competence Explanations of Economic Profits in Strategic Management: Some Policy Implications. In J. Ellig (ed.), *Dynamic Competition and Public Policy: Technology, Innovation and Anti-trust Issues.* New York: Cambridge University Press.

—— (2001*b*). 'Is the Resource-Based "View" a Useful Perspective for Strategic Management Research? Yes', *Academy of Management Review*, 26(1): 41–56.

—— (2002). *Gaining and Sustaining Competitive Advantage*, 2nd edn. Upper Saddle River, NJ: Prentice-Hall.

—— and Arikan, A. (2001). 'The Resource-Based View: Origins and Implications', in M. A. Hitt, R. E. Freeman, and J. S. Harrison (eds.), *The Blackwell Handbook of Strategic Management.* Oxford, UK: Blackwell, pp. 124–88.

——— and Hansen, M. (1994). 'Trustworthiness as a Source of Competitive Advantage', *Strategic Management Journal*, 15: 175–90.

——— and Hesterly, W. (1996). 'Organizational Economics: Understanding the Relationship between Organizations and Economic Analysis', in S. Clegg, C. Hardy, and W. Nord (eds.), *Handbook of Organization Theory*. London: Sage, pp. 115–47.

——— ——— (2005). *Strategic Management and Competitive Advantage.* Text only. Upper Saddle River, NJ: Prentice Hall.

——— ——— (2006). 'Organizational Economics: Understanding the Relationship between Organizations and Economic Analysis', in S. Clegg, C. Hardy, and W. Nord (eds.), *Handbook of Organization Studies*, 2nd edn. London: Sage, pp. 115–47.

——— and Hoskisson, R. (1989). 'Strategic Groups: Untested Assertions and Research Proposals', *Managerial and Decision Economics*, 11: 187–98.

——— and Mackey, T. B. (2005). 'Testing Resource-Based Theory', in D. J. Ketchen and D. D. Bergh (eds.), *Research Methodology in Strategy and Management*, vol. 2. New York: Elsevier, pp. 1–13.

——— and Turk, T. A. (1994). 'Superior Performance from Implementing Merger and Acquisition Strategies: A Resource-based Analysis', in G. Von Krogh, A. Sinatra, and H. Singh (eds.), *The Management of Corporate Acquisitions: International Perspectives*. London: MacMillan Press, pp. 105–27.

——— and Tyler, B. (1991). 'The Prescriptive Limits and Potential for Applying Strategic Management Theory', Working Paper. (Never Published)

——— ——— (1992). 'The Attributes of Top Management Teams and Sustained Competitive Advantage', in M. Lawless and L. Gomez-Mejia (eds.), *Managing the High Technology Firm (II)*. JAI Press, pp. 33–48.

——— and Wright, P. M. (1998). 'On Becoming a Strategic Partner: The Role of Human Resources in Gaining Competitive Advantage', *Human Resource Management*, 37: 31–46.

——— McWillams, A., and Turk, T. (1989). 'On the Relevance of the Concept of Entry Barriers in the Theory of Competitive Strategy', Paper presented at the annual meeting of the Strategic Management Society, San Francisco.

——— Wright, M., and Ketchen Jr., D. J. (2001). 'The Resource-based View of the Firm: Ten Years After 1991', *Journal of Management*, 27: 625–41.

Bates, K. A. and Flynn, E. J. (1995). 'Innovation History and Competitive Advantage: A Resource-based View Analysis of Manufacturing Technology Innovations', *Academy of Management Journal*, 38: 235–9.

Baum, J. and Berta, W. B. (1999). 'Sources, Dynamics, and Speed: A Longitudinal Behavioral Simulation of Interorganizational and Population-level Learning', *Advances in Strategic Management*, 16: 155–84.

Baumol, W. J., Panzar, J. C., and Willig, R. P. (1982). *Contestable Markets and the Theory of Industry Structure.* New York: Harcourt, Brace, and Jovanovich.

Bazerman, M. and Samuelson, W. (1983). 'The Winner's Curse: An Empirical Investigation', *Lecture Notes in Economics and Math. Systems*, 213: 186–200.

Becker, B. and Gerhart, B. (1996). 'The Impact of Human Resource Practices on Organizational Performance: Progress and Prospects', *Academy of Management Journal*, 39: 779–801.

Becker, E. and Lindsay, C. M. (1994). 'Sex-differences in Tenure Profiles—Effects of Shared Firm-specific Investment', *Journal of Labor Economics*, 12(1): 98–118.

Becker, G. S. (1964). *Human Capital*. New York: Columbia.

Beitler, M. A. (2003). *Strategic Organizational Change*. Greensboro, NC: Practitioner Press International.

Benjamin, R. I., Rockart, J. F., Scott Morton, M. S., and Wyman, J. (1984). 'Information Technology: A Strategic Opportunity', *Sloan Management Review*, 25(3): 3–10.

Bennett, N., Ketchen, D. J., and Schultz, E. B. (1998). 'An Examination of Factors Associated with the Integration of Human Resource Management and Strategic Decision Making', *Human Resource Management*, 37(1): 3–16.

Bennis, W. G. (1989). *On Becoming a Leader*. Reading, MA: Addison-Wesley.

—— (2003). *On Becoming a Leader: The Leadership Classic Updated and Expanded*, revised edn. New York: Perseus Publishing.

Benston, G. J. (1980). *Conglomerate Mergers: Causes, Consequences, and Remedies*. Washington, DC: American Enterprise Institute for Public Policy Research.

Berger, P. and Ofek, E. (1999). 'Causes and Effects of Corporate Refocusing', *Review of Financial Studies*, 12: 311–45.

—— —— (1995). 'Diversification's Effect on Firm Value', *Journal of Financial Economics*, 37: 39–65.

Berger, P. L. and Luckman, T. (1967). *The Social Construction of Reality*, Garden City, NY: Anchor.

Bergh, D. D. (2001). 'Diversification Strategy Research at a Crossroad: Established, Emerging and Anticipated Paths', in M. A. Hitt, R. E. Freeman, and J. S. Harrison (eds.), *The Blackwell Handbook of Strategic Management*. Oxford, UK: Blackwell, pp. 362–83.

Berle, A. A. and Means, G. C. (1932). *The Modern Corporation and Private Property*. New York: Corporation Trust.

Berman, S. L., Down, J., and Hill, C. W. L. (2002). 'Tacit Knowledge as a Source of Competitive Advantage in the National Basketball Association', *Academy of Management Journal*, 45: 13–31.

Besanko, D., Dranove, D., and Shanley, M. (2000). *Economics of Strategy*. 2nd Ed. New York: John Wiley & Sons.

Bethel, J. (1999). 'Stabilizing Company Cash Flows: Strategy, Scope, and New Alternatives', Working paper, Babson College.

Bettis, R. (1981). 'Performance Differences in Related and Unrelated Diversified Firms', *Strategic Management Journal*, 2: 379–93.

—— (1983). 'Modern Financial Theory, Corporate Strategy, and Public Policy: Three Conundrums', *Academy of Management Review*, 8: 406–15.

Bharadwaj, A. S. (2000). 'A Resource-based Perspective on Information Technology Capability and Firm Performance: An Empirical Investigation', *MIS Quarterly*, 24: 169–96.

Birkinshaw, J., Hood, N., and Jonsson, S. (1998). 'Building Firm-specific Advantages in Multinational Corporations: The Role of Subsidiary Initiative', *Strategic Management Journal*, 19(3): 221–41.

Bisp, S., Sorrenson, E., and Grunert, K. (1998). 'Using the Key Success Factor Concept in Competitor Intelligence and Benchmarking', *Competitor Intelligence Review*, 9(3): 55–7.

Blackburn, J. D., Hoedemaker, G., and Van Wassenhove, L. N. (1996). 'Concurrent Software Engineering: Prospects and Pitfalls', *IEEE Transactions on Engineering Management*, 43: 179–88.

Blackburn, R. and Rosen, B. (1993). 'Total Quality and Human Resources Management: Lessons Learned from Baldridge Award-winning Companies', *Academy of Management Executive*, 7: 49–66.

Boissueau, C. (1995). 'Morale is Higher as New Managers and a Return to Profitability Give Workers a Reason to Have Hope', *Houston Chronicle*, October 22: 1 D.

Borch, O. J., Huse, M., and Senneseth, K. (1999). 'Resource Configuration, Competitive Strategies, and Corporate Entrepreneurship: An Empirical Examination of Small Firms', *Entrepreneurship Theory & Practice*, 24(1), Fall: 49–70.

Boudreau, J. (1991). 'Utility Analysis for Decisions in Human Resource Management', in M. Dunnette and L. Hough (eds.), *Handbook of Industrial/Organizational Psychology*, vol. 2, 2nd edn. PaloAlto, CA: Consulting Psychologist Press, pp. 621–746.

Bower, J. (1996). 'WPP-Integrating Icons', Harvard Business School Case No. 9-396-249.

Bowman, C. and Amrosini, V. (2000). 'Value Creation Versus Value Capture: Towards a Coherent Definition of Value in Strategy', *British Journal of Management*, 11: 1–15.

Bowman, E. H. (1974). 'Epistemology, Corporate Strategy and Academe', *Sloan Management Review*, 15: 35–50.

Boxall, P. F. (1996). 'The Strategic HRM Debate and the Resource-based View of the Firm', *Human Resource Management Journal*, 6(3): 59–75.

—— (1998). 'Human Resource Strategy and Industry-based Competition: A Conceptual Framework and Agenda for Theoretical Development', in P. M. Wright, L. D. Dyer, J. W. Boudreau, and G. T. Milkovich (eds.), *Research in Personnel and Human Resources Management* (Suppl. 4). Madison, WI: IRRA, pp. 1–29.

—— and Steeneveld, M. (1999). 'Human Resource Strategy and Competitive Advantage: A Longitudinal Study of Engineering Consultancies', *Journal of Management Studies*, 36: 443–63.

Boynton, A. C., Zmud, R. W., and Jacobs, G. C. (1994). 'The Influence of Management Practice on IT Use in Large Organizations', *MIS Quarterly*, 18(3): 299–318.

Bradach, J. L. and Eccles, R. G. (1989). 'Price, Authority, and Trust', *Annual Review of Sociology*, 15: 97–118.

Bradley, M., Desai, A., and Kim, E. (1988). 'Synergistic Gains from Corporate Acquisitions and Their Division between the Stockholders of Target and Acquiring Firms', *Journal of Financial Economics*, 21: 3–40.

Brancheau, J. C. and Wetherbe, J. C. (1987). 'Key Issues in Information Systems Management', *MIS Quarterly*, 11(1): 23–45.

Brandenburger, A. M. and Stuart, H. W. (1996). Value-based Business Strategy, *Journal of Economics and Management Strategy*, 5: 5–24.

Brander, J. A. and Lewis, T. R. (1986). 'Oligopoly and Financial Structure: The Limited Liability Effect', *American Economic Review*, 76: 956–70.

Brews, P. J. and Hunt, M. R (1999). 'Learning to Plan and Planning to Learn: Resolving the Planning School/Learning School Debate', *Strategic Management Journal*, 20(10): 889–913.

Broadbent, M., Weill, P., and Neo, B. S. (1999). 'Strategic Context and Patterns of IT Infrastructure Capability', *Journal of Strategic Information Systems*, 8(2): 157–87.

Bromiley, P. (1991). 'Testing a Causal Model of Risk Taking and Performance', *Academy of Management Journal*, 34(1): 37–59.

____ (2005). *The Behavioral Fundations of Strategic Management*. Malden, MA; Oxford: Blackwell.

Brush, C. G. and Chaganti, R. (1999). 'Businesses Without Glamour? An Analysis of Resources on Performance by Size and Age in Small Service and Retail Firms', *Journal of Business Venturing*, 14(3): 233–57.

Brush, T. H. and Artz, K. W. (1999). 'Toward a Contingent Resource-based Theory: The Impact of Information Asymmetry on the Value of Capabilities in Veterinary Medicine', *Strategic Management Journal*, 20(3): 223–50.

____ and Bromiley, P. (1997). 'What Does a Small Corporate Effect Mean? A Variance Components Simulation of Corporate and Business Effects', *Strategic Management Journal*, 18: 825–35.

Burgelman, R. (1983). 'Corporate Entrepreneurship and Strategic Management: Insights from a Process Study', *Management Science*, 29: 1349–64.

____ and Maidique, M. A. (1988). *Strategic Management of Technology and Innovation*. Homewood, IL: Irwin.

Busenitz, L. and Barney, J. B. (1997). 'Differences between Entrepreneurs and Managers in Large Organizations: Biases and Heuristics in Strategic Decision-making', *Journal of Business Venturing*, 12(1): 9–30.

Cameron, K. S. and Quinn, R. E. (1999). *Diagnosing and Changing Organizational Culture: Based on the Competing Values Framework*. New York: Prentice-Hall.

Campa, J. M. and Kedia, S. (2002). 'Explaining the Diversification Discount', *Journal of Finance*, 57(4): 1731–62.

Capon, N. and Glazer, R. (1987). 'Marketing and Technology: A Strategic Coalignment', *Journal of Marketing*, 51(3): 1–14.

Capron, L. (1999). 'The Long-term Performance of Horizontal Acquisitions', *Strategic Management Journal*, 20(11): 987–1018.

____ and Hulland, J. (1999). 'Redeployment of Brands, Sales Forces, and General Marketing Management Expertise Following Horizontal Acquisitions: A Resource-based View', *Journal of Marketing*, 63(2): 41–54.

____ Dussauge, P., and Mitchell, W. (1998). 'Resource Redeployment Following Horizontal Acquisitions in Europe and North America, 1988–1992', *Strategic Management Journal*, 19(7): 631–61.

Carow, K., Heron, R., and Saxton, T. (2004). 'Do Early Birds Get the Returns? An Empirical Investigation of Early-mover Advantages in Acquisitions', *Strategic Management Journal*, 25: 563–85.

Carr, N. G. (2003). 'IT Doesn't Matter', *Harvard Business Review*, 18(5): 41–9.

Cascio, W. (1987). *Costing Human Resources: The Financial Impact of Behaviour in Organizations*. Boston, MA: Kent.

Cash, J. L. and Konsynski, B. (1985). 'IS Redraws Competitive Boundaries', *Harvard Business Review*, 63(2): 134–42.

Castanias, R. P. and Helfat, C. E. (1991). 'Managerial Resources and Rents', *Journal of Management*, 17(1): 155–71.

____ ____ (2001). 'The Managerial Rents Model: Theory and Empirical Analysis', *Journal of Management*, 27(6): 661–78.

Caves, R. and Williamson, P. (1985). 'What is Product Differentiation, Really?', *The Journal of Industrial Economics*, 34: 113–32.

Caves, R. E. and Porter, M. (1977). 'From Entry Barriers to Mobility Barriers: Conjectural Decisions and Contrived Deterrence to New Competition', *Quarterly Journal of Economics*, 91: 241–62.

Chamberlin, E. H. (1933). *The Theory of Monopolistic Competition*. Cambridge, MA: Harvard University Press.

Chandler, A. D. (1962). *Strategy and Structure: Chapters in the History of the Industrial Enterprise*. Cambridge, MA: MIT Press.

____ (1984). 'Comparative Business History', in D. C. Coleman and P. Mathias (eds.), *Enterprise and History: Essays in Honor of Charles Wilson*. Cambridge: Cambridge University Press, pp. 3–26.

Chang, H. F. (1995). 'Patent Scope, Antitrust Policy, and Cumulative Innovation', *The Rand Journal of Economics*, 26(1): 34–57.

Chatterjee, S. (1986). 'Types of Synergy and Economic Value: the Impact of Acquisitions on Merging and Rival Firms', *Strategic Management Journal*, 7: 119–40.

____ (1990). 'The Gain to Acquiring Firms: The Related Principle Revisited', in L. R. Jauch and J. C. Wall (eds.), *Academy of Management Best Paper Proceedings*, pp. 12–16.

____ and Lubatkin, M. (1990). 'Corporate Mergers, Stockholder Diversification, and Changes', *Strategic Management Journal*, 11: 255–68.

Chatterjee, S. and Singh, J. (1999). 'Are Tradeoffs Inherent in Diversification Moves? A Simultaneous Model for Type of Diversification and Mode of Expansion Decisions', *Management Science*, 45(1): 25–41.

—— and Wernerfelt, B. (1991). 'The Link Between Resources and Type at Diversification: Theory and Evidence', *Strategic Management Journal*, 12: 33–48.

Choi, Y. R. and Shepherd, D. A. (2004). 'Entrepreneurs' Decisions to Exploit Opportunities', *Journal of Management*, 30: 377–95.

Chrisman, J. J. (1999). 'The Influence of Outsider-generated Knowledge Resources on Venture Creation', *Journal of Small Business Management*, 37(4): 42–58.

Christensen, C. M. (1997). *The Innovators' Dilemma: When New Technologies Cause Great Firms to Fail.* Boston, MA: Harvard Business School Press.

—— Anthony, S. D., and Roth, E. A. (2004). *Seeing What's Next: Using the Theories of Innovation to Predict Industry Change.* Boston: Harvard Business School Publishing.

Christie, B. (1985). *Human Factors and Information Technology in the Office.* New York: John Wiley & Sons.

Christofides, L. N. and Oswald, A. J. (1992). 'Real Wage Determination and Rent-sharing in Collective-bargaining Agreements', *Quarterly Journal of Economics*, 107(3): 985–1002.

Clark, B. R. (1970). *The Distinctive College: Antioch, Reed, and Swarthmore.* Chicago, IL: Aldine.

—— (1972). 'The Organizational Saga in Higher Education', *Administrative Science Quarterly*, 17: 178–84.

Clemons, E. K. (1986). 'Information Systems for Sustainable Competitive Advantage', *Information & Management*, 11(3): 131–6.

—— (1991). 'Corporate Strategies for Information Technology: A Resource-based Approach', *Computer*, 24(11): 23–32.

—— and Kimbrough, S. O. (1986). 'Information Systems, Telecommunications, and Their Effects on Industrial Organization', in *Proceedings of the Seventh International Conference on Information Systems*, December, pp. 99–108.

—— and Knez, M. (1988). 'Competition and Cooperation in Information Systems Innovation', *Information & Management*, 15(1): 25–35.

—— and Row, M. (1987). 'Structural Differences among Firms: A Potential Source of Competitive Advantage in the Application of Information Technology', in *Proceedings of the Eight International Conference on Information Systems*, December, 1–9.

—— and Row, M. C. (1991*a*). 'Sustaining IT Advantage: The Role of Structural Differences', *MIS Quarterly*, 15(3): 275–92.

—— —— (1992). 'Information Technology and Industrial Cooperation', in *Proceedings of the Twenty-Fifth Annual Hawaii International Conference on System Sciences*, vol. 4, pp. 644–53.

—— and Row, M. K. (1991*b*). 'Information Technology at Rosenbluth Travel: Competitive Advantage in a Rapidly Growing Service Company', *Journal of Management Information Systems*, 8(2): 53–79.

—— and Weber, B. W. (1990). 'Strategic Information Technology Investments: Guidelines for Decision Making', *Journal of Management Information*, 7(2): 9–28.

Coff, R. (1999). 'When Competitive Advantage Doesn't Lead to Performance: Resource-based Theory and Stakeholder Bargaining Power', *Organization Science*, 10(2): 119–33.

Collins, J. C. and Porras, J. I. (1997). *Built to Last: Successful Habits of Visionary Companies*. New York: HarperCollins.

Collis, D. J. (1986). 'The Value Added Structure and Competition Within Industries', Unpublished Ph.D. dissertation, Harvard University.

—— (1991). 'A Resource-based Analysis of Global Competition: The Case of the Bearings Industry', *Strategic Management Journal*, 12(Summer): 49–68.

—— (1994). 'Research Note: How Valuable are Organizational Capabilities?', *Strategic Management Journal*, 15(Winter Special Issue): 143–52.

—— and Montgomery, C. A. (1995). 'Competing on Resources: Strategy in the 1990s', *Harvard Business Review*, 73(4): 118–28.

—— —— (1997). *Corporate Strategy: Resources and the Scope of the Firm*. Chicago, IL: Irwin.

Combs, J. G. and Ketchen Jr., D. J. (1999). 'Explaining Interfirm Cooperation and Performance: Toward a Reconciliation of Predictions from the Resource-based View and Organizational Economics', *Strategic Management Journal*, 20(9): 867–88.

Comment, R. and Jarrell, G. (1995). 'Corporate Focus and Stock Returns', *Journal of Financial Economics*, 37: 67–87.

Conner, K. R. (1991). 'A Historical Comparison of Resource Based Theory and Five Schools of Thought within Industrial Organization Economics: Do We have a New Theory of the Firm?', *Journal of Management*, 17(1): 121–54.

—— and Prahalad, C. K. (1996). 'A Resource Based Theory of the Firm: Knowledge versus Opportunism', *Organization Science*, 7(5): 477–501.

Cool, K., Dierickx, I., and Jemison, D. (1989). 'Business Strategy, Market Structure and Risk-return Relationships: A Structural Approach', *Strategic Management Journal*, 10(6): 507–22.

Copeland, D. G. and McKenney, J. L. (1988). 'Airline Reservation Systems: Lessons from History', *MIS Quarterly*, 12(3): 353–70.

Copeland, T. and Weston, J. F. (1979). *Financial Theory and Corporate Policy*. Reading, MA: Addison-Wesley.

—— —— (1983). *Financial Theory and Corporate Policy*, 2nd edn. Reading, MA: Addison-Wesley.

—— Koller, T., and Murrin, J. (1995). *Valuation: Measuring and Managing the Value of Companies*. New York: John Wiley & Sons.

Corporate culture: The hard-to-change values that spell success or failure. (1980). *Business Week*, October 27: 148–60.

Covey, S. R. (1989). 'Basic Principles of Total Quality', *Executive Excellence*, 6(5), May: 17–19.

Crozier, M. (1964). *The Bureaucratic Phenomena.* Chicago, IL: University of Chicago Press.

Daft, R. (1983). *Organization Theory and Design.* New York: West.

Daily, C. M., Certo, S. T., and Dalton, D. R. (2000). 'International Experience in the Executive Suite: The Path to Prosperity?', *Strategic Management Journal*, 21(4): 515–23.

Datta, D. K., Rajagopalan, N., and Rasheed, A. M. A. (1991). 'Diversification and Performance: Critical Review and Future Directions', *Journal of Management Studies*, 28: 529–58.

—— Narayanan, V. K., and Pinches, G. E. (1992). 'Factors Influencing Wealth Creation from Mergers and Acquisitions: A Meta-analysis', *Strategic Management Journal*, 13: 67–84.

D'Aveni, R. and Ravenscraft, D. (1994). 'Economics of Integration versus Bureaucracy Costs: Does Vertical Integration Improve Performance?', *Academy of Management Journal*, 37: 1167–206.

David, P. A. (1985). 'Clio and the Economics of QWERTY', *American Economic Review: Proceedings*, 75: 332–7.

Deal, T. and Kennedy, A. E. (1982). *Corporate Cultures.* Reading, MA: Addison-Wesley.

Dean, T. J., Turner, C. A., and Bamford, C. E. (1997). 'Impediments to Imitation and Rates of New Firm Failure', *Academy of Management Proceedings*, pp. 103–7.

Debreu, G. (1991). 'Random Walk and Life Philosophy', *American Economist*, 35(2): 3–8.

De Carolis, D. M. (2003). 'Competencies and Imitability on the Pharmaceutical Industry: An Analysis of Their Relationship with Firm Performance', *Journal of Management*, 29: 27–50.

—— and Deeds, D. L. (1999). 'The Impact of Stocks and Flows of Organizational Knowledge on Firm Performance: An Empirical Investigation of the Biotechnology Industry', *Strategic Management Journal*, 20(10): 953–68.

Deeds, D. L., De Carolis, D., and Coombs, J. (2000). 'Dynamic Capabilities and New Product Development in High Technology Ventures: An Empirical Analysis of New Biotechnology Firms', *Journal of Business Venturing*, 15(3): 211–29.

Deephouse, D. L. (1999). 'To be Different, or to be the Same? It's a Question (and theory) of Strategic Balance', *Strategic Management Journal*, 20(2): 147–66.

—— (2000). 'Media Reputation as a Strategic Resource: An Integration of Mass Communication and Resource-based Theories', *Journal of Management*, 26: 1091–112.

—— and Wiseman, R. M. (2000). 'Comparing Alternative Explanations for Accounting Risk-return Relations', *Journal of Economic Behavior and Organization*, 42: 463–82.

Delaney, J. T. and Huselid, M. A. (1996). 'The Impact of Human Resource Management Practices on Perceptions of Organizational Performance', *Academy of Management Journal*, 39(4): 949–69.

Del Canto, J. G. and Gonzalez, I. S. (1999). 'A Resource-based Analysis of the Factors Determining a Firm's R&D Activities', *Research Policy*, 28(8): 891–905.

Delery, J. and Doty, H. (1996). 'Modes of Theorizing in Strategic Human Resource Management: Tests of Universalistic, Contingency, and Configurational Performance Predictions', *Academy of Management Journal*, 39: 802–35.

Delios, A. and Beamish, P. W. (1999). 'Geographic Scope, Product Diversification, and the Corporate Performance of Japanese Firms', *Strategic Management Journal*, 20(8): 711–27.

Demsetz, H. (1973). 'Industry Structure, Market Rivalry, and Public Policy', *Journal of Law and Economics*, 16: 1–9.

Dent-Micallef, A. and Powell, T. (1998). 'Information Technology: Strategic Necessity of Source of Competitive Advantage? An Empirical Study on the Retail Sector of the United States', *Canadian Journal Of Administrative Sciences-Revue Canadienne Des Sciences De L Administration*, 15(1): 39–64.

Dess, G. G., Gupta, A., Hennart, J.-F., and Hill, C. W. L. (1995). 'Conducting and Integrating Strategy Research at the International, Corporate and Business Levels: Issues and Directions', *Journal of Management*, 21: 357–93.

Dierickx, I. and Cool, K. (1989). 'Asset Stock Accumulation and Sustainability of Competitive Advantage', *Management Science*, 35: 1504–11.

DiMaggio, P. and Powell, W. W. (1983). 'The Iron Cage Revisited: Institutional Isomorphism and Collective Rationality in Organizational Fields', *American Sociological Review*, 4: 147–60.

Donaldson, L. (1990*a*). 'A Rational Basis for Criticisms of Organizational Economics: A Reply to Barney', *Academy of Management Review*, 15: 394–401.

—— (1990*b*). 'The Ethereal Hand: Organizational Economics and Management Theory', *Academy of Management Review*, 15(3): 369–82.

—— and Davis, J. H. (1991). 'Stewardship Theory or Agency Theory: CEO Governance and Shareholder Returns', *Australian Journal of Management*, 16(1): 49–64.

Dougherty, D. and Hardy, C. (1996). 'Sustained Product Innovation in Large, Mature Organizations: Overcoming Innovation-to-Organization Problems', *Academy of Management Journal*, 39(5): 1120–53.

Douglas, T. J. (2003). 'Understanding Competitive Advantage in the General Hospital Industry: Evaluating Strategic Competencies', *Strategic Management Journal*, 24: 333–47.

Dussauge, P., Garrette, B., and Mitchell, W. (2000). 'Learning from Competing Partners: Outcomes and Durations of Scale and Link Alliances in Europe, North America and Asia', *Strategic Management Journal*, 21(2): 9–126.

Dutta, S., Zbaracki, M. J., and Bergen, M. (2003). 'Pricing Process as a Capability: A Resource-based Perspective', *Strategic Management Journal*, 24: 615–30.

—— Narasimhan, O., and Rajiv, S. (2005). 'Conceptualizing and Measuring Capabilities: Methodology and Empirical Application', *Strategic Management Journal*, 26: 277–85.

Dyer, J. (1997). 'Effective Interfirm Collaboration: How Firms Minimize Transactions Costs and Maximize Transaction Value', *Strategic Management Journal*, 18: 535–56.

Dyer, J. and Ouchi, W. (1993). 'Japanese Style Partnerships: Giving Companies a Competitive Edge', *Sloan Management Review*, 35: 51–63.

——— and Singh, H. (1998). 'The Relational View: Corporative Strategy and Sources of Interorganizational Competitive Advantage', *Academy of Management Review*, 23: 660–79.

Eckbo, E. H. (1983). 'Horizontal Mergers, Collusion and Stockholder Wealth', *Journal of Financial Economics*, 11: 241–74.

Eisenhardt, K. M. (1989*a*). 'Agency Theory: An Assessment and Review', *Academy of Management Review*, 14: 57–74.

——— (1989*b*). 'Building Theories from Case Study Research', *Academy of Management Review*, 14: 532–50.

——— and Brown, S. (1998). 'Time Pacing: Competing in Markets that Won't Stand Still', *Harvard Business Review*, March–April: 59–69.

——— and Martin, J. A. (2000). 'Dynamic Capabilities: What Are They?', *Strategic Management Journal*, 21: 1105–21.

Elgers, P. T. and Clark, J. J. (1980). 'Merger Types and Shareholder Returns: Additional Evidence', *Financial Management*, 9: 66–72.

Ellert, J. C. (1976). 'Merger, Antitrust Law Enforcement, and Stockholder Returns', *Journal of Finance*, May: 715–32.

Ellig, J. (2001). *Dynamic Competition and Public Policy: Technology, Innovation and Anti-Trust Issues*. New York: Cambridge University Press.

Elton, E. J. and Gruber, M. J. (1995). *Modern Portfolio Theory and Investment Analysis*, 5th edn. New York: John Wiley & Sons.

Etheridge, J. (1988). 'Sky Wars Over Europe', *Datamation*, 34(3): 84-1–84-5.

Etzioni, E. (1988). *The Moral Dimension: Toward a New Economics*. New York: Free Press.

Fama, E. F. (1970). 'Efficient Capital Markets: A Review of Theory and Empirical Work', *Journal of Finance*, May: 383–417.

Farjoun, M. (1998). 'The Independent and Joint Effects of the Skill and Physical Bases of Relatedness in Diversification', *Strategic Management Journal*, 19: 611–30.

Feeny, D. (1988). 'Creating and Sustaining Competitive Advantage with IT', in M. Earl (ed.), *Information Management: The Strategic Dimension*. Oxford, UK: Oxford University Press, pp. 98–117.

Feeny, D. F. and Ives, B. (1990). 'In Search of Sustainability: Reaping Long-term Advantage from Investments in Information Technology', *Journal of Management Information Systems*, 7(1): 27–46.

Ferris, S., Jayaraman, N., and Makhija, A. (1997). 'The Response of Competitors to Announcements of Bankruptcy: An Empirical Examination of Contagious and Competitive Effects', *Journal of Corporate Finance*, 3: 367–95.

Fey, C. F., Bjorkman, I., and Pavlovskaya, A. (2000). 'The Effect of Human Resource Management Practices on Firm Performance in Russia', *International Journal of Human Resource Management*, 11(1): 1–18.

Field, D., Chan, A., and Akhtar, S. (2000). 'Organizational Contest and Human Resource Management Strategy: A Structural Equation Analysis of Hong Kong Firms', *International Journal of Human Resource Management*, 11(2): 264–77.

Finkelstein, S. (2003). *Why Smart Executives Fail: And What You Can Learn from Their Mistakes*. New York: Portfolio.

—— and Hambrick, D. (1996). *Strategic Leadership: Top Executives and Their Effects on Organizations*. Minneapolis/St. Paul: West.

Fiol, C. M. (1991). 'Managing Culture as a Competitive Resource: An Identity-Based View of Sustainable Competitive Advantage', *Journal of Management*, 17(1): 191–211.

—— (2001). 'Revisiting an Identity-based View of Sustainable Competitive Advantage', *Journal of Management*, 27: 691–9.

Flamholtz, E. and Lacey, J. (1981). *Personnel Management: Human Capital Theory and Human Resource Accounting*. Los Angeles, CA: Institute of Industrial Relations, UCLA.

Floyd, S. and Woolridge, B. (1990). 'Path Analysis of the Relationship between Competitive Strategy, Information, Technology, and Financial Performance', *Journal of Management Information Systems*, 7: 47–64.

Folta, T. (1998). 'Governance and Uncertainty: The Tradeoff Between Administrative Control and Commitment', *Strategic Management Journal*, 19(11): 1007–29.

Foss, N. J. and Knudsen, T. (2003). 'The Resource-based Tangle: Towards a Sustainable Explanation of Competitive Advantage', *Managerial and Decision Economics*, 24: 291–307.

Frank, R. H. (1988). *Passions within Reason*. New York: W. W. Norton.

Fredrickson, J. (1984). 'The Comprehensiveness of Strategic Decision Processes: Extension, Observations, Future Directions', *Academy of Management Journal*, 27: 445–66.

—— and Mitchell, T. R. (1984). 'Strategic Decision Processes: Comprehensiveness and Performance in an Industry with an Unstable Environment', *Academy of Management Journal*, 27: 399–423.

Freiberg, K. and Freiberg, J. (1996). *Nuts! Southwest Airlines Crazy Recipe for Business and Personal Success*. Austin, TX: Bard Press.

Fuld, L. M. (1995). *The New Competitor Intelligence: The Complete Resource for Finding, Analyzing, and Using Information About Your Competitors*. New York: John Wiley & Sons.

Gainey, T. W. and Klaas, B. S. (2003). 'The Outsourcing of Training and Development: Factors Impacting Client Satisfaction', *Journal of Management*, 29: 207–29.

Gale, B. (1972). 'Market Share and Rate of Return', *Review of Economics and Statistics*, 412–23.

Gambetta, D. (1988). *Trust: Making and Breaking Cooperative Relations*. New York: Basil Blackwell.

Gatignon, H., Robertson, T. S., and Fein, A. J. (1997). 'Incumbent Defense Strategies Against New Product Entry', *International Journal of Research in Marketing*, 14(2): 163–76.

Gerhart, B., Trevor, C., and Graham, M. (1996). 'New Directions in Employee Compensation Research', in G. Ferris (eds.), *Research in Personnel and Human Resource Management*, 143–203.

Geringer, J. M., Tallman, S., and Olsen, D. M. (2000). 'Product and International Diversification among Japanese Multinational Firms', *Strategic Management Journal*, 21(1): 51–80.

Gerstein, M. and Reisman, H. (1983). 'Strategic Selection: Matching Executives to Business Conditions', *Sloan Management Review*, 24(2): 33–49.

Ghemawat, P. (1986). 'Wal-Mart Stores Discount Operations, Operations', Harvard Business School Case 9-387-018, Harvard Business School Publishing Division, Boston, MA.

Ghingold, M. and Johnson, B. (1997). 'Technical Knowledge as Value Added in Business Markets', *Industrial Marketing Management*, 26(3): 71–280.

Gimeno, J. (1999). 'Reciprocal Threats in Multimarket Rivalry: Staking Out "spheres of influence" in the U.S. Airline Industry', *Strategic Management Journal*, 20(2): 101–28.

Glunk, U. and Wilderom, C. P. M. (1998). 'Predictors of Organizational Performance in Small and Medium-sized Professional Service Firms', *International Journal of Technology Management*, 16(1–3): 23–36.

Godfrey, P. and Hill, C. W. L. (1995). 'The Problem of Observables in Strategic Management Research', *Strategic Management Journal*, 16: 519–33.

Goffman, E. (1959). *The Presentation of Self in Everyday Life*. New York: Doubleday.

Gomes, J. and Livdan, D. (2004). 'Optimal Diversification: Reconciling Theory and Evidence', *Journal of Finance*, 59(2): 507–35.

Gong, Y. (2003). 'Subsidiary Staffing in Multinational Enterprises: Agency, Resources, and Performance', *Academy of Management Journal*, 46: 728–39.

Goold, M. and Campbell, A. (1998). 'Desperately Seeking Synergy', *Harvard Business Review*, Sept–Oct: 131–43.

Gordon, R. A. and Howell, J. E. (1959). *Higher Education for Business*. New York: Columbia University Press.

Gort, M. (1962). *Diversification and Integration in American Industry*. Princeton, NJ: Princeton University Press.

Graham, J. R., Lemmon, M. L., and Wolf, J. G. (2002). 'Does Corporate Diversification Destroy Value?', *Journal of Finance*, 57(2): 695–721.

Granovetter, M. (1985). 'Economic Action and Social Structure: The Problem of Embeddedness', *American Journal of Sociology*, 91(3): 481–510.

Grant, R. M. (1988). 'On "Dominant Logic" Relatedness and the Link between Diversity and Performance', *Strategic Management Journal*, 9: 639–42.

____ (1991). 'The Resource-based Theory of Competitive Advantage: Implications for Strategy Formulation', *California Management Review*, Spring: 114–35.

____ (1996). 'Toward a Knowledge-based Theory of the Firm', *Strategic Management Journal*, 17(Winter Special Issue): 109–22.

Gregory, K. L. (1983). 'Native-view Paradigms: Multiple Cultures and Culture Conflicts in Organizations', *Administrative Science Quarterly*, 28: 359–76.

Greve, H. R. (1999). 'Branch Systems and Nonlocal Learning in Populations', *Advances in Strategic Management*, 16: 57–80.

Grossman, S. J. and Hart, O. (1986). 'The Costs and Benefits of Ownership: A Theory of Vertical and Lateral Integration', *Journal of Political Economy*, 97(4): 691–719.

Gulati, R. (1999). 'Network Location and Learning: The Influence of Network Resources and Firm Capabilities on Alliance Formation', *Strategic Management Journal*, 20(5): 97–420.

—— Khana, T., and Nohira, N. (1994). 'Unilateral Commitments and the Importance of Process in Alliances', *Sloan Management Review*, Spring, 35(3): 61–9.

Gunther, R. (1988). 'Chemical Bank, AT&T to Scrap Home-bank Service', *Wall Street Journal*, December 5: C21.

Gupta, A. K. (1984). 'Contingency Linkages between Strategy and General Manager Characteristics: A Conceptual Examination', *Academy of Management Review*, 9: 399–412.

—— and Govindarajan, V. (1984). 'Business Unit Strategy, Managerial Characteristics, and Business Unit Effectiveness at Strategy Implementation', *Academy of Management Journal*, 27: 25–41.

—— —— (2000). 'Knowledge Flows within Multinational Corporations', *Strategic Management Journal*, 21(4): 473–96.

Guthrie, J. and Olian, J. (1991). 'Does Context Affect Staffing Decisions? The Case of General Managers', *Personnel Psychology*, 44: 263–92.

—— Grimm, C., and Smith, K. (1991). 'Environmental Change and the Top Management Teams', *Journal of Management*, 17: 735–48.

Hall, R. (1992). 'The Strategic Analysis of Intangible Resources', *Strategic Management Journal*, 13(2): 35–144.

—— (1993). 'A Framework for Linking Intangible Resources and Capabilities to Sustainable Competitive Advantage', *Strategic Management Journal*, 18: 607–18.

Halpern, P. J. (1973). 'Empirical Estimates of the Amount and Distribution of Gains to Companies in Mergers', *Journal of Business*, 1973: 554–75.

—— (1983). 'Corporate Acquisitions: A Theory of Special Cases? A Review of Event Studies Applied to Acquisitions', *Journal of Finance*, 38: 297–317.

Hambrick, D. (1987). 'Top Management Teams: Key to Strategic Success', *California Management Review*, 30: 88–108.

Hamermesh, R. and Rosenbloom, R. S. (1989). 'Crown Cork & Seal, Inc.', Harvard Business School Case Number 9-388-096.

Hannan, M. T. and Freeman, J. (1977). 'The Population Ecology of Organizations', *American Journal of Sociology*, 82: 929–64.

Hansen, G. S. and Wernerfelt, B. (1989). 'Determinants of Firm Performance: The Relative Importance of Economic and Organizational Factors', *Strategic Management Journal*, 10: 399–411.

Hansen, M. H., Hoskisson, R. E., and Barney, J. B. (2000). 'Resolving the Opportunism Minimization-opportunity Maximization Paradox', Academy of Management paper presentation, 1999.

____ Perry, L. T., and Reese, C. S. (2004). 'A Bayesian Operationalization of the Resource-based View', *Strategic Management Journal*, 25: 1279–95.

Harel, G. H. and Tzafrir, S. S. (1999). 'The Effect of Human Resource Management Practices on the Perceptions of Organizational and Market Performance of the Firm', *Human Resource Management*, 38(3): 85–199.

Harrigan, K. R. (1983). *Strategies for Vertical Integration.* Lexington MA: Lexington Books.

____ (1985). 'Vertical Integration and Corporate Strategy', *Academy of Management Journal*, 2: 397–425.

____ (1986). 'Matching Vertical Integration Strategies to Competitive Conditions', *Strategic Management Journal*, 7: 535–55.

____ (2001). 'Strategic Flexibility in the Old and New Economies', In M. A. Hitt, R. E. Freeman, and J. S. Harrison (eds.), *The Blackwell Handbook of Strategic Management.* Oxford UK: Blackwell, pp. 97–123.

Harris, M. and Raviv, A. (1988). 'Corporate Control Contests and Capital Structure', *Journal of Financial Economics*, 20: 55–86.

Harrison, J. S., Hitt, M. A., Hoskisson, R. E., and Ireland, R. D. (1991). 'Synergies and Post-acquisition Performance: Differences versus Similarities in Resource Allocations', *Journal of Management*, 17: 173–90.

____ Hall Jr., E. H., and Nargundkar, R. (1993). 'Resource Allocation as an Outcropping of Strategic Consistency: Performance Implications', *Academy of Management Journal*, 36(5): 1026–51.

Hart, O. D. (1995). *Firms, Contracts, and Financial Structure.* Oxford: Clarendon Press.

____ and Moore, J. (1990). 'Property Rights and the Nature of the Firm', *Journal of Political Economy*, 98(6): 1119–58.

Hashimoto, M. (1981). 'Firm-specific Human Capital as a Shared Investment', *American Economic Review*, 71: 475–82.

Haspeslagh, P. C. and Jemison, D. (1987). 'Acquisitions—Myths and Realities', *Sloan Management Review*, 28: 53–8.

____ ____ (1991). *Managing Acquisitions: Creating Value through Corporate Renewal.* New York: Free Press.

Hatch, N. W. and Dyer, J. H. (2004). 'Human Capital and Learning as a Source of Sustainable Competitive Advantage', *Strategic Management Journal*, 25: 1155–78.

Hatten, K. J. and Hatten, M. L. (1987). 'Strategic Groups, Asymmetrical Mobility Barriers and Contestability', *Strategic Management Journal*, 8: 329–42.

Haunschild, P. R. and Miner, A. S. (1997). 'Modes of Interorganizational Imitation: The Effects of Outcome Salience and Uncertainty', *Administrative Science Quarterly*, 42(3): 72–500.

Hayes, R. H. and Wheelwright, S. (1984). *Restoring Our Competitive Edge.* New York: John Wiley & Sons.

Helfat, C. E. (1997). 'Know-how and Asset Complementarity and Dynamic Capability Accumulation: The Case of R&D', *Strategic Management Journal*, 18(5): 339–60.

Henderson, A. D. (1999). 'Firm Strategy and Age Dependence: A Contingent View of the Liabilities of Newness, Adolescence, & Obsolescence', *Administrative Science Quarterly*, 44(2): 281–314.

Henderson, B. D. (1979). *Henderson on Corporate Strategy.* New York: Mentor.

Henderson, J. C. and Venkatraman, N. (1993). 'Strategic Alignment: Leveraging Information Technology for Transforming Organizations', *IBM Systems Journal*, 32: 4–16.

Henderson, R. and Cockburn, I. (1994). 'Measuring Competence? Exploring Firm Effects in Pharmaceutical Research', *Strategic Management Journal*, 15: 63–84.

—— —— (1996). 'Scale, Scope and Spillovers: The Determinants of Research Productivity in Drug Discovery', *RAND Journal of Economics*, 27(1): 32–59.

Hennart, J.-F. (1988). 'A Transaction Costs Theory of Equity Joint Ventures', *Strategic Management Journal*, 9: 361–74.

Hill, C. W. L. (1990). 'Cooperation, Opportunism, and the Invisible Hand: Implications for Transaction Cost Theory', *Academy of Management Review*, 15(3): 500–13.

—— and G. R. Jones (1992). *Strategic Management Theory: An Integrated Approach.* Boston: Houghton Mifflin.

—— Hitt, M. A., and Hoskisson, R. E. (1992). 'Cooperative versus Competitive Structures in Related and Unrelated Diversified Firms', *Organization Science*, 3(4): 501–21.

Hirshleifer, J. (1980). *Price Theory and Applications*, 2nd edn. Englewood Cliffs, NJ: Prentice-Hall.

—— (1988). *Price Theory and Applications*, 4th edn. Englewood Cliffs, NJ: Prentice-Hall.

—— and Hirshleifer, D. (1998). *Price Theory and Applications*, 6th edition, Upper Saddle River, New Jersey: Prentice-Hall International Inc.

Hitt, M. A. and Ireland, R. D. (1985*a*). 'Corporate Distinctive Competence, Strategy, Industry and Performance', *Strategic Management Journal*, 6(3): 273–93.

—— —— (1985*b*). 'Strategy, Contextual Factors, and Performance', *Human Relations*, 38(8): 79–812.

—— —— (1986). 'Relationships among Corporate Level Distinctive Competencies, Diversification Strategy, Corporate Strategy and Performance', *Journal of Management Studies*, 23: 401–16.

—— Hoskisson, R. E., and Kim, H. (1997). 'International Diversification: Effects on Innovation and Firm Performance in Product-diversified Firms', *Academy of Management Journal*, 40(4): 767–98.

—— Ireland, R. D., and Hoskisson, R. E. (1997). *Strategic Management: Competitiveness and Globalization*, 2nd edn. New York: West.

Hitt, M. A., Dacin, M. T., Levitas, E., Arregle, J.-L., and Borza, A. (2000). 'Partner Selection in Emerging and Developed Market Contexts: Resource-based and Organizational Learning Perspectives', *Academy of Management Journal*, 43(3): 449–67.

——Bierman, L., Shimizu, K., and Kochhar, R. (2001). 'Direct and Moderating Effects of Human Capital in Professional Service Firms: A Resource-based Perspective', *Academy of Management Journal*, 44(1): 13–28.

——Harrison, J. S., and Ireland, R. D. (2001). *Mergers and Acquisitions.* New York: Oxford University Press.

——Ireland, R. D., and Harrison, J. S. (2001). 'Mergers and Acquisitions: A Value Creating or Destroying Strategy?', in M. A. Hitt, R. E. Freeman, and J. S. Harrison (eds.), *The Blackwell Handbook of Strategic Management.* Oxford, UK: Blackwell, pp. 384–408.

Hofer, C. and Schendel, D. (1978). *Strategy Formulation: Analytical Concepts.* St. Paul, MN: West.

Holmstrom, B. (1979). 'Moral Hazard and Observability', *Bell Journal of Economics*, 10: 74–91.

——and Milgrom, P. (1987). 'Aggregation and Linearity in the Provision of Intertemporal Incentives', *Econometrica*, 55: 303–28.

Hooley, G., Cox, T., Shipley, D., Fahy, J., Beracs, J., and Kolos, K. (1996). 'Foreign Direct Investment in Hungary: Resource Acquisition and Domestic Competitive Advantage', *Journal of International Business Studies*, 27(4): 683–709.

Hooley, G. J., Greenley, G. E., Cadogan, J. W., and Fahy, J. (2003). 'The Performance Impact of Marketing Resources', Working paper.

Hoopes, D. G. and Postrel, S. (1999). 'Shared Knowledge, "Glitches," and Product Development Performance', *Strategic Management Journal*, 20(9): 837–65.

Hopper, M. D. (1990). 'Rattling SABRE—New Ways to Compete on Information', *Harvard Business Review*, 68(3): 118–25.

Hoskisson, R. and Hitt, M. (1990). 'Antecedents and Performance Outcomes of Diversification: Review and Critique of Theoretical Perspectives', *Journal of Management*, 16: 461–509.

——Johnson, R., and Moesel, D. (1994). 'Corporate Divestiture Intensity in Restructuring Firms: Effects of Governance, Strategy, and Performance', *Academy of Management Journal*, 37: 1207–51.

Howell, W. C. and Fleishman, E. A. (1982). *Information Processing and Decision Making.* Hillsdale, NJ: L. Erlbaum.

Hrebiniak, L. G. and Snow, C. C. (1982). 'Top-Management Agreement and Organizational Performance', *Human Relations*, 35(12): 1139–57.

Hsu, J. and Wang, H. X. (2005). 'On Welfare under Cournot and Bertrand Competition in Differentiated Oligopolies', *Review of Industrial Organization*, 27(2): 185–96.

Hubbard, R. G. and Palia, D. (1999). 'A Reexamination of the Conglomerate Merger Wave in the 1960s: An Internal Capital Markets View', *Journal of Financial Economics*, LIV(3).

Huey, J. (1989). 'Wal-Mart: Will It Take the World?', *Fortune*, 119(3) January 30: 52–61.

Hult, G. T. M. and Ketchen, D. J. (2001). 'Does Market Orientation Matter? A Test of the Relationship between Positional Advantage and Performance', *Strategic Management Journal*, 22: 899–906.

——— and Nichols, E. L. (2002). 'An Examination of Cultural Competitiveness and Order Fulfillment Cycle Time within Supply Chains', *Academy of Management Journal*, 45: 577–86.

——— and Slater, S. F. (2004). 'Market Orientation and Performance: An Integration of Disparate Approaches', *Strategic Management Journal*, 26: 1173–81.

Human Resource Management, Spring 1998, 37(1): 31–46. John Wiley & Sons.

Huselid, M. A. (1995). 'The Impact of Human Resource Management Practices on Turnover, Productivity, and Corporate Financial Performance', *Academy of Management Journal*, 38: 635–72.

—— and Becker, B. E. (1997). 'The Impact of High Performance Work Systems, Implementation Effectiveness, and Alignment with Strategy on Shareholder Wealth', *Academy of Management Proceedings*, 1997: 144–8.

—— Jackson, S. E., and Schuler, R. S. (1997). 'Technical and Strategic Human Resource Management Effectiveness as Determinants of Firm Performance', *Academy of Management Journal*, 40: 171–88.

Ingham, H. and Thompson, S. (1995). 'Deregulation, Firm Capabilities and Diversifying Entry Decisions: The Case of Financial Services', *The Review of Economics and Statistics*, 77(1): 177–83.

Ingram, P. and Baum, J. A. C. (1997). 'Opportunity and Constraint: Organizations' Learning from the Operating and Competitive Experience of Industries', *Strategic Management Journal*, 18(Summer Special Issue): 75–98.

Irwin, J. G., Hoffman, J. J., and Lamont, B. T. (1998). 'The Effect of the Acquisition of Technological Innovations on Organizational Performance: A Resource-based View', *Journal of Engineering and Technology Management*, 15(1): 25–54.

Itami, H. (1987). *Mobilizing Invisible Assets.* Cambridge, MA: Harvard University Press.

Jackson, B. B. (1985). *Winning and Keeping Industrial Customers: The Dynamics of Customer Relationships.* Lexington, MA: Lexington Books.

Jackson, S. and Schuler, R. (1995). 'Understanding Human Resource Management in the Context of Organizations and Their Environments', *Annual Review of Psychology*, 46: 237–64.

Jacobsen, R. (1988). 'The Persistence of Abnormal Returns', *Strategic Management Journal*, 9: 41–58.

Jakes, J. M. and Yoches, E. R. (1989). 'Legally Speaking: Basic Principles of Patent Protection for Computer Software', *Communications of the ACM*, 32(8): 922–4.

Jarvenpaa, S. L. and Ives, B. (1990). 'Information Technology and Corporate Strategy: A View from the Top', *Information Systems Research*, 1(4): 351–76.

Jarvenpaa, S. L. and Leidner, D. E. (1999). 'An Information Company in Mexico: Extending the Resource-based View of the Firm to a Developing Country Context', *Information Systems Research.*

Jensen, M. C. (1986). 'Agency Costs of Free Cash Flows, Corporate Finance and Takeovers', *American Economic Review*, 76(2): 323–30.

—— (1988). 'Takeovers: Their Causes and Consequences', *Journal of Economic Perspectives*, 2: 21–48.

—— and Meckling, W. H. (1976). 'Theory of the Firm: Managerial Behavior, Agency Costs, and Ownership Structure', *Journal of Financial Economics*, 3: 305–60.

—— and Ruback, R. (1983). 'The Market for Corporate Control: The Scientific Evidence', *Journal of Financial Economics*, 11: 5–50.

Johnson, J. L. (1999). 'Strategic Integration in Industrial Distribution Channels: Managing the Interfirm Relationship as a Strategic Asset', *Journal of the Academy of Marketing Science*, 27(1): 4–18.

Jones, C. and Wright, P. (1992). 'An Economic Approach to Conceptualizing the Utility of Human Resource Management Practices', in K. Rowland and C. Ferris (eds.), *Research in personnel and human resource management*, 10: 271–99.

Jones, N. (1986). 'The Hallow Corporation', *Business Week*, March 3: 56–9.

Johnston, H. P. and Vitale, M. R. (1988). 'Creating Competitive Advantage with Interorganizational Information Systems', *MIS Quarterly*, 12(2): 153–65.

Judge, W. Q. and Douglas, T. J. (1998). 'Performance Implications of Incorporating Natural Environmental Issues into the Strategic Planning Process: An Empirical Assessment', *Journal of Management Studies*, 35(2): 241–62.

Kanter, R. M. (1993). 'FCB and Publicis (A): Forming the Alliance', Harvard Business School Case 9-393-099.

—— Stein, B. A., and Jick, T. D. (1992). *The Challenge of Organizational Change: How Companies Experience it and Leaders Guide it.* New York: Free Press.

Karagozoglu, N. and Lindell, M. (1998). 'Internationalization of Small and Medium-sized Technology-based Firms: An Exploratory Study', *Journal of Small Business Management*, 36(1): 44–59.

Karnoe, P. (1995). 'Competence as Process and the Social Embeddedness of Competence Building', *Academy of Management Journal*, 38: 427–31.

Katz, R. L. (1974). 'Skills of an Effective Administrator', *Harvard Business Review*, 52(5): 90–102.

Keller, J. J. and Wilson, J. W. (1986). 'Why ZapMail Finally Got Zapped. *Business Week*, 2968, October 13: 48–9.

Kennedy, A. (2000). *The End of Shareholder Value.* London: Orion Business Books.

Kettinger, W., Grover, V., Guha, S., and Segars, A. (1994). 'Strategic Information Systems Revisited: A Study in Sustainability and Performance', *MIS Quarterly*, 18(1): 31–58.

Khatri N. (2000). 'Managing Human Resource for Competitive Advantage: a Study of Companies in Singapore', *International Journal of Human Resource Management*, 11(2): 336–65.

Kimberly, J., Miles, R., and Associates (eds.) (1981). *Organizational Life Cycles*. San Francisco, IL: Jossey-Bass.

Kissler, C. (1994). 'The New Employment Contract', *Human Resource Management Journal*, 33: 335–52.

Klaas, B. S., McClendon, J., and Gainey, T. W. (1999). 'HR Outsourcing and Its Impact: The Role of Transaction Costs', *Personnel Psychology*, 52(1):13–136.

Klassen, R. D. and Whybark, D. C. (1999). 'The Impact of Environmental Technologies on Manufacturing Performance', *Academy of Management Journal*, 42(6): 599–615.

Klein, B. and Leffler, K. (1981). 'The Role of Price in Guaranteeing Quality', *Journal of Political Economy*, 89: 615–41.

—— Crawford, R. G., and Alchian, A. (1978). 'Vertical Integration, Appropriable Rents, and the Competitive Contracting Process', *Journal of Law and Economics*, 21: 297–326.

Knights, D. and McCabe, D. (1997). 'How Would You Measure Something Like That? Quality in a Retail Bank', *The Journal of Management Studies*, 34(3): 71–388.

Koch, M. J. and McGrath, R. G. (1996). 'Improving Labor Productivity: Human Resource Management Policies Do Matter', *Strategic Management Journal*, 17(5): 335–54.

Kogut, B. (1988). 'Joint Ventures: Theoretical and Empirical Perspectives', *Strategic Management Journal*, 9: 319–32.

—— (1991). 'Joint Ventures and the Option to Expand and Acquire', *Management Science*, 37(1): 19–33.

—— and Zander, U. (1992). 'Knowledge of the Firm, Combinative Capabilities, and the Replication of Technology', *Organization Science*, 3: 383–97.

—— —— (1993). 'Knowledge of the Firm and the Evolutionary Theory of the Multinational Corporation', *Journal of International Business Studies*, 24(4): 625–45.

—— —— (1996). 'What Firms Do? Coordination, Identity, and Learning', *Organization Science*, 7: 502–18.

Kohlberg, L. (1969). 'Stage and Sequence: The Cognitive-Developmental Approach to Socialization', in D. A. Goslin (ed.), *Handbook of Socialization*. New York: Rand McNally.

—— (1971). 'From Is to Ought', in T. Mischel (ed.), *Cognitive Development and Epistemology*. New York and London: Academic Press.

Kor, Y. Y. and Leblebici, H. (2005). 'How Do Interdependencies among Human Capital Deployment, Development and Diversification Strategies Affect Firm's Financial Performance?', *Strategic Management Journal*, 26: 96–985.

Kotha, S. and Nair, A. (1995). 'Strategy and Environment as Determinants of Performance: Evidence from the Japanese Machine Tool Industry', *Strategic Management Journal*, 16(7): 497–518.

Kotter, J. P. (1996). *Leading Change*. Boston, MA: Harvard Business School Press.

Kotter, J. P. and Cohen, D. S. (2002). *The Heart of Change: Real-life Stories of How People Change Their Organizations.* Boston, MA: Harvard Business School Press.

—— and Heskett, J. L. (1992). *Corporate Culture and Performance.* New York: Free Press.

Kudla, R. J. (1980). 'The Effects of Strategic Planning on Common Stock Returns', *Academy of Management Journal*, 23: 5–20.

Kuhn, T. S. (1970). *The Structure of Scientific Revolutions.* Chicago, IL: University of Chicago Press.

Kupfer, A. (1997). 'Is Lucent Really As Good As It Seems?', *Fortune.* May 26, 1997.

Labich, K. and Ballen, K. (1988). 'The Seven Keys to Business Leadership', *Fortune*, 1198(9), Oct. 24.

Lado, A. and Wilson, M. (1994). 'Human Resource Systems and Sustained Competitive Advantage: A Competency-based Perspective', *Academy of Management Review*, 19: 699–727.

Laffer, A. (1969). 'Vertical Integration by Corporations: 1929–1965', *Review of Economics and Statistics*, 51: 91–3.

Lafferty, M. (2005). 'Home PCs May Prove Point for Einstein, *Columbus Dispatch*, Tuesday, February 22: A1+.

Lamont, O. (1997). 'Cash Flow and Investment: Evidence from Internal Capital Markets', *Journal of Finance*, 52: 83–109.

Landro, L. (1995). 'Giants Talk Synergy But Few Make It Work', *Wall Street Journal*, September 25: B1+.

Lane, P. J. and Lubatkin, M. (1998). 'Relative Absorptive Capacity and Interorganizational Learning', *Strategic Management Journal*, 19(5): 461–77.

Lang, H. P. and Stulz, R. (1994). 'Tobin's q, Corporate Diversification, and Firm Performance', *Journal of Political Economy*, 102: 1248–80.

Learned, E. P., Christensen, C. R., Andrew, K. R., and Guth, W. (1969). *Business Policy.* Homewood, IL: Irwin.

Lee, J. and Miller, D. (1999). 'People Matter: Commitment to Employees, Strategy and Performance in Korean Firms', *Strategic Management Journal*, 20(6): 579–93.

Lei, D., Hitt, M. A., and Bettis, R. A. (1996). 'Dynamic Core Competences through Meta-learning and Strategic Context', *Journal of Management*, 22: 549–69.

Leiblein, M. (2003). 'The Choice of Organizational Governance Form and Performance: Predictions from Transaction Cost, Resource-based and Real Options Theories', *Journal of Management*, 29: 937–61.

—— and Miller, D. J. (2003). 'An Empirical Examination of Transaction- and Firm-level Influences on the Vertical Boundaries of the Firm', *Strategic Management Journal*, 24: 839–59.

Lenz, R. T. (1980). 'Strategic Capability: A Concept and Framework for Analysis', *Academy of Management Review*, 5: 225–34.

Leonard-Barton, D. (1990). 'A Dual Methodology for Case Studies: Synergistic Use of a Longitudinal Single Site with Replicated Multiple Sites', *Organization Science*, 1: 248–65.

Leontiades, M. and Tezel, A. (1980). 'Planning Perceptions and Planning Results', *Strategic Management Journal*, 1: 65–79.

Lepak, D. P. and Snell, S. A. (1999). 'The Human Resource Architecture: Toward a Theory of Human Capital Allocation and Development', *Academy of Management Review*, 24: 31–48.

Levine, D. I. (1993). 'Worth Waiting for Delayed Compensation, Training, and Turnover in the United States and Japan', *Journal of Labor Economics*, 11(4): 724–52.

Lewicki, R. J. and Bunker, B. B. (1994). 'Trust in Relationships: A Model of Trust Development and Decline', Working paper, Department of Management and Human Resources, The Ohio State University.

Li, M. and Ye, L. R. (1999). 'Information Technology and Firm Performance: Linking with Environmental, Strategic and Managerial Contexts', *Information & Management*, 35(1): 3–51.

Li, T. and Calantone, R. J. (1998). 'The Impact of Market Knowledge Competence on New Product Advantage: Conceptualization and Empirical Examination', *Journal of Marketing*, 62(4): 3–29.

Lieberman, M. B. (1982). 'The Learning Curve, Pricing and Market Structure in the Chemical Processing Industries', Unpublished Doctoral Dissertation, Harvard University.

—— (1987). 'The Learning Curve, Diffusion, and Competitive Strategy', *Strategic Management Journal*, 8: 441–52.

—— and Montgomery, D. B. (1988). 'First Mover Advantages', *Strategic Management Journal*, 9: 41–58.

Liebeskind, J. P. (1996). 'Knowledge, Strategy, and the Theory of the Firm', *Strategic Management Journal*, 17(Winter Special Issue): 93–107.

Lindbolm, C. (1959). 'The Science of Muddling Through', *Public Administration Review*, 19: 79–88.

Linnehan, F. and De Carolis, D. (2005). 'Strategic Frameworks for Understanding Employer Participation in School-to-Work Programs', *Strategic Management Journal*, 26: 523–39.

Lippman, S. and Rumelt, R. (1982). 'Uncertain Imitability: An Analysis of Interfirm Differences in Efficiency under Competition', *Bell Journal of Economics*, 13: 418–38.

—— —— (2003*a*). 'The Payments Perspective: Micro-foundations of Resource Analysis', *Strategic Management Journal*, 24(10): 903–27.

—— —— (2003*b*). 'A Bargaining Perspective on Resource Advantage', *Strategic Management Journal*, 24(11): 1069–86.

Lorange, P. (1980). *Corporate Planning: An Executive Viewpoint*. Englewood Cliffs, NJ: Prentice-Hall.

Lorenzoni, G. and Lipparini, A. (1999). 'The Leveraging of Interfirm Relationships as a Distinctive Organizational Capability: A Longitudinal Study', *Strategic Management Journal*, 20(4): 317–38.

Louis, M. (1983). 'Culture: Yes. Organization: No', Paper presented at the annual meeting of the Academy of Management, Dallas.

Lubatkin, M. (1983). 'Merger and the Performance of the Acquiring Firm', *Academy of Management Review*, 8: 218–25.

—— (1987). 'Merger Strategies and Stockholder Value', *Strategic Management Journal*, 8: 39–53.

—— and Chatterjee, S. (1994). 'Extending Portfolio Theory into the Domain of Corporate Diversification: Does It Apply?', *Academy of Management Journal*, 37(1): 109–36.

—— and O'Neil, H. (1987). 'Merger Strategies and Capital Market Risk', *Academy of Management Journal*, 30(4): 665–84.

Luo, Y. D. (1999). 'The Structure-performance Relationship in a Transitional Economy: An Empirical Study of Multinational Alliances in China', *Journal of Business Research*, 46(1): 15–30.

Luo, Y. and Peng, M. W. (1999). 'Learning to Compete in a Transition Economy: Experience, Environment, and Performance', *Journal of International Business Studies*, 30(2): 269–96.

MacDuffie, J. (1995). 'Human Resource Bundles and Manufacturing Performance: Organizational Logic and Flexible Production Systems in the World Auto Industry', *Industrial and Labor Relations Review*, 49: 197–221.

Mackey, A. (2006). 'Dynamics in Executive Labor Markets: CEO Effects, Executive-firm Matching, and Rent Sharing', The Ohio State University: Unpublished doctoral dissertation.

Mackey, T. B. and Barney, J. B. (2006). 'Is There a Diversification Discount? Diversification, Payout Policy, and the Value of a Firm', Unpublished working paper, The Ohio State University.

Maddigan, R. (1979). 'The Impact of Vertical Integration on Business Performance', Unpublished Doctoral Dissertation, Indiana University at Bloomington.

Mahmood, M. and Soon, S. K. (1991) 'A Comprehensive Model for Measuring the Potential Impact of Information Technology on Organizational Strategic Variables', *Decision Sciences*, 22: 869–97.

Mahoney, J. T. (1992). 'The Choice of Organizational Form: Vertical Financial Ownership versus Other Methods of Vertical Integration', *Strategic Management Journal*, 13: 559–84.

—— (1993). 'Strategic Management and Determinism: Sustaining the Conversation', *The Journal of Management Studies*, 30(1): 173–91.

—— (2001). 'A Resource-based Theory of Sustainable Rents', *Journal of Management*, 27(6): 651–61.

—— and Pandian, J. R. (1992). 'The Resource-based View within the Conversation of Strategic Management', *Strategic Management Journal*, 13: 363–80.

—— Huff, A. S., and Huff, J. O. (1993). 'Toward a New Social Contract Theory in Organization Science', Working paper 93-0136, Department of Management, University of Illinois at Urbana-Champaign.

Maignan, I., Ferrell, O. C., and Hult, G. T. M. (1999). 'Corporate Citizenship: Cultural Antecedents and Business Benefits', *Journal of the Academy of Marketing Science*, 27(4): 455–69.

Maijoor, S. and van Witteloostuijn, A. (1996). 'An Empirical Test of the Resource-based Theory: Strategic Regulation in the Dutch Audit Industry', *Strategic Management Journal*, 1: 549–69.

Makadok, R. (1998). 'Can First-mover and Early-mover Advantages Be Sustained in an Industry with Low Barriers to Entry/Imitation?', *Strategic Management Journal*, 19(7): 683–96.

—— (1999). 'Interfirm Differences in Scale Economies and the Evolution of Market Shares', *Strategic Management Journal*, 20(10): 935–52.

—— (2001). 'Towards a Synthesis of the Resource-based and Dynamic-capability Views of Rent Creation', *Strategic Management Journal*, 22: 387–401.

—— and Barney, J. B. (2001). 'Strategic Factor Market Intelligence: An Application of Information Economics to Strategy Formulation and Competitor Intelligence', *Management Science*, 47: 1621–38.

Makhija, M. (2003). 'Comparing the Resource-based and Market-based Views of the Firm: Empirical Evidence from Czech Privatization', *Strategic Management Journal*, 24: 433–51.

Malone, T. W., Yates, J., and Benjamin, R. I. (1989). 'The Logic of Electronic Markets', *Harvard Business Review*, 67(3): 166–70.

Mancke, R. (1974). 'Causes of Interfirm Profitability Differences: A New Interpretation of the Evidence', *Quarterly Journal of Economics*, 88: 181–93.

Mandelker, G. (1974). 'Risk and Return: The Case of Merging Firms', *Journal of Financial Economics*, 1974: 303–35.

Mansfield, E. (1985). 'How Rapidly Does New Industrial Technology Leak Out?', *Journal of Industrial Economics*, 34: 217–33.

—— Schwartz, M., and Wagner, S. (1981). 'Imitation Costs and Patents: An Empirical Study', *Economic Journal*, 91: 907–18.

Marcus, A. and Geffen, D. (1998). 'The Dialectics of Competency Acquisition: Pollution Prevention in Electric Generation', *Strategic Management Journal*, 19(12): 1145–68.

Maritan, C. A. (2001). 'Capital Investment as Investing in Organizational Capabilities: An Empirically Grounded Process Model', *Academy of Management Journal*, 44: 513–31.

Markides, C. and Williamson, P. J. (1994). 'Related Diversification, Core Competencies, and Corporate Performance', *Strategic Management Journal*, 15: 149–65.

—— —— (1996). 'Corporate Diversification and Organization Structure: A Resource-based View', *Academy of Management Journal*, 39: 340–67.

Martin, J., Feldman, M. S., Hatch, M. J., and Sitkin, S. (1983). 'The Uniqueness Paradox in Organizational Stories', *Administrative Science Quarterly*, 28: 438–53.

Maskell, P. (1998). 'Low-tech Competitive Advantages and the Role of Proximity: The Danish Wooden Furniture Industry', *European Urban And Regional Studies*, 5(2): 99–118.

Maskell, P. and Malmberg, A. (1999). 'Localised Learning and Industrial Competitiveness', *Cambridge Journal of Economics*, 23(2): 167–85.

Mata, F. J., Fuerst, W. L., and Barney, J. B. (1995). 'Information Technology and Sustained Competitive Advantage: A Resource-based Analysis', *MIS Quarterly*, 19(4): 487.

Matsusaka, J. G. (1993). 'Takeover Motives During Conglomerate Merger Wave', *RAND Journal of Economics*, 24: 357–9.

Mauri, A. J. and Michaels, M. P. (1998). 'Firm and Industry Effects within Strategic Management: An Empirical Examination', *Strategic Management Journal*, 19(3): 211–19.

Mayer, K. J. and Argyres, N. S. (2004). 'Learning to Contract: Evidence from the Personal Computer Industry', *Organization Science*, 15(4): 394–410.

McEvily, B. and Zaheer, A. (1999). 'Bridging Ties: A Source of Firm Heterogeneity in Competitive Capabilities', *Strategic Management Journal*, 20(12): 1133–56.

McFarlan, F. W. (1981). 'Portfolio Approach to Information Systems', *Harvard Business Review*, 59(5): 142–50.

—— (1984). 'Information Technology Changes the Way You Compete', *Harvard Business Review*, 62(3, May–June 1984): 98–103.

—— and Stoddard, D. (1986). 'OTISLINE', Harvard Business School Case 9-186-304, Harvard Business School Publishing Division, Boston, MA.

McGahan, A. M. and Porter, M. E. (1997). 'How Much Does Industry Matter, Really?', *Strategic Management Journal*, 18 (Special Issue): 15–30.

McGaughey, S. L., Liesch, P. W., and Poulson, D. (2000). 'An Unconventional Approach to Intellectual Property Protection: The Case of an Australian Firm Transferring Shipbuilding Technologies to China', *Journal of World Business*, 35(1): 1–20.

McGee, J. and Thomas, H. (1986). 'Strategic Groups: Theory, Research and Taxonomy', *Strategic Management Journal*, 7: 141–60.

McGee, J. E., Dowling, M. J. and Megginson, W. L. (1995). 'Cooperative Strategy and New Venture Performance: The Role of Business Strategy and Management Experience', *Strategic Management Journal*, 16(7): 565–80.

McGrath, R. G., MacMillan, I. C., and Venkataraman, S. (1995). 'Defining and Developing a Competence: A Strategic Process Paradigm', *Strategic Management Journal*, 16(4): 251–75.

—— Tsui, M.-H., Venkataraman, S., and MacMillan, I. C. (1996). 'Innovation, Competitive Advantage and Rent: A Model and Test', *Management Science*, 42(3): 389–403.

McGuire, J. (2000). 'Corporate Governance and Growth Potential: An Empirical Analysis', *Corporate Governance-An International Review*, 8(1): 32–42.

McKelvey, W. (1982). *Organizational Systematics: Taxonomy, Evolution, and Classification.* Los Angeles: University of California Press.

McMahan, C. and Woodman, R. (1992). 'The Current Practice of Organization Development within the Firm: A Survey of Large Industrial Corporations', *Group and Organization Studies*, 17: 117–34.

McMahan, G. C., Virick, M., and Wright, P. M. (1999). 'Alternative Theoretical Perspective for Strategic Human Resources Management Revised; Progress, Problems, and Prospects', in P. M. Wright, L. D. Dyer, J. W. Boudreau, and G. T. Milkovich (eds.), *Research in Personnel and Human Resources Management* (Suppl. 4). Greenwich, CT: JAI Press, pp. 99–122.

Menon, A., Bharadwaj, S. G., Adidam, P. T., and Edison, S. W. (1999). 'Antecedents and Consequences of Marketing Strategy Making: A Model and a Test', *Journal of Marketing*, 63(2): 8–40.

Merton, R. K. (1957). 'Manifest and Latent Functions', In *Social Theory and Social Structure.* New York: Free Press, 5–10.

Michael, S. C. and Robbins, D. K. (1998). 'Retrenchment among Small Manufacturing Firms During Recession', *Journal of Small Business Management*, 36(3): 5–45.

Miles, R. and Cameron, K. (1982). *Coffin Nails and Corporate Strategy.* Englewood Cliffs, NJ: Prentice-Hall.

Milgrom, P. and Roberts, J. (1992). *Economics, Organization and Management.* Englewood Cliffs, NJ: Prentice-Hall.

Miller, D. (1996). 'A Preliminary Typology of Organizational Learning: Synthesizing the Literature', *Journal of Management*, 22(3): 485–505.

____ and Shamsie, J. (1996). 'The Resource-based View of the Firm in Two Environments: The Hollywood Film Studios from 1936 to 1965', *Academy of Management Journal*, 39: 519–43.

____ and Toulouse, J.-M. (1998). 'Quasi-rational Organizational Responses: Functional and Cognitive Sources of Strategic Simplicity', *Revue Canadienne des Sciences de l'Administration*, 15(3): 230–44.

Miller, D. J. (2000). 'Corporate Diversification, Relatedness, and Performance', Unpublished dissertation, Fisher College of Business, The Ohio State University, 171 pages.

____ (2004). 'Firms' Technological Resources and the Performance Effects of Diversification: A Longitudinal Study', *Strategic Management Journal*, 25: 1097–119.

Miller, K. D. (1992). 'A Framework for Integrated Risk Management in International Business', *Journal of International Business Studies*, 23: 311–31.

____ (1998). 'Economic Exposure and Integrated Risk Management', *Strategic Management Journal*, 19: 497–514.

____ and Chen, W. (2003). 'Risk and Firms' Costs', *Strategic Organization*, 1(4): 335–82.

Mintzberg, H. (1978). 'Patterns in Strategy Formation', *Management Science*, 24: 934–48.

____ and McHugh, A. (1985). 'Strategy Formation in Adhocracy', *Administrative Science Quarterly*, 30: 160–97.

Mishra, A. and Mishra, K. (1994). 'The Role of Trust in Effective Downsizing Strategies', *Human Resource Management*, 33: 261–80.

Moingeon, B., Ramanantsoa, B., Metais, E., and Orton, J. D. (1998). 'Another Look at Strategy-structure Relationships: The Resource-based View', *European Management Journal*, 16(3): 297–305.

Montgomery, C. A. (1979). 'Diversification, Market Structure and Firm Performance: An Extension of Rumelt's Model', Unpublished dissertation, Purdue University.

—— (1994). 'Corporate Diversification', *Journal of Economic Perspectives*, 8(3): 163–78.

—— and Wernerfelt, B. (1988). 'Diversification, Ricardian Rents, and Tobin's q', *Rand Journal of Economics*, 19: 623–32.

Morita, M. and Flynn, E. J. (1997). 'The Linkage among Management Systems, Practices and Behaviour [sic.] in Successful Manufacturing Strategy', *International Journal of Operations & Production Management*, 17(10): 967–93.

Morris, S. A. (1997). 'Environmental Pollution and Competitive Advantage: An Exploratory Study of U.S. Industrial-goods Manufacturers', *The Academy of Management Proceedings*, 1997: 411–15.

Mosakowski, E. (1998). 'Managerial Prescriptions under the Resource-based View of Strategy: The Example of Motivational Techniques', *Strategic Management Journal*, 19: 1169–82.

Mossin, J. (1973). *Theory of Financial Markets*. Englewood Cliffs, NJ: Prentice-Hall.

Mowery, D. C., Oxley, J. E., and Silverman, B. S. (1998). 'Technological Overlap and Interfirm Cooperation: Implications for the Resource-based View of the Firm', *Research Policy*, 27(5): 507–23.

Mutinelli, M. and Piscitello, L. (1998). 'The Entry Mode Choice of MNEs: An Evolutionary Approach', *Research Policy*, 27(5): 491–506.

Myers, S. C. and Majluf, N. S. (1984). 'Corporate Financing and Investment Decisions When Firms Have Information That Investors Do Not Have', *Journal of Financial Economics*, 13: 187–221.

Nachum, L. and Rolle, J. D. (1999). 'The National Origin of the Ownership Advantages of Firms', *Service Industries Journal*, 19(4): 17–48.

Nayyar, P. (1990). 'Information Asymmetries: A Source of Competitive Advantage for Diversified Service Firms', *Strategic Management Journal*, 11: 513–19.

Nelson, R. and Winter, S. (1982). *An Evolutionary Theory of Economic Change*. Cambridge, MA: Belknap Press.

Neo, B. S. (1988). 'Factors Facilitating the Use of Information Technology for Competitive Advantage: An Exploratory Study', *Information and Management*, 15: 191–201.

Nickerson, J. A. and Silverman, B. S. (1998). 'Economic Performance, Strategic Position, and Vulnerability to Ecological Pressures among US Interstate Motor Carriers', *Advances in Strategic Management*, 15: 37–61.

Niederman, F., Brancheau, J. C., and Wetherbe, J. C. (1991). 'Information Systems Management Issues for the 1990s', *MIS Quarterly*, 15(4): 475–95.

O'Brien, J. (1983). *Computers and Information Processing in Business*. Homewood, IL: Irwin.

Oktemgil, M., Greenley, G. E., and Broderick, A. J. (2000). 'An Empirical Study of Isolating Mechanisms in UK Companies', *European Journal of Operational Research*, 122(3): 638–55.

Oliver, C. (1997). 'Sustainable Competitive Advantage: Combining Institutional and Resource Based Views', *Strategic Management Journal*, 18: 697–713.

Ouchi, W. G. (1980). 'Markets, Bureaucracies, and Clans', *Administrative Science Quarterly*, 25: 121–41.

—— (1981). *Theory* Z. Reading, MA: Addison-Wesley.

Palepu, K. (1985). 'Diversification Strategy, Profit Performance and the Entropy Measure', *Strategic Management Journal*, 6: 239–55.

Palich, L. E., Cardinal, L. B., and Miller, C. C. (2000). 'Curvilinearity in the Diversification Performance Linkage: An Examination of over Three Decades of Research', *Strategic Management Journal*, 21: 155–74.

Park, N. K., Mezias, J. M., and Song, J. (2004). 'A Resource-based View of Strategic Alliances and Firm Value in the Electronic Marketplace', *Journal of Management*, 30: 7–27.

Pearce, I. A., Freeman, E. B., and Robinson, R. B. (1987). 'The Tenuous Link between Formal Strategic Planning and Financial Performance', *Academy of Management Review*, 12: 658–75.

Peffer, J. and Salanak, G. R. (1978). *The External Control of Organizations: A Resource Dependence Perspective*. New York: Harper and Row.

Pennings, J. M., Lee, K., and van Witteloostuijn, A. (1998). 'Human Capital, Social Capital, and Firm Dissolution', *Academy of Management Journal*, 41(4): 425–40.

Penrose, E. T. (1959). *The Theory of the Growth of the Firm*. New York: John Wiley & Sons.

Perrow, C. (1986). *Complex Organizations. A Critical Essay*, 3rd edn. New York: Random House.

Perry, M. K. (1989). 'Vertical Integration: Determinants and Effects', in R. Schmalensee and R. Willg (eds.), *The Handbook of Industrial Organization*. Amsterdam: Elsevier Science, pp. 189–235.

Peteraf, M. A. (1993). 'The Cornerstones of Competitive Advantage: A Resource-based View', *Strategic Management Journal*, 14: 179–91.

—— (2001). 'Of Cornerstones and Building Blocks: Resource-based Theory in Perspective', Working paper.

—— and Barney, J. B. (2003). 'Unraveling the Resource-based Triangle', *Managerial and Decision Economics*, 24: 309–23.

Peters, T. J. (1978). 'Symbols, Patterns, and Settings: An Optimistic Case for Getting Things Done', *Organizational Dynamics*, 7(2): 2–23.

—— and Waterman, R. H. (1982, 2004). *In Search of Excellence*. New York: Harper and Row.

Pettigrew, A. M. (1979). 'On Studying Organizational Cultures', *Administrative Science Quarterly*, 24: 570–81.

Pettus, M. L. (2001). 'The Resource-based View as a Developmental Growth Process: Evidence from the Deregulated Trucking Industry', *Academy of Management Journal*, 44: 878–96.

Pfeffer, J. (1994). *Competitive Advantage through People: Unleashing the Power of the Workforce*. Boston, MA: Harvard Business School Press.

Pierson, F. C. (1959). *The Education of American Businessmen: A Study of University-College Programs in Business Administration*. New York: McGraw-Hill.

Pisano, G. P. (1994). 'Knowledge, Integration, and the Locus of Learning: An Empirical Analysis of Process Development', *Strategic Management Journal*, 15(Winter Special Issue): 85–100.

Pisano, G. (1995). 'The New Logic of High Tech R&D', *Harvard Business Review*, Sept–Oct.: 93–7.

Polanyi, M. (1958). *Personal Knowledge*. Chicago, IL: University of Chicago Press.

____ (1962). *Personal Knowledge: Towards a Post Critical Philosophy*. London: Routledge.

Poppo, L. and Zenger, T. (1995). 'Opportunism, Routines, and Boundary Choices: A Comparative Test of Transaction Cost and Resource-based Explanations for Make-or-Buy Decisions', *Academy of Management Journal*, 38(1): 42–6.

____ ____ (1998). 'Testing Alternative Theories of the Firm: Transaction Cost, Knowledge-based, and Measurement Explanations for Make-or-Buy Decisions in Information Services', *Strategic Management Journal*, 19(9): 853–78.

Porras, J. and Berg, P. O. (1978*a*). 'Research Methodology in Organization Development: An Analysis and Critique', *Journal of Applied Behavioral Science*, 14(2): 151–74.

____ ____ (1978*b*). 'The Impact of Organization Development', *Academy of Management Review*, 3: 249–66.

Porter, M. E. (1979). 'How Competitive Forces Shape Strategy', *Harvard Business Review*, March–April: 137–56.

____ (1980). *Competitive Strategy*. New York: Free Press.

____ (1981). 'The Contribution of Industrial Organization to Strategic Management', *Academy of Management Review*, 6: 609–20.

____ (1985). *Competitive Advantage*. New York: Free Press.

____ (1987). 'From Competitive Advantage to Corporate Strategy', *Harvard Business Review*, May–June: 43–59.

____ (1990). 'Why Are Firms Successful?', Paper presented at the Fundamental Issues in Strategy Conference, Napa, CA.

____ (1991). 'Towards a Dynamic Theory of Strategy', *Strategic Management Journal*, 12: 95–118.

____ and Millar, V. E. (1985). 'How Information Gives You Competitive Advantage', *Harvard Business Review*, 63(4): 149–60.

____ and Wayland, R. (1991). 'Coca-Cola vs Pepsi and the Soft Drink Industry', Harvard Business School Case no. 9-391-179.

Postin, M. (1988). 'The Hallow Corporation', *Executive Excellence*, 5: 11–12.

Postrel, S. (2002). 'Islands of Shared Knowledge: Specialization and Mutual Understanding in Problem-Solving Teams', *Organization Science*, 13(3): 303–20.

—— (2004). 'Competitive Advantage: A Synthesis', Southern Methodist University working paper.

Powell, T. C. (1995). 'Total Quality Management as Competitive Advantage: A Review and Empirical Study', *Strategic Management Journal*, 16(1): 15–37.

—— and Dent-Micallef, A. (1997). 'Information Technology as Competitive Advantage: The Role of Human, Business, and Technology Resources', *Strategic Management Journal*, 18: 375–405.

Prahalad, C. K. and Bettis, R. A. (1986). 'The Dominant Logic: A New Linkage between Diversity and Performance', *Strategic Management Journal*, 7: 485–501.

—— and Hamel, G. (1990). 'The Core Competence of the Corporation', *Harvard Business Review*, June: 79–91.

Priem, R. L. and Butler, J. E. (2001). 'Is the Resource-based "View" a Useful Perspective for Strategic Management Research?', *Academy of Management Review*, 26(1): 22–40.

Quick, J. C. (1992). 'Crafting an Organizational Culture: Herb's Hand at Southwest Airlines', *Organizational Dynamics*, 21: 45–56.

Quinn, J. B. (1980). *Strategies for Change*. Homewood, IL: Irwin.

Rajan, R. G. and Zingales, L. (1998). 'Power in a Theory of the Firm', *The Quarterly Journal of Economics*, 387–432.

—— —— (2001). 'The Firm as a Dedicated Hierarchy: A Theory of the Origin and the Growth of Firms', *The Quarterly Journal of Economics*, 805–51.

—— Servaes, H. and Zingales, L. (2000). 'The Cost of Diversity: The Diversification Discount and Inefficient Investment', *Journal of Finance*, 55: 35–80.

Ramanujam, V. and Varadarajan, P. (1989). 'Research on Corporate Diversification: A Synthesis', *Strategic Management Journal*, 10: 523–51.

Rao, H. (1994). 'The Social Construction of Reputation—Certification Contests, Legitimation, and the Survival of Organizations in the American Automobile-Industry, 1895–1912', *Strategic Management Journal*, 15(Special Winter Issue): 29–44.

Rangone, A. (1999). 'A Resource-based Approach to Strategy Analysis in Small-Medium Sized Enterprises', *Small Business Economics*, 12(3): 233–48.

Rasmussen, J. (1986). *Information Processing and Human Machine Interaction*. New York: North Holland.

Ray, G. (2000). 'Information Systems and Competitive Advantage: A Process Oriented Theory', Unpublished dissertation, Fisher College of Business, The Ohio State University.

—— Barney, J. B., and Muhanna, W. A. (2004). 'Capabilities, Business Processes, and Competitive Advantage: Choosing the Dependent Variable in Empirical Tests of the Resource-based View', *Strategic Management Journal*, 25: 23–37.

—— Muhanna, W. A., and Barney, J. B. (2005). 'Information Technology and the Performance of the Customer Service Process: A Resource-based Analysis', *MIS Quarterly*, 29: 625–52.

Reed, R. and DeFillippi, R. (1990). 'Causal Ambiguity, Barriers to Imitation, and Sustainable Competitive Advantage', *Academy of Management Review*, 15: 88–102.

Reed, R., Lemak, D. J., and Montgomery, J. C. (1996). 'Beyond Process: TQM Content and Firm Performance', *The Academy of Management Review*, 21(1): 173–202.

Reich, B. H. and Benbasat, I. (1990). 'An Empirical Investigation of Factors Influencing the Success of Customer-Oriented Strategic Systems', *Information Systems Research*, 1(3): 325–47.

Reichheld, F. (1996). *The Loyalty Effect: The Hidden Force Behind Growth, Profits, and Lasting Value*. Boston, MA: Harvard Business School Press.

Rhyne, L. C. (1986). 'The Relationship of Strategic Planning to Financial Performance', *Strategic Management Journal*, 7: 423–36.

Ricardo, D. (1817). *Principles of Political Economy and Taxation*. London: J. Murray.

—— (1966). *Economic Essays*. New York: A.M. Kelly.

Richard, O. C. (2000). 'Racial Diversity, Business Strategy, and Firm Performance: A Resource-based View', *Academy of Management Journal*, 43(2): 164–77.

Riley, P. (1983). 'A Structurationist Account of Political Cultures', *Administrative Science Quarterly*, 28: 414–37.

Ring, P. and Van de Ven, A. (1994). 'Developmental Processes of Cooperative Interorganizational Relationships', *Academy of Management Review*, 19: 90–118.

Riorden, M. and Williamson, O. (1985). 'Asset Specificity and Economic Organization', *International Journal of Economic Organization*, 3: 365–78.

Robins, J. and Wiersema, M. F. (1995). 'A Resource-based Approach to the Multi-business Firm: Empirical Analysis of Portfolio Interrelationships and Corporate Financial Performance', *Strategic Management Journal*, 16: 277–99.

Roll, R. (1985). 'The Hubris Hypothesis', Unpublished, Graduate School of Management, UCLA.

Ross, J. W., Beath, C. M., and Goodhue, D. L. (1996). 'Develop Long-term Competitiveness through IT Assets', *Sloan Management Review*, 38: 31–43.

Rouse, M. J. and Dallenbach, U. S. (1999). 'Rethinking Research Methods for the Resource-based Perspective: Isolating Sources of Sustainable Competitive Advantage', *Strategic Management Journal*, 20: 487–94.

Rousseau, D. and Greller, M. (1994). 'Guest Editors; Overview: Psychological Contracts and Human Resource Practices', *Human Resource Management Journal*, 33: 383–4.

Ruback, R. (1982). 'The Conoco Takeover and Stockholder Returns', *Sloan Management Review*, 23: 13–33.

Ruiz-Navarro, J. (1998). 'Turnaround and Renewal in a Spanish Shipyard', *Long Range Planning*, 31(1): 51–9.

Rukstad, M. G. and Horn, J. (1989). 'Caterpillar and the Construction Equipment Industry in 1988', Harvard Business School Case No.9-389-097, Boston, MA.

Rumelt, P. P. (1987). 'Theory, Strategy, and Entrepreneurship', in D. J. Teece (ed.), *The Competitive Challenge*. Cambridge, MA: Ballinger Publishing, pp. 137–58.

Rumelt, R. (1974). *Strategy, Structure, and Economic Performance.* Cambridge, MA: Harvard University Press.

—— (1982). 'Diversification Strategy and Profitability', *Strategic Management Journal*, 3: 359–69.

—— (1984). 'Towards a Strategic Theory of the Firm', in R. Lamb (ed.), *Competitive Strategic Management.* Englewood Cliffs, NJ: Prentice-Hall, pp. 556–70.

—— (1991). 'How Much Does Industry Matter?', *Strategic Management Journal*, 12: 167–85.

—— and Wensley, J. R. C. (1981*a*). 'Market Share and the Rate of Return: Testing the Stochastic Hypothesis', Unpublished, Graduate School of Management, UCLA.

—— and Wensley, R. (1981*b*). 'In Search of the Market Share Effect', in K. Chung (ed.), *Academy of Management Proceedings*, 1981: 2–6.

—— Schendel, D., and Teece, D. (1991). 'Strategic Management and Economics', *Strategic Management Journal*, 12: 5–29.

Russo, M. V. and Fouts, P. A. (1997). 'A Resource-based Perspective on Corporate Environmental Performance and Profitability', *Academy of Management Journal*, 40(3): 534–59.

Sabel, C. F. (1993). 'Studied Trust: Building New Forms of Cooperation in a Volatile Economy', *Human Relations*, 46(9): 1133–70.

Sakakibara, M. (1997). 'Heterogeneity of Firm Capabilities and Cooperative Research and Development: An Empirical Examination of Motives', *Strategic Management Journal*, 18 (Special Summer Issue): 143–64.

Salter, M. and Weinhold, W. (1979). *Diversification through Acquisition: Strategies for Creating Economic Value.* New York: Free Press.

Sarasvathy, S. D. (2001). 'Causation and Effectuation: Toward a Theoretical Shift from Economic Inevitability to Entrepreneurial Contingency', *Academy of Management Review*, 26(2): 243–88.

Sargent, T. J. (1987). *Macroeconomic Theory*, 2nd edn. Academic Press.

Schall, L. D. (1972). 'Asset Valuation, Firm Investment, and Firm Diversification', *Journal of Business*, 1972: 11–28.

Schankerman, M. (1998). 'How Valuable is Patent Protection? Estimates by Technology Field', *The Rand Journal of Economics*, 29(1): 77–107.

Schein, E. H. (1983). 'The Role of the Founder in Creating Organizational Culture', *Organizational Dynamics*, 12(1): 13–28.

—— (1999). *The Corporate Culture Survival Guide.* New York: Jossey-Bass.

Scherer, F. M. (1980). *Industrial Market Structure and Economic Performance*, 2nd edn. Boston, MA: Houghton-Mifflin.

Schipper, K. and Thompson, R. (1983). 'Evidence on the Capitalized Value of Merger Activity for Merging Firms', *Journal of Financial Economics*, 11: 85–119.

Schlesinger, L. and Zornitsky, J. (1991). 'Job Satisfaction, Service Capability, and Customer Satisfaction: An Examination of Linkages and Management Implications', *Human Resource Planning*, 14: 141–50.

Schmalensee, R. (1985). 'Do Markets Differ Much?', *American Economic Review*, 75: 341–51.

Schmit, M. and Allscheid, S. (1995). 'Employee Attitudes and Customer Satisfaction: Making Theoretical and Empirical Connections', *Personnel Psychology*, 48: 521–36.

Schneider, B. and Bowen, D. (1985). 'Employee and Customer Perceptions of Service in Banks: Replication and Extension', *Journal of Applied Psychology*, 70: 423–33.

Schoenecker, T. S. and Cooper, A. C. (1998). 'The Role of Firm Resources and Organizational Attributes in Determining Entry Timing: A Cross-industry Study', *Strategic Management Journal*, 19(12): 1127–43.

Schroeder, R. G., Bates, K. A., and Junttila, M. A. (2002). 'A Resource-based View of Manufacturing Strategy and the Relationship to Manufacturing Performance', *Strategic Management Journal*, 23: 105–17.

Schuler, R. S. (1992). 'Strategic Human Resource Management: Linking the People with the Strategic needs of the Business', *Organizational Dynamics*, Summer: 18–31.

—— and Jackson, S. E. (1987). 'Linking Competitive Strategies with Human Resource Management Practices', *Academy of Management Executive*, 1: 200–19.

—— and MacMillan, I. (1984). 'Gaining Competitive Advantage through Human Resource Practices', *Human Resource Management*, 23: 241–56.

Schumpeter, J. (1934). *The Theory of Economic Development*. Cambridge: Harvard University Press.

—— (1950). *Capitalism, Socialism and Democracy*, 3rd edn. New York: Harper and Row.

Schwartz, H. and Davis, S. (1981). 'Matching Corporate Culture and Business Strategy', *Organizational Dynamics*, 10(3): 30–48.

Scott, J. H. (1977). 'On the Theory of Conglomerate Mergers', *Journal of Finance*, 32(4): 1235–50.

Segal, I. R. (1998). 'Monopoly and Soft Budget Constraint', *Rand Journal of Economics*, 29(3): 596–609.

Segev, E., Raveh, A. and Farjoun, M. (1999). 'Conceptual Maps of the Leading MBA Programs in the United States: Core Courses, Concentration Areas, and the Ranking of the School', *Strategic Management Journal*, 20(6): 549–65.

Selznick, P. (1957). *Leadership in Administration*. New York: Harper and Row.

Senge, P. (1990). *The Fifth Discipline*. New York: Doubleday.

Shamsie, J. (2003). 'The Context of Dominance: An Industry-driven Framework for Exploiting Reputation', *Strategic Management Journal*, 24: 199–215.

—— Phelps, C., and Kuperman, J. (2004). 'Better Late Than Never: A Study of Late Entrants in Household Electrical Equipment', *Strategic Management Journal*, 25: 69–84.

Shane, S. 2004. *A General Theory of Entrepreneurship: The Individual-Opportunity Nexus*. Northampton, MA: E. Elgar.

—— and Venkataraman, S. (2000). 'The Promise of Entrepreneurship as a Field of Research', *Academy of Management Review*, 25(1): 217–26.

Sharma, S. and Vredenburg, H. (1998). 'Proactive Corporate Environmental Strategy and the Development of Competitively Valuable Organizational Capabilities', *Strategic Management Journal*, 19: 729–53.

Shavell, S. (1979). 'Risk Sharing and Incentives in the Principal and Agent Relationship', *Bell Journal of Economics*, Spring: 55–73.

Shenkar, O. and Li, J. T. (1999). 'Knowledge Search in International Cooperative Ventures', *Organizational Science*, 10(2):134–43.

Sherer, P. D., Rogovsky, N., and Wright, N. (1998). 'What Drives Employment Relationships in Taxicab Organizations? Linking Agency to Firm Capabilities and Strategic Opportunities', *Organization Science*, 9(1): 34–48.

Sherman, S. (1992). 'Are Strategic Alliances Working?', *Fortune*, September 21: 77–8.

Shin, H. and Stulz, R. (1998). 'Are Internal Capital Markets Efficient?', *Quarterly Journal of Economics*, 113: 532–51.

Shleifer, A. (2000). *Inefficient Markets: An Introduction to Behavioral Finance*. New York: Oxford University Press.

Short, H., Keasey, K., Wright, M., and Hull, A. (1999). 'Corporate Governance: From Accountability to Enterprise', *Accounting and Business Research*, 29: 337–52.

Shroeder, R. G., Bates, K. A., and Junttila, M. A. (2002). 'A Resource-based View of Manufacturing Strategy and the Relationship to Manufacturing Performance', *Strategic Management Journal*, 23: 105–17.

Silverman, B. (1999). 'Technological Resources and the Direction of Corporate Diversification: Toward an Integration of the Resource-based View and Transactions Cost Economics', *Management Science*, 45: 1109–24.

Simon, H. A. (1976). *Administrative Behavior*, 3rd edn. New York: Macmillan.

Singh, H. (1984). 'Corporate Acquisitions and Economic Performance', Unpublished doctoral dissertation, University of Michigan.

—— and Montgomery, C. (1987). 'Corporate Acquisition Strategies and Economic Performance', *Strategic Management Journal*, 8: 377–86.

Smircich, L. (1983). 'Concepts of Culture and Organizational Analysis', *Administrative Science Quarterly*, 28: 339–58.

Smythe, D. and Zhao, J. (2006). 'The Complete Welfare Effects of Cost Reductions in a Cournot Oligopoly', *Journal of Economics*, 87(2): 181–93.

Snell, S., Youndt, M., and Wright, P. (1996). 'Establishing a Framework for Research in Strategic Human Resource Management: Merging Resource Theory and Organizational Learning', in G. Ferris (ed.), *Research in Personnel and Human Resource Management*, 14: 61–90.

Spanos, Y. E. and Lioukas, S. (2001). 'An Examination into the Causal Logic of Rent Generation: Contrasting Porter's Competitive Strategy Framework and the Resource-based Perspective', *Strategic Management Journal*, 22: 907–34.

Spence, A. M. (1973). *Market Signaling: Information Transfer in Hiring and Related Processes*. Cambridge, MA: Harvard University Press.

Spender, J. C. (1983). 'The Business Policy Problem and Industry Recipes', in R. Lamb (ed.), *Advances in Strategic Management*, vol. 2. Greenwich, CT: JAI Press, pp. 211–29.

—— (1996). 'Making Knowledge the Basis of a Dynamic Theory of the Firm', *Strategic Management Journal*, 17(Winter Special Issue): 109–22.

—— and Grant, R. (1996). 'Knowledge and the Firm: Overview', *Strategic Management Journal*, 17(Winter Special Issue): 5–10.

Stalk, G., Evans, P., and Shulman, L. E. (1992). 'Competing on Capabilities: The New Rules of Corporate Strategy', *Harvard Business Review*, 70(2): 57–69.

Staw, B. M. (1981). 'The Escalation of Commitment to a Course of Action', *Academy of Management Review*, 6: 577–87.

Steffy, B. and Maurer, S. (1988). 'Conceptualizing and Measuring the Economic Effectiveness of Human Resource Activities', *Academy of Management Review*, 13: 271–86.

Steven, L. (1992). 'Front Line Systems', *Computerworld*, 26(March 2): 61–3.

Stevens, J. M. and Bagby, J. W. (1999). 'Intellectual Property Transfer from Universities to Business: Requisite for Sustained Competitive Advantage?', *International Journal of Technology Management*, 18(5–8): 688–704.

Stevenson, H. (1976). 'Defining Corporate Strengths and Weaknesses', *Sloan Management Review*, 17(3): 51–68.

Stillman, R. (1983). 'Examining Anti-trust Policy Toward Horizontal Mergers', *Journal of Financial Economics*, 11: 225–40.

Stinchcombe, A. L. (1965). 'Social Structure and Organizations', in J. G. March (ed.), *Handbook of Organizations*. Chicago, IL: Rand-McNally, pp. 142–93.

Stogdill, R. M. (1974). *Handbook of Leadership: A Survey of Theory and Research*. New York: Free Press.

Stuart, T. E. and Podolny, J. M (1996). 'Local Search and the Evolution of Technological Capabilities', *Strategic Management Journal*, 17(Special Summer Issue): 21–38.

Stulz, R. M. (1990). 'Managerial Discretion and Optimal Financing Policies', *Journal of Financial Economics*, 26: 3–27.

Swaminathan, A. (1996). 'Environmental Conditions at Founding and Organizational Mortality: A Trial-by-Fire Model', *Academy of Management Journal*, 39(5): 1350–77.

Tallman, S. B. (1991). 'Strategic Management Models and Resource-based Strategies among MNEs in a Host Market', *Strategic Management Journal*, 12(Special Summer Issue): 69–82.

Teece, D. J. (1980). 'Economy of Scope and the Scope of the Enterprise', *Journal of Economic Behavior and Organization*, 1: 223–45.

—— (1982). 'Toward an Economic Theory of Multiproduct Firm', *Journal of Economic Behavior and Organization*, 3(1): 39–63.

—— (1988). 'Capturing Value from Technological Innovation: Integration, Strategic Partnering, and Licensing Decisions', *Interfaces*, 18(3): 46–61.

—— Pisano, G., and Shuen, A. (1997). 'Dynamic Capabilities and Strategic Management', *Strategic Management Journal*, 18: 509–33.

Templin, N. (1992). 'A Decisive Response to Crisis Brought Ford Enhanced Productivity', *Wall Street Journal*, Dec. 15: A1, A13.

—— (1994). 'Auto Plants, Hiring Again, Are Demanding Higher-skilled Labour', *Wall Street Journal*, March 10: Al, A4.

Terpstra, D. and Rozzell, E. (1993). 'The Relationship of Staffing Practices to Organizational Level Measures of Performance', *Personnel Psychology*, 46: 27–48.

Tichy, N. M. (1983). *Managing Strategic Change: Technical, Political, and Cultural Dynamics.* New York: John Wiley & Sons.

—— and Devanna, M. A. (1986). *The Transformational Leader*. New York: John Wiley & Sons.

Tippens, M. J. and Sohi, R. S. (2003). 'IT Competency and Firm Performance: Is Organizational Learning a Missing Link?', *Strategic Management Journal*, 24: 745–61.

Titman, S. (1984). 'The Effect of Capital Structure on a Firm's Liquidation Decision', *Journal of Financial Economics*, 13(1): 137–51.

Thompson, A. A. and Strickland, A. J. (1980). *Strategy Formulation and Implementation.* Dallas: Business Publications.

—— —— (1983). *Strategy Formulation and Implementation*, Revised edn. Dallas: Business Publications.

Tomer, J. F. (1987). *Organizational Capital: The Path to Higher Productivity and Well-being.* New York: Praeger.

Tornow, W. and Wiley, J. (1991). 'Service Quality and Management Practices: A Look at Employee Attitudes, Customer Satisfaction, and Bottom Line Consequences', *Human Resource Planning*, 14: 105–15.

Trigeorgis, L. (ed.) (1995). *Real Options in Capital Investment: Models, Strategies, and Applications*. Westport, CT: Praeger.

—— (1996). *Real Options: Managerial Flexibility and Strategy in Resource Allocation.* Cambridge, MA: MIT Press.

Tripsas, M. (1997). 'Unraveling the Process of Creative Destruction: Complementary Assets and Incumbent Survival in the Typesetter Industry', *Strategic Management Journal*, 18(Special Summer Issue): 119–42.

Truss, C., Gratton, L., Hope-Hailey, V., McGovern, P., and Stiles, P. (1997). 'Soft and Hard Models of Human Resource Management: A Reappraisal', *The Journal of Management Studies*, 34(1): 53–73.

Tucker, I. and Wilder, R. P. (1977). 'Trends in Vertical Integration in the US Manufacturing Sector', *Journal of Industrial Economics*, 26: 81–94.

Turk, T. (1987). 'The Determinants of Management Responses to Interfirm Tender Offers and Their Effect on Shareholder Wealth', Unpublished dissertation, Graduate School of Management, University of California at Irvine.

Tyler, B. B. and Steensma, H. K. (1995). 'Evaluating Technological Collaborative Opportunities: A Cognitive Modeling Perspective', *Strategic Management Journal*, 16: 43–70.

——— (1998). 'The Effects of Executives' Experiences and Perceptions on Their Assessment of Potential Technological Alliances', *Strategic Management Journal*, 19(10): 939–65.

Ulrich, D. (1997). *Human Resource Champions*. Boston, MA: Harvard Business School Press.

—— Halbrook, R., Meder, D., Stuchlik, M., and Thorp, S. (1991). 'Employee and Customer Attachment: Synergies for Competitive Advantage', *Human Resource Planning*, 14: 8–104.

Varadarajan, P. R. and Ramanujam, V. (1987). 'Diversification and Performance: A Reexamination Using a Two Dimensional Conceptualization of Diversity in Firms', *Academy of Management Journal*, 30: 380–93.

Venkatraman, N. and Short, J. E. (1992). 'Baxter Healthcare: Evolution from ASAP to ValueLink in the Hospital Supplies Marketplace', *Proceedings of the Twenty-Fifth Annual Hawaii International Conference on System Sciences*, 4(January): 666–77.

Vicente-Lorente, J. D. (2001). 'Specificity and Opacity as Resource-based Determinants of Capital Structure: Evidence for Spanish Manufacturing Firms', *Strategic Management Journal*, 22: 157–77.

Villalonga, B. (2004*a*). 'Diversification Discount or Premium? New Evidence from the Business Information Tracking Series', *Journal of Finance*, 59(2): 479–506.

—— (2004*b*). 'Does Diversification Cause the Diversification Discount?', *Financial Management*, 33(2): 5–27.

Vitale, M. R. (1986). 'The Growing Risks of Information Systems Success', *MIS Quarterly*, 10(4): 327–34.

—— and Konsynski, B. (1991). 'Baxter Healthcare Corporation: ASAP Express', Harvard Business School Case 9-188-080, Revision 2/11/91, Harvard Business School Publishing Division, Boston, MA.

Vives, X. (ed.) (2000). *Corporate Governance: Theoretical and Empirical Perspectives*. New York: Cambridge Press.

Walston, S. L., Burns, L. R., and Kimberly, J. R. (2000). 'Does Reengineering Really Work? An Examination of the Context and Outcomes of Hospital Reengineering Initiatives', *Health Services Research*, 34(6): 1363–88.

Walter, G. A. and Barney, J. B. (1990). 'Management Objectives in Mergers and Acquisitions', *Strategic Management Journal*, 11: 79–86.

Wang, H. C. and Barney, J. B. (2006). Employee Incentives to Make Firm-specific Investments: Implications for Resource-based Theories of Corporate Diversification', *Academy of Management Review*, 31(2): 466–76.

—— and Lim, S. Y. (2001). 'Stakeholder Firm Specific Investments, Financial Hedging, and Corporate Diversification', Unpublished, Departments of Management & Human Resources and Finance, The Fisher College of Business, The Ohio State University.

Waterman, R. H. (1994). *Frontiers of Excellence.* London: Nicholas Brealey.

Welbourne, T. and Andrews, A. (1996). 'Predicting the Performance of Initial Public Offerings: Should Human Resource Management be in the Equation?', *Academy of Management Journal*, 39: 891–919.

Wernerfelt, B. (1984). 'A Resource-based View of the Firm', *Strategic Management Journal*, 5: 171–80.

—— (1989). 'From Critical Resources to Corporate Strategy', *Journal of General Management*, 14: 4–12.

—— and Montgomery, C. A. (1986). 'What Is an Attractive Industry?', *Management Science*, 32(10): 1223–30.

—— —— (1988). 'Tobin's *q* and the Importance of Focus in Firm Performance', *American Economic Review*, 78: 246–50.

Who's Excellent Now: Some of the Best-seller's Picks Haven't Been Doing so Well Lately. (1984). *Business Week*, November 5: 76–8.

Wilkins, A. (1989). *Developing Corporate Character.* San Francisco: Jossey-Bass.

Williamson, O. E. (1975). *Markets and Hierarchies: Analysis and Antitrust Implication.* New York: Free Press.

—— (1979). 'Transaction-cost Economics: The Governance of Contractual Relations', *Journal of Law & Economics*, 22: 233–61.

—— (1985). *The Economic Institutions of Capitalism.* New York: Free Press.

—— (1989). 'Transaction Cost Economics', in R. Schmalensee and R. D. Willig (eds.), *Handbook of Industrial Organization*, vol. 1. Amsterdam: Elsevier Science, pp. 36–182.

—— (1999). 'Strategy Research: Governance and Competence Perspectives', *Strategic Management Journal*, 20: 1087–108.

Will Regulators Get Tougher on M & A (1996). *Mergers and Acquisitions*, 31 (1): 42–51.

Winter, S. G. (1987). 'Knowledge and Competence as Strategic Assets,' in D. Teece (ed.), *The Competitive Challenge.* Cambridge, MA: Ballinger, pp. 159–84.

—— (2003). 'Understanding Dynamic Capabilities', *Strategic Management Journal*, 24: 991–5.

Wiseman, C. (1988). *Strategic Information Systems.* Homewood, IL: Irwin.

Womack, J. P., Jones, D. I., and Roos, D. (1990). *The Machine That Changed the World.* New York: Harper Perennial.

Wright, P. M. and McMahan, G. C. (1992). 'Alternative Theoretical Perspectives for Strategic Human Resource Management', *Journal of Management*, 18: 295–320.

—— and Snell, S. A. (1991). 'Toward an Integrative View of Strategic Human Resource Management', *Human Resource Management Review*, 1: 203–25.

—— McMahan, G. C., and McWilliams, A. (1994). 'Human Resources as a Source of Sustained Competitive Advantage', *International Journal of Human Resource Management*, 5: 299–324.

Wright, P. M., McCormick, B., and Sherman, W. S. (1998). 'Strategy, Core Competence, and HR Involvement as Determinants of HR Effectiveness and Refinery Performance', *Human Resource Management*, 37(1): 17–29.

—— Dunford, B. B., and Snell, S. A. (2001). 'Human Resources and the Resource-based View of the Firm', *Journal of Management*, 27: 701–21.

—— McCormick, B., Sherman, S., and McMahan, G.C. (1996). 'The Role of Human Resource Practices in Petro-chemical Refinery Performance', Paper presented at the 1996 Academy of Management meeting, Cincinnati, OH.

Yeoh, P. L. and Roth, K. (1999). 'An Empirical Analysis of Sustained Advantage in the US Pharmaceutical Industry: Impact of Firm Resources and Capabilities', *Strategic Management Journal*, 20: 637–53.

Youndt, M., Snell, S., Dean, J., and Lepak, D. (1996). 'Human Resource Management, Manufacturing Strategy, and Firm Performance', *Academy of Management Journal*, 39: 836–66.

Yukl, G. (1989). 'Managerial Leadership: A Review of Theory and Research', *Journal of Management*, 15(2): 251–89.

Zajac, E. and Olsen, C. P. (1993). 'From Transaction Cost to Transaction Value Analysis: Implications for the Study of Interorganizational Strategies', *Journal of Management Studies*, 30: 131–45.

Zander, U. and Kogut, B. (1995). 'Knowledge and the Speed of the Transfer and Imitation of Organizational Capabilities: An Empirical Test', *Organization Science*, 6(1): 76–92.

Zenger, J. H. and Folkman, J. (2002). *The Extraordinary Leader: Turning Good Managers into Great Leaders*. New York: McGraw-Hill Trade.

Zou, S. and Ozsomer, A. (1999). 'Global Product R & D and the Firm's Strategic Position', *Journal of International Marketing*, 7(1): 57–76.

Zucker, L. (1977). 'The Role of Institutionalization in Cultural Persistence', *American Sociological Review*, 42: 726–43.

Zucker, L. G. (1987). 'Institutional Theories of Organization', *Annual Review of Sociology*, 13, 443–64.

INDEX